RICK PITINO'S FAST BREAK

When Rick Pitino accepted the job as New York Knicks head coach, he inherited a team that had averaged just 24 wins a season for the past three years. He faced a New York crowd that regularly booed their home team. And he confronted the New York sports columnists, most of whom predicted that Pitino's college style would bomb in the press. He asked for 30 games to prove himself. He did it in less.

Searingly honest, *Born to Coach* is a riveting portrait of a man obsessed with basketball, a man pushing himself in a way the television cameras can never show. It's a book that captures all the drama of a team, a season, and a coach who dared to reach for the stars.

"Cager fans will find this a stirring saga of losers who became winners."
—*Publishers Weekly*

"Thought-provoking and insightful."
—John R. Thompson Jr., Georgetown University

RICK PITINO is the head coach at the University of Kentucky and the former head coach of the New York Knickerbockers.

BILL REYNOLDS is a sports columnist with the *Providence Journal-Bulletin*

BORN TO COACH

A Season with the New York Knicks

Updated Edition

RICK PITINO
and Bill Reynolds

A SIGNET BOOK

NEW AMERICAN LIBRARY
A DIVISION OF PENGUIN BOOKS USA INC.

NAL BOOKS ARE AVAILABLE AT QUANTITY DISCOUNTS WHEN USED
TO PROMOTE PRODUCTS OR SERVICES. FOR INFORMATION PLEASE
WRITE TO PREMIUM MARKETING DIVISION, NEW AMERICAN LIBRARY,
1633 BROADWAY, NEW YORK, NEW YORK 10019.

This book previously appeared in an NAL Books edition published by New
American Library and simultaneously in Canada by Penguin Books Canada
Limited.

SIGNET TRADEMARK REG. U.S. PAT. OFF. AND FOREIGN COUNTRIES
REGISTERED TRADEMARK—MARCA REGISTRADA
HECHO EN DRESDEN, TN, U.S.A.

SIGNET, SIGNET CLASSIC, MENTOR, ONYX, PLUME, MERIDIAN
and NAL BOOKS are published by New American Library, a division of
Penguin Books USA Inc., 1633 Broadway, New York, New York 10019

First Signet Printing, October, 1989

1 2 3 4 5 6 7 8 9

PRINTED IN THE UNITED STATES OF AMERICA

To Joanne, Michael, Christopher, and little Ricky. Without their love, dedication and support, the opportunity to pursue a dream would not have been possible.

R.P.

To my mother, Marion Coleman, who's always been able to make the three-point shot.

B.R.

ACKNOWLEDGMENTS

I want to thank John Simpson, the former Boston University athletic director, who gave me my first head coaching opportunity. Hubie Brown, who gave me a chance to get into the NBA, and who taught me so many things. Richard Evans, Jack Diller, and Al Bianchi, who gave me the opportunity to fulfill every New York hoop junkie's dream. Father John Cunningham and John Marinatto, two friends who went beyond the call of duty to help a friend in need. Lou Lamoriello, who not only gave me the opportunity to coach at Providence College, but also helped my wife and me through so many difficult times. Fred and Ann, who have meant so much to me and my family. And, finally, I want to publicly thank all my former players and assistant coaches—from Boston University to Providence College to the New York Knickerbockers—without whom none of this would be possible.

—Rick Pitino

So many people contribute to the shaping of a book. Here are a special few: David Vigliano, a great agent, who had the idea for this book and was there all along the way. Wayne Worcester, Chris Zarcadoolas, Jim Cox, and Ann Kellan, all of whom read portions of the manuscript. John

Cirillo and Dennis D'Agostino of the Knicks staff, who always made me feel welcome. Stu Jackson, Jim O'Brien, Brendan Malone, Ralph Willard, Mike Saunders, Tim Walsh, Dick McGuire, all were great to me, and have my thanks. Fred Kerber, Suzyn Waldman, and Tom Kertes, who went out of their way to be helpful. My colleagues in the *Providence Journal* sports department—especially Dave Reid and Dave Bloss—who were understanding and supportive. Kevin Mulroy, whose editorial hand is all over this book. And most of all, Rick and Joanne Pitino, who let me enter their lives for a year I'll always treasure.

—Bill Reynolds

INTRODUCTION

My first vivid recall of Rick Pitino dates back to a January night in 1973 when as the coach of Providence my team was playing UMass in the Providence Civic Center. Number twenty-two on the UMass roster was junior guard Rick Pitino, whom I had been slightly aware of as a high school player on Long Island. An hour or so before the game I was sitting at courtside watching various players on both teams informally shooting around. Rick wandered by and we began to talk. I asked him how things were going. He replied not very well, that he wasn't satisfied with his playing time and was thinking of transferring after the season. I asked him what he wanted to do after college. His reply was quick and unhesitant, "I want to coach". I told him that being the case he should stay right where he was because a good program and solid academic experience would serve him well in the long run.

More on Rick Pitino, the player, later. But Rick Pitino—coach, indeed. As they say in the trade, "This man can flat-out coach."

My first sighting of Rick as a coach was at Madison Square Garden when he was an assistant at Hawaii. I recall how terribly young he looked and that he was wearing a pair of hideous, shiny white shoes. Come to think of it, he still looks awfully young, but fortunately his taste in footwear has improved greatly over the years.

After a short stint at Syracuse, Rick became the head coach at Boston University. I recall hearing some coaching chatter around New England about him being aggressive, brash, and competitive. I was curious to see his team play. When I did on television one evening, I was most impressed. He obviously had a great feel for the game, managed the game very well from the bench, and his players hustled and executed very well. A short time later I was on a clinic program with Rick in Boston. He had some of his BU players with him, and I came away very impressed with the obvious respect and closeness that his players had for him.

A couple of years later Lou Lamoriello needed to hire a coach at Providence. Lou and I had been connected for twenty years. He is a hockey man and a good one. He is also as competitive a guy as you'll ever meet. He wanted P.C. to be competitive and to compete for the top rung in the Big East. He called me and said, "I need to educate myself about basketball coaches so I'll know who is who." I told him I'd give him a list and a bio of every coach who might possibly be interesting. I further told him I'd give him a much shorter list of people in whom he should have interest. Rick Pitino's name was at the top of that list with the following comments: "He has been a successful head coach and coming out of the NBA will help him in many ways, particularly recruiting. I don't think there is any question he'll get the job done. You need to be sure you're comfortable with him."

Lou called me once more. In the interim, one can only guess how many Knick games he wandered into. He said to me, "What do you think the reaction in the league would be if we hired Pitino?" I replied, "The other coaches would raise their eyes and you'd get their attention because they will feel he'll be a new force." Lou later said he kept coming back to this conversation as assuring him he had his man.

I underestimated by a big margin the extent to which Rick

Pitino would become a force at Providence. Quite simply, what he accomplished in his two years was close to miraculous in my opinion. And I'm not speaking so much about March 1987 and the run to the Final Four. That story has been well documented. What amazes me is his first year. He came in positive and confident. He then proceeded to take a team that perhaps had slightly underachieved the previous year, and transformed them through his own design and energy into a team that physically bore no resemblance to the year past. They became a team that improved every day of his two-year tenure. It was quite a remarkable thing to watch.

If you've sensed by now that I think Rick Pitino is quite gifted in his chosen profession, you're right. His past year was no surprise to me. In the fall when he was privately showing concern about his personnel (while destroying yet another golf course with a swing that is so bad that a one-foot-long and one-foot-deep divot is a clean hit), I told him I picked him to win 34–36 games and make the playoffs. I based my feeling that Rick would improve the Knicks from their mid-20-level wins the previous two years primarily on two strong areas of his coaching strength. First, the ability to motivate. He can motivate his players to compete when many other clubs are struggling in the NBA dog days. Secondly, his analytical ability which gives him the sense to change and adapt as the season progresses.

I'm sure this book on a season with the Knicks will be most enjoyable reading. Co-author Bill Reynolds was a fine basketball player in his college days at Brown. He earned his nickname "Shooter" by possessing a soft, true jump shot, and by passing the ball only when all attempts to shoot had been exhausted. His love and knowledge of the game are unusual for one so gifted of pen.

And, oh yes, lest I not forget one final comment on Rick Pitino as a player. Though he may choose to deny it, the record will reflect that he played substantial minutes the next year and played well in a game between UMass and Providence. However, he did miss the front end of a one-and-one with :07 on the clock, which the Friars rebounded and pulled out a one-point victory on a Kevin Stacom jumper at the buzzer.

Unlike that errent free throw, this book can't miss being most entertaining and interesting to all basketball fans. Enjoy.

—Dave Gavitt,
Commissioner of the
Big East Conference.
Coach of the 1980
Olympic Team

PROLOGUE

Sometimes I think none of this would have ever happened if not for that five minutes last spring in Birmingham.

It was the second round of the NCAA tournament, and my Providence College team was playing Austin Peay. With five minutes left, we were down 10 points. All afternoon we had been a little out of synch. All afternoon it had been like Sisyphus climbing the hill. I could see we were starting to get frustrated, beginning to think we couldn't win. So I called a timeout. As the team gathered around me, tired, the panic becoming visible in their eyes, I knew I needed something special to spur them on. I began talking calmly, in a very low voice.

"We probably are going to have to congratulate Austin Peay, so you better start getting ready for it. They have outplayed you all afternoon. They have beaten your press. They have shut down your offense. They have been in control the entire game. They have been the better team.

"Some days it just doesn't happen," I continued, beginning to raise my voice. "Some days you try as hard as you can try and you do everything right, but it's just not to be. It looks like this is one of those days.

"But there's one thing left you can do. Just one." By this time I was screaming. "For the next five minutes we can rip our hearts out of our chests and just throw them on the floor.

1

Just open up your chest and grab your heart and just throw it on the floor. Just throw it on the floor and see what happens!"

What happened? We made a miracle comeback and won the game in overtime. When we came into the locker room we knew something special had occurred. We had reached down and found something few teams ever find. Two weeks later we were in New Orleans in the Final Four.

The Knicks first contacted me in early April, right after I returned from New Orleans. They had just fired coach Bob Hill and general manager Scotty Stirling, and I met with Knick president Richard Evans and Jack Diller, vice-president of the Madison Square Garden sports group, at a restaurant in Rockefeller Center. As we talked about what I thought the Knicks should do, the papers were already draping me in Knickerbocker orange and blue. That night when Diller and I got out of the cab to meet Arthur Barron, the chairman of the board at Gulf & Western, I saw the headline in the New York *Post*: "KNICKS PICK RICK." The next morning the *Providence Journal* ran a front-page story saying I was all set to leave Providence and become the head coach of the Knicks.

It simply wasn't true.

No offer was ever made. In fact, my wife, Joanne, and I soon went to Phoenix to interview with Jerry Colangelo for the Suns job. Jerry had called me before the Final Four to wish me luck, and ask if we could talk after I got back about the coaching vacancy in Phoenix. At the time I said yes, but after I started talking with the Knicks, I knew I didn't want to go to Phoenix. And my agent, Gary Wichard, was dead-set against me going while we were negotiating with the Knicks. On the other hand, I had made a commitment to Colangelo, and it already had been publicized I was going out there. The funny thing is, after visiting Phoenix I began being interested. Their drug scandal didn't bother me. The job had potential. I felt the Suns could turn a real adverse situation into a positive one. That appealed to me: turning negatives into positives has been the theme of my coaching career.

When Joanne and I returned to Providence, I told the Knicks I thought the next coach should have full control of the basketball operations. The back-biting and turf wars between Hubie Brown and Dave DeBusschere (the general manager before Stirling) weren't for me. What I really wanted was a division of labor. I believed the general manager should be a businessman dealing with salaries and the NBA's salary cap, while the coach should control the team. So I wanted to be either coach and general manager, or else a coach dealing directly with player-personnel director Dick McGuire.

I think I would have been hired if the Don Nelson rumors hadn't started in the newspapers. Several stories in the New York papers were asking: what's the rush? It seems my whole life was being scheduled by the papers. Mike Stanton, a writer for the *Providence Journal*, had written a story a few weeks earlier that I was signing with the Knicks, after I had specifically told him I had not been offered the job. On the morning it appeared my kids were harassed in school, and I resented him for it. So when he persisted and asked if I had a personal deadline, I said May Day just to get rid of him.

After I saw the date in print, though, I thought, Why not? I wasn't going to wait forever. I was perfectly happy in Providence. A few days before May 1, I met again with Evans and Diller. They asked me if I would extend my personal deadline. I said, "No, I want to have my personal situation resolved by May 1. Everything has dragged on too long already." The meeting lasted five minutes.

When May 1 came without an offer from the Knicks, I held a press conference in Providence and said I would soon sign a new five-year contract at Providence College. "My wife and family are adamant about me not going to the Knicks, and if I do, I'll probably second-guess myself for the rest of my life."

I also said that day the new contract would not contain a

buy-out clause, so I would have no legal way to get out of my contract. That was my idea. Originally, Lou Lamoriello, the athletic director, had presented me with a first draft of a contract that contained a buy-out clause, just in case I wanted to get into the NBA. I told Lou I didn't want one. With a buy-out I would always be keeping one eye out on NBA openings, and I didn't want to be like that. I wanted to have my full attention on Providence.

That day I truly believed I was going to be at Providence College for at least the next five years. My new contract provided security for my family and all the perks that go with being a coach in a major college program. I knew I might never have a situation this good again.

So when the Knicks came back in July, it couldn't have come at a worse time. My summer camp at Providence College had started, and for the first time in a long while I was starting to relax. I had signed a new five-year contract at Providence. My wife was ecstatic. I felt I had the best college job in America. The turmoil of the spring—the death of my infant son, Daniel, the Final Four, the question of whether I was leaving for the Knicks or staying at Providence—I felt was all behind me.

I was at the dentist when my wife calls. I mean, I'm in the dentist's chair with my mouth open wide. "It's Jack Diller, and it's important." Thankful for any opportunity to stay out of that chair, I call Jack, and he says the Knicks have just hired Al Bianchi as their new general manager. "That's great," I said, but I'm thinking, "Why is he calling me at the dentist to tell me this?" Then he says that they want to take the shuttle up tonight and talk to me.

"You don't understand, Jack," I said. "I just signed a new five-year contract at Providence, and there's no way I can get out of it."

"I talked to Father Cunningham [the president of·Providence College] and got permission to talk to you." I was stunned. My first thought was Father Cunningham was upset with me about something.

I met with Diller, Evans, and Bianchi that night at an out-of-the way hotel about a half hour north of Providence, the same hotel where I had had secret negotiations with Providence College two years earlier. The next day I went to see Father Cunningham, because I didn't understand why he was letting me out of the contract. I told him, "You don't have to let me go. If there's the slightest inkling you're uncomfortable with it, don't do it. I love my job here, and you won't be hurting me if you don't. Maybe it's best for me to stay here."

"Rick, I want you to do what's best for your family. If this is what you want, you should go for it."

The next afternoon I started negotiating with the Knicks at the Hilton at Logan Airport in Boston. In the next room was John Marinatto, the Providence sports information director, who had become a sort of little brother to me. That night I was scheduled as the main speaker at the Bay State Games at the Boston Garden. I spent all day in contract negotiations with the Knicks, but broke it off because I had this commitment to speak. So who should shake my hand but Ray Flynn, the mayor of Boston and a former basketball star at Providence. When he introduced me, he said my decision to remain at Providence College had made him one very happy man. I felt sick to my stomach. I wanted to slink into the floor.

After the speech I went back to the hotel, and we continued ironing out the contract. Mitch Dukov, a Chicago-based financial adviser who handles financial interests for many college coaches, was with me. But I didn't have Gary Wichard with me, because when he had negotiated for me with the Knicks the first time, he had asked for a four-year salary that started at five hundred and went up to eight hundred thousand a year, plus a million-dollar interest-free loan, a New York apartment, and bonuses that could have led into the millions. It had made me uncomfortable. I thought that if I made more than the players, it would come back to haunt me.

They wanted me to sign then, but I told them I would let them know in two days. At about one in the morning John and I drove back to Providence. I began having doubts as soon as we got in the car. It made more sense economically to stay at Providence. And though I never had made a career decision based on money, I didn't like this deal economically. We got back to Providence about three, and I called Lou Lamoriello, the man who had hired me. Lou was someone I always went to for advice. He has very high standards, and possesses as much integrity as anyone I've ever met in sports. I told him I was confused.

"What do you want to do with your life?" Lou asked.

"I'm really not sure."

"Rick, do what's best for you and your family."

We spoke for two hours, and after leaving his office I felt better about going. Then I woke up the next morning and went through all the doubts all over again. I called Lou and met with him again. I told him, "I feel very guilty, like I'm letting everyone down. There probably couldn't be a better situation than to be the basketball coach at Providence College."

This time he told me I was too concerned with what people might think. The people who really cared for me would understand, and who cared about the rest of them?

I went to see Father Cunningham again. "I don't think you understand the ramifications of what you are doing," I told him. "You are going to take a lot of heat for this."

"Rick, I would never stand in the way of anyone's professional advancement, be it a history or an English professor. And I have very thick skin."

"But, Father, I'm not sure I really want to go. It might be in *my* best interest if you didn't let me leave."

"Rick, that's your call. You have to do what's best. But we'll be all right here. I don't think we'll lose a step."

I hoped the father was right, but I wasn't sure. A little

voice was telling me that it wasn't going to be as easy as he thought.

I was up all Saturday night agonizing about the decision. The next morning Joanne and I went out for breakfast with our next-door neighbors, the Duchins, and Gloria Duchin said something that made a real impression on me. "Thirty-four years old is not the time of life to choose being comfortable. At thirty-four you should go for the challenge." To me, the challenge was trying to rebuild the Knicks.

Jack Diller came by that afternoon, brought Joanne some roses, and I signed the contract.

In many ways, though, I was still distraught about it. My family didn't want me to go. People in Providence were going to think I betrayed them. Morally, I feel down about it to this day. I really do. It's not right to break an obligation. Without question, it's wrong. On the other hand, though, it's not earth-shattering when a basketball coach leaves a college. Let's put things in their proper perspective. I don't think when I meet the Almighty Father someday, He'll say to me, "No, you can't come in because you left Providence College."

If I hadn't accepted this job, I would have looked at myself in the mirror for the rest of my life, and said: You didn't accept the challenge. And that's what it's all about for me. People think I did it for the money. That's ludicrous. I was losing on the deal.

Later in the summer, John Marinatto became the new Providence athletic director after Lamoriello left for the New Jersey Devils. When he called me in New York, he said, "Rick, if you had stayed, you would have owned Rhode Island."

"But I don't want to own Rhode Island," I said. "I'm not Donald Trump. I'm a basketball coach."

✝✝✝✝✝✝✝✝✝

It's the press conference in Madison Square Garden's Hall of Fame room announcing Pitino's hiring, complete with the inevitable hoopla. In one corner of the room, amid the minicams and media hordes, Pitino is saying that this is the one job he always wanted. Plaques memorializing some of the greatest names in the history of American sports stare down from the paneled walls. "I went to P.S. 147 in Queens, where I dreamed every kid's playground dream of playing one day for the Knicks. I was in the Garden that night when Willis Reed dragged his leg on the court in the seventh game for the 1970 title. When I was an assistant coach here, I used to get a thrill every time I came through the tunnel into the Garden and heard John Condon announce my name."

A few tables away sits his wife, Joanne. It is not an easy time for her. She loved living in Rhode Island: the pace was slower, she had made several close friends. The family was still grieving over Daniel's death. She did not want to move again so soon, and start a new life in a new town. "The three most difficult things in life are death, divorce, and moving, and in the past four months I've experienced two of them. I know Rick wasn't going to stay at Providence forever, but I had hoped it would be longer. We both needed to slow down the pace. Too much has happened in the past couple of months. It's the worst possible time for us to be making an important decision.

"Yet I also know Rick. He had to take this job, or regret it the rest of his life."

That morning, in the limo that had taken them from their Rhode Island home to midtown Manhattan, she had felt physically ill. As the limo pulled in front of the Garden, she vomited.

"It's an omen," she told her husband.

So as she watches her husband at the height of his professional life, his longtime dream finally realized, she's not happy.

"Why did it all have to happen so soon?"

This is a question her husband will ask himself many times in the months ahead.

1 | Great Expectations

The basic premise of my system is to fatigue your opponents with constant pressure defensively and constant movement offensively. You're trying to get up more shots than your opponents by forcing more turnovers. By using multiple substitutions and ten to eleven players, you go into the final five minutes of play as the superior-conditioned team.

In the pros you have to do things differently than you do in college. In college you use the building block method: you build up to the number of offenses and defenses you want overall. Here you have to put in the whole right away. You allow for the mistakes, which for a coach is difficult, and as time goes on you work on those mistakes. But you got to get the whole in. In one week everything must be in place, because one week is all the time you have before the exhibition games start.

Some veterans will come in great shape. Others will come in and say this is my time to get in shape. We have to be careful with that, because the one thing you don't do is chastise a pro for not arriving in shape. In college you'd be upset. You can't do that in the pros. Your job is to get the most value out of a player.

The key to coaching is not what you do, but the way you do it. The intangibles, the motivational parts of the game are the most important facets of it. That's what gets your team to a different level. I don't have to be motivated. You see, my life is basketball. My family's involved in basketball. I can't wait to get at it. That's not true of the people you're coaching. Practice ends in college and they go eat, they want a social life, they want to study. In the pro ranks they get their fill of basketball. They're not going to go home and watch films.

My ability to motivate stems from doing so much speaking to a variety of groups. You have to read the mood of your audience. With a team you know the mood. If they've lost, they have low self-esteem, so you build it up. If they have high self-esteem, you bring them down a notch, force them to understand why they won. Tell them it wasn't because they were great, but because collectively they did great things.

The first time I ever spoke in public was at the Five Star basketball camp when I was still in college. I was very nervous and spent a lot of time looking down at my notes. Afterward, I wasn't happy with my performance, and I've never looked at lecture notes again. I compose a few general themes, and then read the mood of the audience, whether it's my team in the locker room or a room full of people. If you constantly look down at notes, it will be boring. You can be a lot of things when you speak in public, but you can't be boring.

Near the end of my first year of coaching at Boston University, I started reading about Vince Lombardi. I saw one of those NFL flashback programs and the Green Bay Packer glory days. Then I watched a film on Lombardi with Ernest Borgnine, and really got turned on by him. I started reading all about him. I was fascinated by him: the way he spoke, the way he demanded things. I started adopting many of the principles he taught. Developing character. That was his whole thing: character as an attitude.

A lot of coaches motivate, but they do it differently. I want my players to reflect my personality on the court. Not off the court, on the court. That's what happened at Providence. The players were meek and mild off the court, but once they crossed the lines they became killers. That's what I want to happen here.

I've already told the team I expect them to have a boyish enthusiasm for this game. When I'm playing in the Y, I want to be jumping up and slapping high-fives, even now when I'm over the hill. I told them they have to have that. I think they all want to be that way. Everybody strives for that boyish enthusiasm. Who wants to grow old? You have to show them that they can have that enthusiasm, and it doesn't have to be embarrassing.

True motivation is not getting people to play to their potential. It's getting people to play beyond their potential.

✝✝✝✝✝✝✝✝✝✝

October 11

It is the third day of training camp. Outside, it is raining, the sky gray and overcast. Already camp has become a world unto itself. Practice in the morning, return to the hotel, then back to the gym a couple of hours later to start preparing for the evening workout. The talk is all basketball: who is looking good and who is struggling, the upcoming season, other teams, other players. The baseball playoffs and the second week of the replacement games in the NFL might as well be happening on the moon.

The New York Knickerbockers are practicing a pressing defense in a large gym at SUNY Purchase, a state university set amid the monied greenery of suburban Westchester County. Already the Knicks are playing a different style of basketball than they did the year before. It is the frantic, all-court style Pitino patented at Providence College. Defensive players play all over the court, trapping the man with the ball with two men whenever possible. This style of play has never been attempted in the NBA. Traditional thinking holds that the season is simply too long to press every game; the players will get too worn out.

Midway through morning practice, the players are obviously winded. Pitino blows the whistle. "Will you guys get to where you're supposed to be?" he shouts. "Don't tell me you're tired. Get there. I know you're tired. So are the other guys. You have to be tougher than the other guys. That's the sign of a good team. And we *are* a team. If someone gives Patrick Ewing a cheap shot, he is giving all of us a cheap shot. We are a *team*. It doesn't matter who scores the points. It's not Rory Sparrow fighting Gerald Henderson for who starts. None of that matters anymore."

It's the beginning of trying to create a team, not just twelve players using the same locker room, a collection of stars all spinning in their own orbits.

When Pitino first came to Providence College, he did the same thing. On a blackboard in the front of the room he listed four categories: basketball, school, work ethic, family. The four things that made up his players' lives.

"How many of you want to be professional basketball players some day?" he asked.

Virtually every hand in the room shot up.

"Well, since you had a losing season last year and there is no one here in this room who averaged in double figures, it's obvious you are not a success in the basketball part of your lives," he said, erasing one fourth of the blackboard. "And since I've seen your grade-point averages, it's also obvious that you aren't successes in school either."

The room was silent as he erased another quarter of the blackboard. Then he turned to the team's trainer, "Fast" Eddie Jamiel. "Fast, how many of these guys have been in the gym every day since the season working on their games, trying to improve?"

The room was silent. Jamiel shrugged. "No one, Coach."

"So it's also obvious that you don't work hard either." Pitino erased another part of the blackboard. His voice rising, he noted, "Let's see. You aren't successful in basketball and you aren't successful in school and you don't work hard. What's left?"

Building the suspense, he paused for a minute, as if trying to think of anything that could salvage something for these players who were meeting their new coach for the first time and seeing their collective self-esteem shrinking with each passing sentence.

"Well, hopefully you are a close team," he said finally. "Hopefully you care about each other."

"Oh, we do, Coach," said a player named Harold Starks, one of the upper classmen.. "We're a close team."

Pitino pretended to think for a second. "Okay, Harold, how many brothers does Steve Wright have?"

Starks slowly shook his head.

"What does Billy Donovan's father do?"

Starks shook his head some more.

"So you don't really know anything about each other, do you?"

No one spoke.

So he made each player stand up and talk about themselves and their families. What had been twelve individuals began the transformation into a team. Twenty-two months later they were in the Final Four.

The New York Knicks have averaged only 24 wins for the past three seasons. The once proud franchise that Mike Lupica will call in *Esquire* magazine "the dumbest in sports," has fallen on hard times.

Will Pitino's almost evangelical style work with professional athletes, supposedly jaded and overpaid, on cruise control to their next paycheck? Can he re-create the close, almost family atmosphere he had in college in a city universally known as cold and impersonal? Will his unique style of play be as successful in the National Basketball Association as it was in college? Can any coach survive the New York media? They are questions whose answers will determine Rick Pitino's fate in New York.

The night before camp opened, he met the Knicks in the locker room, the first time he had addressed them collectively. "All I've heard ever since getting this job are the negatives. Patrick Ewing can't rebound or block shots. Kenny Walker can't shoot. Gerald Wilkins and Pat Cummings can't pass. All I've heard is what you can't do, and I'm sick of it. I don't want to hear how many games you didn't win. I don't want to hear what other coaches think of you. I don't want to hear what you can't do. It's no one's fault. It's not your fault, not your coaches' fault. It's losing's fault. That all comes with losing. And that's all over now."

After the meeting he shook everyone's hand.

In the early Seventies, Madison Square Garden rang with the cheers that showered on Reed, Frazier, Bradley, and the Miracle on 33rd Street: two world championships in four years. They were a symbol of NBA excellence, the epitome of teamwork. Now the cheers are only echoes. Everything seems rooted in the past tense. Since 1973 there only have been five winning seasons. In a revolving door of players, the faces changed, but the losing tradition remained the same. All the while management kept throwing good money after bad in a futile attempt to resurrect the past, as if the Knicks were just a bad Broadway show you could close down after a week and bring in another one.

The past three years the Garden has become a tomb. The banners immortalizing the great Knicks of the past hang from the Garden rafters and seem to stare down accusingly, as if the current Knicks are their wastral sons.

In 1984 they took the Celtics to the seventh game of the Eastern Finals. They seemed on the threshold of one day challenging Boston and Philadelphia's dominance in the East. Pitino was an assistant to Hubie Brown that year, and the future looked bright. The following season Bill Cartwright got hurt, and the slide started. By the end of 1987 the Knicks were in shambles; a victim of injuries and poor management. They stood for everything that's wrong with the NBA: a collection of overpriced athletes who resembled an all-star team thrown together on the spur of the moment.

Their offense degenerated into a me-shoot, you-shoot. The big men often didn't get back defensively, giving opponents too many easy transition baskets.

Who were these wounded warriors of this hapless team?

Cartwright has become the designated scapegoat. Once he was seen as the young center who would carry the Knicks up in the Atlantic Division standings. Now he is perceived, in NBA parlance, as "too soft," someone who wants to shoot foul-line jumpers instead of living in the low post. He is negatively called Mr. Bill in the New York tabloids. He is the subject of virtually every trade rumor that surfaces, the thinking being that most of the Knicks' problems will be solved if only Cartwright is shipped somewhere, anywhere.

"After the first meeting I asked Billy how he was doing," says Pitino. "It was the first time I had talked to him in nearly three years. He said he was feeling fine, but he wanted to be traded. 'I've had enough of New York. I'm tired of being called Medibill, and Invisibill. It's been very traumatic for me and my family, and I want to end my career somewhere else.' I asked him to give me some time."

Then there was Bernard King. Three years before, King was a folk hero in New York, the city kid who had dribbled over the Brooklyn Bridge to lead the NBA in scoring. Outside on 33rd Street vendors sold St. Bernard hats. Inside, Bernard put on a nightly clinic on how to score on the baseline. He was filled with explosive energy and an iron will nurtured in the city's mean streets. He lusted for points, was possessed by points. Then had come the knee injury that sidelined him for two full seasons. King retreated into a cocoon, hiding out in his New Jersey home, not attending games, working out in seclusion, a King in exile. What better symbol of the Knicks' demise?

The prodigal son returned for the last six games of the 1987 season, complete with a five-minute ovation, the only thing the Garden crowd had had to cheer for since he had gone down with his knee injury in a nothing game in March

1985. In the offseason he has been demanding a multiyear guaranteed contract. He wants to be treated as the great player he was three years earlier, instead of a thirty-one-year-old small forward trying to come back from a knee injury no one has ever come all the way back from. The Knicks are refusing to offer him a contract.

When Patrick Ewing came out of Georgetown in 1985, he was the most celebrated college basketball player of his generation, billed as the next Bill Russell. When the Knicks won the right to select him in the NBA's first lottery, a televised event that showed general manager Dave DeBusschere all but drooling, Ewing was perceived as the NBA's next dominant center. He was given a ten-year contract in the vicinity of thirty million, and Knick fans waited for St. Patrick to resurrect the glory days.

But the Ewing of the pros seemed a parody of the Ewing at Georgetown. Not only did he miss fifty-one games in two years, due to cranky knees, he showed a marked propensity to take fall-away jump shots. At Georgetown he had been a menacing presence, the cornerstone of a style that often relied on intimidation. In his first two years with the Knicks he has seemed almost petulant on the court.

It was a team Pitino didn't like watching. He considered them selfish, a team that never made the extra pass, a team full of guys blowing solo, lacking any real chemistry, and having no idea how to win. At this first practice session, his first goal is to begin changing that.

"See the ball." "React." "See the ball." "Hands up in the press."

A large body sprawls on the floor and Pitino blows his whistle. "So, we have one guy here who wants to play basketball." He blows his whistle and play starts again. One team in white jerseys brings the ball up the court against a team in blue jerseys. "You got to move your feet, Blue," he yells. "You got to react. See the ball. We are not going to allow a team to run one play that they practice. Not one."

Under severe pressure in the backcourt, veteran guard Gerald Henderson throws a pass into the forecourt. His teammate Gerald Wilkins catches it going to his left, tries to avoid two men in blue jerseys who come frantically rushing at him, and throws a pass that's intercepted.

"See?" Pitino yells excitedly. "See what you're doing? You're making them make four or five decisions every time they catch the ball, and they can't do it. Can you see what you're doing?"

The blue team brings the ball up the court, and the white team presses them all over the court, expensive sneakers squeaking on the polished floor. "Hands up in the press," he yells, again stopping the practice. "That's not a small thing. It's a major thing. The number one thing in our press is deflections."

The message that this is a new era is already apparent on the strained faces. The pace is frantic and charged. Bodies sprawl onto the court. The blue team takes the ball out-of-bounds again, and this time beats the white press for an easy layup. Pitino blows his whistle. "See, White, you didn't talk. And if you don't talk, I'm going to think it's because you're tired. You determine fatigue, not me. So don't come to me when you come out of the game after only thirty seconds."

Pitino is nonstop energy, all but running up and down the sideline. Energy seems to run off him as easily as sweat runs off the players. Again the blue team takes the ball out-of-bounds. This time everyone on the white team is talking. They swarm all over the ball near midcourt, and force a turnover. "In ten seconds you've gone from a passive team that didn't talk to an aggressive, talking, trapping team."

It keeps going, the players visibly winded, the play ragged. Pitino blows the whistle. Many of the players lean over, hands on their knees, their shirts stained with sweat. They came to training camp expecting to ease back into work, talk to the press, smile for the camera, a basketball version of back-to-scool days. Here they are looking as if they were in the fourth quarter at the end of a ten-day road trip.

Pat Cummings bends over, holds the bottom of his shorts, and takes a deep breath. "No," yells Pitino. "You're telling your opponent you're tired. Any time we saw opponents like that we pounced on them. *Don't tire on us.* We're playing this way for 82 games, plus the playoffs. And the team standing at the end wins. Our whole system is predicated on fatigue. Your opponent will get tired. You will be in great physical condition because of our style of play. You will still have something left at the end of the game. The other team will beg to get out of the game. Beg to get out, I guarantee it."

From the moment the first practice started two days earlier, Pitino has been as intense as his reputation. That first morning they practiced for two hours, and the players gasped for breath. "Is it going to be this way all the time?" Ewing asked, a certain concern in his voice, as Pitino blew the whistle ending practice.

"Tonight will be a tough practice. This was easy. When we get into it, this will seem like a walk-through."

The players laughed, sort of.

For already there is a legend surrounding Pitino. Had he really told his mother at age twelve that she should think of sending him to a summer basketball camp as an investment in his future? Had he really postponed his honeymoon while an assistant coach at Syracuse to recruit Louis Orr? Did he really practice three times on Thanksgiving at Boston University? Did he really used to have his players run around the gym carrying bricks?

He had taken a Providence College program that had been on life-support systems to the Final Four in two years. He had taken a bunch of kids who had known only failure in their college careers, and made them believe in themselves, both individually and collectively. He had been named Coach of the Year. Along the way he had challenged the conventional wisdom. You can't press all over the court with slow players? Pitino did. You can't play an up-tempo game with players not as physically talented as your opponents? Pitino did it all the time. Sure, he held early-morning practices and worked eighteen-hour days, but he also did it with a certain amount of magic. Pitino had come up with a wholly new blueprint for the game.

By the time Pitino became the new coach of the Knicks on July 13, he had created a legend. Fiction sprinkled in with truth to form the Pitino Mystique. It first began at Syracuse as an assistant coach. He had been a tireless recruiter, the epitome of the slick new breed of fast-talking basketball salesmen who were changing the game. At Boston University he was the personification of the driven young coach, building a program out of the ashes. It had blossomed the past two years at Providence, one of the greatest resurrection stories in recent college basketball history.

He inherited a program that had been 11–65 in the history of the Big East Conference. Once one of the top basketball schools in the East, the Friars had fallen into mediocrity. They seemed mired in their storied past. Was Providence, a small Catholic school, no longer capable of playing big-time college basketball?

Pitino swept into Providence like Elmer Gantry. He promised to wake up the ghosts. He promised his team would be the hardest-working in America, and then instituted a running, pressing style played with all the intensity of Marines following Teddy Roosevelt up San Juan Hill. He made kids lose weight. He practiced three times a day. In his first year he won 17 games. Excitement returned to Providence as the Friars went to the National Invitational Tournament, their first postseason tournament in nine years.

In 1986–87 the pace intensified. Providence broke into the Top Twenty in January. The national press began focusing on the amazing Rick Pitino. In March the Friars qualified for the NCAA tournament, and the magic carpet ride began. They were sent to Birmingham, where they trounced favored University of Alabama at Birmingham. Two days later they beat Austin Peay in overtime. Five days later they beat heavily favored Alabama in Louisville. Two days after that they beat Georgetown in the finals of the Southeast regional and advanced to the Final Four.

It was a three-week whistle-stop tour. Pitino started out the month known only to basketball fans. He ended it the hottest college coach in the country.

A week later he was named Coach of the Year.

"Is this a Cinderella story?" he was asked.

"No, because Cinderella never worked this hard."

Out with the old, ring in the new. Two days earlier, after the first workout, was the Knicks' first public moment. As the players went to change into their game uniforms for pictures, Cartwright was asked about King's absence from camp.

"The things King gives a team are irreplaceable," he said, towering over five sports writers.

"So if you were the general manager, you wouldn't have gotten rid of King?" he was asked.

He hesitated a second, knowing this is a sensitive subject. "I would have found a way to stretch the salary cap," he said finally.

Fifteen yards away Ewing is saying, "I'm ready to run and do what it takes to win." What he doesn't say is that shortly after Pitino was hired, the two of them had dinner in Washington.

"Patrick basically was concerned about two things. He was concerned because I had once been Hubie's assistant. The problem was not so much how Hubie treated him, but how he treated some of the other guys. Plus, he was concerned that practices might be too tough. He remembered me from Boston University, because we tried to recruit Patrick back then, and he had come to a couple of practices.

I told him, 'Don't worry, we aren't going to practice like I did at BU. But we are going to work hard and I expect you to practice. One of the problems with the Knicks the past couple of years has been that everyone was always getting out of practice. You'll see, you're going to want to practice, it's going to be fun. And you're going to want to work because you want to be the best center in basketball, and we're going to use repetition over and over, to make you become that. I expect you to be a leader each day.'

"I also asked him what the best time in his life had been. He said Georgetown. I asked him why. He said because it had been like a family, everyone had cared about each other. I told him that was what I wanted to re-create with the Knicks, the type of close support group John Thompson has with his players at Georgetown and I had at Providence. 'There are going to be times in practice when my enthusiasm is going to pick you up, but there also are going to be days when I'm going to be down and I'll expect you to pick me up.'

"I also told him that at Georgetown he had been a power player, not the finesse player he was in his first two years with the Knicks, and that I wanted him to be a power player again. Wanted him to go toward the basket offensively, not fall away from it. Then I said I wanted him to lose twenty pounds to take advantage of his athletic ability against more immobile centers."

Losing weight is another theory of Pitino's. His belief that many players carry too many pounds that hinder their quickness is a carryover from his own experience as a player at the University of Massachusetts. The first thing he did at Providence was to tell ineffective guard Billy Donovan to lose twenty pounds. Two years later Donovan was All-Big East. In addition to Ewing, Pitino in July also told first-round draft pick Mark Jackson to lose twelve pounds.

"How much weight have you lost?" someone asks Ewing, noticeably thinner than he was last year.

"What weight?" he says with a wide smile. "I'm not going to talk about how much I weigh."

"What do you think of the new coach?"

"He is intense, he wants things done right, and he works hard. All the things you want. I'm looking forward to playing for him, and I'm looking forward to winning."

Coming from Ewing, this is almost a major address. His first year with the Knicks he said little to the media, not even to the beat writers who traveled with the team. One writer attempting to make small talk was told, "I only give interviews after games." Last year he had been better, but still was regarded as the worst interview on the team.

Ewing was protected at Georgetown by John Thompson, as he had been protected in high school in Cambridge, Massachusetts. Taunts had dogged him throughout his career. In high school he was big, he was black, and he came of age at a time when Boston was going through its traumatic years of school busing, an experience that dramatically increased racial tensions. Ewing was a victim of this, as he was a victim of being a twelve-year-old immigrant from Jamaica and having to adapt from an island culture to an American city, all the while towering over his peers. During high school games he had bananas thrown at him. While at Georgetown he played in gyms that had signs saying "EWING CAN'T READ THIS" and "PEKING MAN." Was it any wonder that he was wary with people he didn't know, and offered little more than perfunctory comments?

On the main court Pitino is quickly surrounded by a dozen members of the New York media. Standing in his blue warmup suit, he is choirboy handsome, a young thirty-five, with dark hair that is thick and full in the front, but starting to thin in the back. This is the first time he has met the press en masse since the day in the Garden's Hall of Fame room. He knows this is a big part of his job, and might just be the barometer of whether he succeeds or fails in New York.

The New York media are a Greek chorus. The daily media blitz is unlike any other city's in the country. The *Post*, *Daily News*, and *Newsday* are all tabloids, complete with screaming headlines and the belief that controversy sells papers. Anything a New York team does is magnified. New York teams are either great or horrible. Every coach is dragged through their mill, drawing raves or calls for his head.

"In my two years as a Knick assistant I had a firsthand look at how the media destroyed Hubie Brown. A jab here, a volley there, then more jabs, until at the end Hubie was all but reeling from the constant verbal body punches. Hubie was affected by it: it damaged his family and continually frustrated him. For any coach to survive in New York, he must be able to handle the New York media. In fact, my one real fear about being the Knick coach is that my family will be affected by the daily media pressure. I've made a vow to myself not to read the New York tabloids. That's not only to spare myself from the inevitable criticism and second-guessing, but also because I want to be able to deal objectively with the writers who cover the Knicks, and not be influenced by what they might have written the day before."

It didn't take long to get his baptism. The day after his hiring, he was reportedly "going into his weasel mode" after a falling-out with his agent over the Knick deal. "He'll climb anybody to get where he wants to go," Peter Vecsey quoted an anonymous source in the *Post*, "and ditch you in a second once you've outlived your usefulness. He's only out for himself and will bleep anybody along the way who gets in his way. He would have buried Hubie when he was his assistant if it meant getting to the top quicker. This guy is not a real person, he's a rattlesnake."

2 | "We Want Bernard"

New York's the kind of town that will give you bad publicity on your wedding night. In New York you have to win, and it's not even a matter of getting fired if you don't. If you don't win, you don't want to live in the town.

I told my players that if you're bothered by people knocking you, if you are bothered by people making up things, then you cannot play in New York. You can choose to go two ways: not to read the papers, or take the philosophy I've always believed in—minimalize the bad and maximize the good.

I think I really know the New York press and how they react. And they do react. The biggest shock to me—and it was sad for me because I'm a New York coach—was the Davey Johnson situation with the Mets. Five or six years ago the Mets are at the bottom, doing about as poorly as they could do as a baseball team. Then along comes Davey Johnson. He has built them up to world champions, has had a tremendous year with the injuries he's had. Then he asks for a one-year extension and gets turned down. To me, that was frightening.

I've always believed if you lose, you're going to be fired, even if it's not your fault. It goes with the territory. Everyone in pro sports is living on borrowed time: coaches and players. On the other hand, when you win that's when you should get rewarded. That's what is scary about Davey Johnson.

Look at the Yankees. Look at what is starting to happen to Bill Parcells with the Giants. More and more it seems that the New York media is going to get any coach here. I don't know if there's any way around that. What you try to remember when someone in the media knocks you is all the good things that are written. It's like the guy that returns from the race track and says, "I lost by a nose. That's just my luck." But he never remembers all the ones he won by a nose. Or the coach that says we lost by one, but doesn't remember all the ones he won by one. A lot of good things have been written about me in my twelve years in coaching. In fact, I've had more things written negatively about me in the past six months than in the entire twelve years. Now, if I get seventy percent good publicity, it's better than anyone's gotten since Red Holtzman.

It was different in Holtzman's time; I've talked with him about this. Back then the writers were rooting for them. By the time Hubie arrived, all that had changed. Now people make reputations by being negative. Now there are writers who are paid to be negative, and there are others, fearful of being called homers, who go overboard the other way. The idea that writers are basically going to be on your side because you're the hometown team is in the past, at least in New York.

When it started going bad for him, Hubie read everything, and it ate him up inside. Someone would question him and it would bother him, for he knew he was right from a coaching standpoint. You can't answer writers. They are like echoes.

Hubie took it too hard. I understand why he took it hard, because it's not nice to have it written about you. But if you're going to coach in New York, it's a lot different than coaching in Indiana. Things are written about you that are not true; people take shots at you. It comes with the territory, and you have to understand that.

October 11–14

SUNY Purchase is modern, impersonal, suburban. It all seems a long way from the City Game. But the gym has three full courts, and a new weight room. The past few years the Knicks practiced at Upsala College in New Jersey, close to where many of the players live. But it only had one court, was old and dark, didn't have a good weight room. As trainer Mike Saunders says, "Every time I went in there early in the morning, I made a lot of noise first to scare away the mice." And Evans, a Gulf & Western trouble-shooter brought over from Radio City Music Hall to handle the troubled Knicks, wanted them to practice in New York.

The coaching staff are overjoyed with training camp. Unlike the end of last year, when the Knicks were a team going through the motions, everyone is working hard.

"I am elated," says Pitino. "I expected more resistance, more evidence of what I called the pro attitude. So far there's been none. Even Cartwright and Pat Cummings, the two players who are the subjects of trade rumors and whose individual games are most likely to suffer in this new style, appear to be into it."

Cartwright would like to go off somewhere and make a fresh start, preferably out West. He is seven feet, wide through the hips, thin shoulders. His oval face is dominated by a trim goatee and large eyes that somehow always seem sad. Once the most highly touted high school player in the country (at Elk Grove, California, just outside of Sacramento), his career, both in college at the University of San Francisco and with the Knicks, has been one of unfulfilled potential.

He's said he's not overly thrilled with being Ewing's backup, the role Pitino envisions for him. Pitino says that unlike Hubie Brown the year before, he will not play Ewing and Cartwright together, a tactic Ewing rebelled against and was instrumental in costing Hubie his job. For a while in the summer it had appeared Cartwright would be off to Atlanta, but at the last minute the deal fell through, leaving the Hawks without any offense at center and Cartwright here in limbo. He's so sure he's going to be traded, he's had his family remain in California.

"I've already talked with him. I've told him he's a valuable commodity, and while he might still be traded, we have no intention of giving him away. I also told him to give the new system a try. Even playing behind Ewing he will get a lot of minutes. The new, fast-paced style will provide ample playing time for everyone."

The opening drills have almost become routine by now, drills that come directly from Pitino's experiences at summer basketball camps. Most NBA teams do few individual drills. The Knicks do them daily, instead of the casual layup lines most teams open practice with.

The big people work on two post-up moves at the beginning of every practice. At Providence Pitino called the moves by the names of the NBA players who popularized them. The step-back move is called the Sikma Move, for Milwaukee center Jack Sikma. The up-and-under, in which a player gets the ball, turns, fakes as if shooting, then steps under and around his opponent is the McHale Move, for Celtic forward Kevin McHale. If the names are not used here, the moves are.

Assistant coach Stu Jackson, holding what resembles a large seat cushion, leans against the players, jockeys with them for position. The players in turn receive a pass and use one of the moves.

The guards are taught to always fake with the ball before trying to go around their man. "Now I want you to give a good ball fake, then use a crossover dribble, and take a jump shot," says Pitino to guard Gerald Wilkins. Wilkins fakes, dribbles, shoots.

"More of a fake," says Pitino. "Again."

Wilkins does it better, but misses the shot.

"Don't move your head. That's the key to shooting. Don't move your head. Do it again."

It is Pitino's defensive philosophy, though, that sets him apart. It started back at Five Star, the showcase summer basketball camp run by Howard Garfinkel. Garfinkel, a Damon Runyon character who never met a jump shot he didn't remember, has long been regarded as one of the top evaluators of high school talent in the country. While Pitino was still a student at the University of Massachusetts, Garfinkel gave him a team to coach, the youngest ever to coach a team at the prestigious camp. The first thing Pitino did was fullcourt press for the entire game.

"He always was yelling to get a fingertip on the ball," remembers Garfinkel. "You don't have to steal it, he used to say. Just get a fingertip on it. That was his trademark. And that first year he got to the championship game of the camp. He had Danny Callendrillo, the Seton Hall kid, and four kids you never heard of. Callendrillo never played harder in his life."

When Pitino got his first head coaching job at Boston University in 1978, he brought that camp experience with him. BU was considered a coach's graveyard, and Pitino quickly realized if he didn't try something different, his BU Terriers were going to have a lot of Three Dog Nights. So he went back to his Five Star coaching experience. Get a fingertip on the ball. "I thought of it like being a boxer. If you are in the ring with someone better, you can't stand there and slug it out with them. You have to make them do something they don't want to do."

So he pressed. Get a fingertip on the ball. His teams swarmed all over opponents, tried to upset their rhythm, made them more concerned with beating his press than running their offense. Gordie Chiesa, his assistant at Providence, labeled it the "mother-in-law" defense, because it was built around "constant pressure and harassment."

Pitino wasn't the first to bring pressure defense to college basketball. Jack Ramsey did variations of it at St. Joe's in the Sixties. John Wooden pressed with his first championship team at UCLA, the one that featured Walt Hazzard, Gail Goodrich, and Keith Erickson. Tom Davis, now at Iowa, has done it extensively in his college career, as has Gary Williams, now at Ohio State. John Thompson often uses fullcourt man-to-man defense. Kevin Mackey does it at Cleveland State, calling it his "run and stun" defense. Traditionally used as an act of desperation, these coaches used pressure defense to control tempo, to make other teams play the full 94 feet.

But not many teams pressed like Providence pressed. They had a manic quality to their pressure defense, making the game helter-skelter, rarely letting opponents gain any offensive flow. At first glance it all seemed chaotic, but there was a method to the apparent madness. "I used two basic fullcourt presses: a 1-2-1-1, or white press, when the man taking the ball out-of-bounds is played. The 2-2-1, or black press, concedes the inbounds pass and the goal is to trap the dribbler near midcourt on either sideline. If we scored on an inside shot, or a foul shot, we were in the white press. If it was a jump shot, we were in black.

"It's based on the theory that as the game has become more physical, passing the basketball has become a lost art. For all the attention given Larry Bird and Magic Johnson for their great passing ability, most teams, at every level of basketball, have two or three players who don't pass well. We ran four presses at Providence, but we lived and died with our matchup press. This one works on box-and-diamond principles to contain the ball. We never trapped a control dribbler or a stationary passer. What we wanted was to trap the speed dribbler, constantly forcing the ball handler to make decisions and adjustments on the run. Our matchup press reacted to what the offense did, and to beat us the offense had to react to us. That's why it was difficult to prepare for our defenses. Instinct works better against the matchup press than complicated concepts and designs."

By now this pressure defense is his personal trademark.

"Swing the ball." "Move it." "Box out." "Get back." "Deny the ball." "Swing it." He is in nonstop motion. He prowls the sidelines, the energy all but steaming out of him, constantly offering commentary on what is happening on the court. He rarely stops moving, and never just sits and watches.

He's also incredibly upbeat. Wilkins and Walker will be "unbelievable in this new system. The greatest injustice I've seen is the way the fans and writers have perceived Bill Cartwright. If I had one wish right now, he'd get a standing ovation in Madison Square Garden." He tells the players he can spot a playoff team when he sees one. "Just like I told my Providence before last year that we would go to the Final Four, if you work hard, you will not only make the playoffs, you will go far in them. If you work hard, I know we're going to win. I know a playoff team when I see it, and you are it."

His favorite word is "positive." Long ago he broke the world into two categories, positive and negative. He looks at things positively. When told someone has written something about his team, his first question often is "Is it positive?" Above all else, he believes a coach must remain positive, because a team basically reflects the coach's attitude.

What happens on the court—the workouts, Pitino and his staff implementing his system, the players trying to adjust—is offset, though, by the intrigue that constantly swirls around offcourt. Every time new general manager Al Bianchi arrives and huddles with Pitino, rumors fly everywhere. Is Cartwright going to the Hawks? The New York *Post* has Henderson being shopped. The Knicks are talking about Sidney Green, but Piston general manager Jack McCloskey says they are offering him nothing of any value.

"I really don't worry about trades. That's really Al's job. Sure, I have major input, but Al's the guy who has to put them together. I have to get a team that's trying to learn an entirely new system ready to play in three weeks. That's my major concern. What's that line? You have to 'dance with who brung you.' "

He is used to this. In college he had to play with the players he inherited. He is used to having to play with what everyone else considers inferior talent. It is, after all, how he made his coaching reputation. "You go into battle with who is behind you, not who you wish was behind you."

At the moment, he does not have a lot of guns behind him. Among the veteran also-rans are Jawann Oldham, Bob Thornton, and Chris McNealy. Oldham is the most intriguing of the three. While he sees himself as another Abdul-Jabbar, many of his teammates call him ALF, for the TV show *Alien Life Form*. He came over to the Knicks the year before in a deal that sent a number one draft choice to Chicago, one of the deals that ultimately cost general manager Scotty Stirling his job. He has the reputation of someone dancing to the beat of his own drum. After his first game as a Knick, he came into the locker room, took off his sneakers and socks, and walked into the shower with his uniform on. Hearing in the spring the Knicks were looking for a new general manager, Oldham said, "I can't wait for a new general manager, so I can demand to be traded."

Thornton is 6–10, slow, limited skills, hanging on the team because of his desire and work ethic. McNealy is 6–6, a great physical specimen with no discernible skills. Both are overachievers from small schools, players who never really expected to get to the NBA.

Ron Moore is a second-round draft pick, a 6–10 forward from West Virginia State who showed up at Pitino's unofficial rookie camp in Providence in late July fat and out of shape. The free agents include Ray Tolbert, a former first-round pick who played on a national championship team at Indiana. He spent last year in the Continental Basketball Association, and knows this is probably his last chance.

As for guards, veterans Henderson and Sparrow team with offguard Gerald Wilkins, younger brother of Dominique Wilkins of the Atlanta Hawks. A former second-round draft pick who averaged 19 points a game last year in his second season, he has the reputation of being selfish and undisciplined. Also here is Geoff Huston, a former NBA player trying to resurrect his career, and Leo Rautins, a former NBA fringe player who spent last year as a color man for the TV broadcasts of Syracuse University basketball games. The rookie guards are fourth-round pick Mike Morgan out of Drake, and fifth-rounder Glenn Clem from Vanderbilt.

Huston, Rautins, Clem, Morgan, Moore, and Tolbert are all survivors from the three-day rookie camp that preceded training camp. In a sense rookie camp is a world unto itself. There are no guaranteed contracts, no visible egos. This is the last roundup; everyone is fighting for their careers. If once the players all had known basketball fame, now they seem as unsure as junior high kids at their first tryout. There are no high-fives, no showy moves. At each practice the players' moods constantly swing between elation and despair.

"You root for these guys because they all play so hard, and you know how much it means to them. Your heart breaks a little bit for them because this is the last chance. This is where their dream dies."

One of the players Pitino did not invite back from rookie camp was Tony Simms, one of his first players at Boston University. At this level you have little room for sentimentality.

The Knicks' staff at these practice sessions include Pitino's two new assistants, Stu Jackson and Jim O'Brien; Brendan Malone, an assistant coach last year; Ralph Willard, a volunteer assistant; and top scout Dick McGuire and his assistant Fuzzy Levane. Stu Jackson was with Pitino the two years at Providence. O'Brien, the son-in-law of Indiana coach Jack Ramsey, was hired largely because Ramsey had called Pitino and told him he'd love to hire O'Brien himself, but it would seem like nepotism. Willard is a former high school coach at St. Dominic's, Pitino's old high school in Oyster Bay, Long Island.

The links to the Knicks past, McGuire and Levane are products of an era before the mega-salaries and agents and salary caps and the NBA on CBS, when the NBA was a barnstorming league played in cramped, drafty gyms where the locker rooms always were too small and there was never enough hot water to go around. Levane, who starred at St. John's in the Forties, grew up in New York. After the war he joined the Rochester Royals because the owner, thinking he was Jewish, thought he would appeal to the team's Jewish fans. He bounced around the league for a while, and became the Knicks' coach in 1958. Let go during the next season, he has been scouting for the Knicks, off and on, ever since. A large, friendly man with a full head of white hair, his distinguishing characteristic is an occasional stutter. Once, as the story goes, he met the Celtics' Frank Ramsey, who also had a slight stutter. "How are you, F-F-F-uzzy?" said Ramsey. "What are you, a f-f-fucking wise guy?" he snapped back.

McGuire, the older brother of former Marquette coach and current media star, Al McGuire, has been the one constant throughout the Knick turmoil; first a player, then a coach, now the Knicks' director of scouting. Until just a few years ago McGuire still played pickup games in the playgrounds, just as he used to do in the Rockaways in the Forties when the players were Irish and Italian and Jewish sons of immigrants. He coached the Knicks for a while in the Sixties before Red Holtzman took over, but McGuire never wanted to be a general manager, never wanted "to have to fire people." He was content to be a scout, to be around the game he always had loved.

When Pitino was an assistant with the Knicks, he and McGuire often played one-on-one, and got along well together. One reason is because McGuire is eminently likeable, a no-pretense basketball lifer. Another is that Pitino is comfortable around other basketball people, a legacy of all the time he spent as a kid at Five Star. Throughout training camp the coaching staff would meet in Pitino's hotel suite to plan the next day, then invariably play cards. Eventually, all the other coaches would drift off to sleep, leaving Pitino and McGuire, both insomniacs, to play gin long into the night.

"My insomnia started my first year as a head coach at Boston University. I'd wake up in the middle of the night and wouldn't be able to get back to sleep. I would lie there and think about the team, or strategies. So I started getting up and going downstairs and looking at film. Now it's long been a way of life. At Providence my assistants and I would play halfcourt basketball at midnight, then go sit in the sauna, and talk about the next day's practice. Every year when practice starts, I can feel myself getting run down physically. I'm taking milligrams of every megavitamin known to man, vitamins the size of baked potatoes."

Not only are the late-night meetings and the card playing a way to pass the time at training camp, they also are Pitino's way of bringing the staff together. "It's the same attitude I'm trying to get across to the players. We're all in this together. In this system it doesn't matter who scores, doesn't matter who stars, doesn't matter who gets the most minutes. The only thing that matters is winning, and the only way that gets accomplished is by togetherness."

One morning he sits down with Louis Orr, whom he's known since Orr was a high school player in Cincinnati, to stress this theme. "You have to have more fun in the game. You listen to Dick and Fuzzy talk about the old days, and what comes through is how much fun they had. The camaraderie, the togetherness. Are you guys going to have the same memories?"

Between practices McGuire and Malone, who first met Pitino years ago at Five Star, sit in the hotel lobby in their blue Knick warmup suits. McGuire goes off to jog his daily mile and a half around the parking lot, and Malone settles deeper into his chair. "Already things are better than they were last year," he says. "Rick has a philosophy of how the game should be played. Last year, after Hubie got fired, Bob Hill wanted to open things up offensively. He didn't like Hubie's set offense. And to keep Ewing and Wilkins happy, he gave them the ball a lot. But we were not a good defensive team. By the end of the year the big men weren't getting back. We were getting killed in transition defense. Just by getting back on defense this year, we will be a better team."

It is three-thirty and already the rookies start assembling in the lobby to go over to practice. One of them is Rautins, who was at Syracuse when Malone was an assistant there. A former number one draft choice of the Philadelphia 76ers, he told Malone the day before he had been praying Pitino wouldn't call his name when three players had been cut.

"I feel for these guys," Malone says, pointing to the rookies, "but it's hard to make a team when the guys ahead of you have guaranteed contracts."

At the night session Mark Jackson arrives with his agent, Don Cronson. The first-round draft choice from St. John's, Jackson was enthusiastically cheered by the crowd at the Felt Forum on draft day when the Knicks selected him. For Jackson it was the culmination of a playground fantasy: the local kid who gets a chance to play for the Knicks. Growing up in Queens, he went to St. John's, and his first two years he was a backup point guard on teams dominated by Chris Mullin. He came into his own his junior year, teaming with Walter Berry to lead the Redmen high in the national rankings. His senior year, with Berry off to the NBA, it became Jackson's team and he emerged as one of the top-rated point guards in the country. Though some scouts thought him as a step slow, McGuire and Malone liked his ability to pass the ball.

Jackson has already rejected the Knicks' initial offer of a

one-year contract for the NBA minimum, $75,000. He is a victim of the salary cap, the NBA's complicated structure for making every team live within a certain collective salary limit. The Knicks know he is worth far more than the minimum. Cronson certainly knows it. As of now, though, there is no more money available, so Jackson is a holdout. Pitino, who has known Jackson since he was a camper at Five Star, walks over to him. Concerned that he is missing too much training camp, he's invited him to come and watch. "I am not the kind of coach who will hold it against you for holding out, but I don't want you to fall too far behind."

Dressed in a shiny blue warmup suit, Jackson stands to one side and watches the Knicks go through their drills. At 6–3, with a strong upper body, thick neck, large head, hair cropped close to his scalp, he looks like a linebacker. A few minutes later McGuire comes over, extending his hand to Cronson.

"I hope you're not angry with us," Cronson says.

McGuire waves his hand. "You have to do what you have to do." McGuire's been around the NBA long enough to know business is business.

Veteran Trent Tucker, also a holdout, sits in one corner of the gym in a blue warmup suit. He is an outstanding long-range shooter who averaged 11 points a game last year, but has the reputation of a one-dimensional player and someone who put a silent knife into the backs of Hubie Brown and Bob Hill.

Veteran Louis Orr, recovering from disc surgery over the summer, trots on a far court, slowly working his way back in shape. Six–eight and thin enough to be known as both Biafra and Ghandi, his production slumped to just seven points a game last year. In the last year of his contract and trying to come back from a serious injury, his career is in jeopardy.

The night sessions are open to the public, and every night there are a few hundred people. Sitting on the first row of bleachers are twenty or so high school and college assistant coaches with clipboards. Every session they take notes, never talking, watching what Pitino is doing: acolytes sitting at the feet of the professor, as if basketball success can be franchised like some fried-chicken recipe. When Indiana won the national title in 1976 with a motion offense, it seemed every college team in the country began using a motion offense. When Villanova won the national title in 1985 with a matchup zone, everyone used a matchup zone. Now everyone is thinking fullcourt pressure, and the young assistant coaches are here to learn Pitino's blueprint.

The first official intra-squad game is Tuesday night, and about one thousand people show up. So do most of the Knicks beat writers and Peter Vecsey, the *Post*'s NBA columnist. Vecsey is the godfather of the NBA writers in New York; his NBA column is full of notes, rumors about trades, all indelibly stamped by a stiletto-sharp wit that spares no one. In his column Cartwright is Billy Idle, Cummings is Shortcummings. Walker, known at Kentucky as Sky Walker, is soon to become Street Walker. A former beat writer for the old New York Nets, Vecsey is universally regarded as having the best sources in the NBA, and his column is the first thing the NBA fraternity turns to each morning to see what's on the grapevine. As Pitino says, "Peter is very funny and entertaining until he's talking about you."

This is the first time the Pitino system is on display. It's quickly obvious Ewing is better than the year before: thinner, more active, more outward enthusiasm. He is called Beast by his teammates, and he has been playing like one in camp. "I'm delighted with Patrick. He's turning out to be one of the favorite players I've ever coached. He's so different than what I had been warned about. I'll tell you, my biggest concern in taking this job was what some people said about Patrick."

On the flip side, Kenny Walker is struggling. A tall, wiry man whose face is dominated by a goatee, he plays the

entire scrimmage with not much to show for it. He seems
tentative, unsure, nothing like the fifth player selected in
the 1986 draft. A post-up player in college, he's now being
asked to be a small forward, someone who must play on the
perimeter, and he's like a stranger in a strange land. Right
from the beginning things hadn't gone right. Shortly after he
was drafted, Bernard King said he didn't think Walker was
a very good pick. When King got hurt again in training
camp, Walker was suddenly thrust into the role of the new
Bernard, and was no way ready to handle that. He was a
rookie joining a bad team, whose coach would be fired
shortly into the season. He's also had to adjust to New
York, light-years away from the rural Georgia town he grew
up in, a town with two traffic lights. Some people in the
Knick organization believe Walker would be a better player
outside of New York, away from the boos and the unfulfilled expectations. Pitino wants him to gain ten pounds.
"We're going to show him some of Ron Moore's restaurants," he quips.

Outside of Ewing, the two most impressive players in the
scrimmage are perhaps Morgan and Clem. Morgan is the
most active in the press. "He plays the game like Joe Frazier
is in the ring with him, and it's like he's going to play pro
basketball or give up on life." Clem is a textbook example
of how to play the game. He passes, hits the open jumper,
blocks two of Gerald Wilkins' shots.

"He's the only one who knows how to play the game, and
he can't play in the league," mutters Howard Garfinkel. It's
the Garf's second trip to training camp. On his first, he
walked in, took one quick look at the Knicks doing their
various drills, and said, in obvious glee, "This is just like
Five Star. This is all very familiar to me."

The next morning Kevin Kernan writes in the *Post*, that
if Pitino really believes Cartwright should get a standing
ovation, then "this team is in more trouble than anyone
thought. Why should Bill Cartwright get a standing ovation?

Because he made more than two million the past two years?
Because he played 60 games in three years? Because he's
finally in shape after eight years in the NBA? Pitino can't
afford to fall into the same trap that cost Hubie Brown his
job. It's time to face facts. Cartwright is 30 years old. The
Knicks are going nowhere in his playing lifetime. Get rid of
the excess baggage before it's too late."

Welcome home, Rick.

"I didn't see it," Pitino says when someone brings the quote
to his attention. "That's why I don't want to read the tabloids.
I don't want to know what Kevin Kernan says, or what anyone of them say. But it's obvious that I don't agree with him
about Billy Cartwright. Every time Billy's been healthy, this
franchise has won. When he's been hurt, it's struggled."

One of the concerns after the scrimmage is Walker, who
threw several passes away. In one of the first drills the next
morning Pitino has Walker on the wing, guarded by the
smaller Geoff Huston, passing the ball to the rest of the
players who, not guarded by anyone, cut to the foul line and
take jump shots. "You do so many things well, Kenny, that
when you learn how to do this you will be terrific."

It is quickly evident, though, that Walker is having diffi-
culty even making these practice passes to teammates who
are not being guarded. He constantly holds the ball over his
head, like some kid in a high school gym class unfamiliar
with basketball. Virtually every third pass he throws Huston
deflects. More than that, Walker keeps shuffling his feet, an
obvious violation.

"Kenny, keep your pivot foot still," says Pitino.

The drill continues. Walker still keeps shuffling his feet.

"Kenny," says Pitino, an edge in his voice. "You can't
move your pivot foot."

Walker looks confused.

Pitino pauses, and motions for Brendan Malone and Huston
to go over to the side court and show Kenny Walker, a
former All-American at Kentucky, what a pivot foot is.

October 15

Minutes before the Knicks are to play the New Jersey Nets, Al Bianchi stands in the runway outside the locker rooms in the Brendan Byrne Arena in the Meadowlands Complex, and says the Knicks have just traded Oldham to Sacramento for a second-round pick in 1988. Bianchi is in a brown suit and carrying a tan briefcase, face tanned, wire-rim glasses, wavy gray hair. "The whole thing is playing time, and with Cartwright and Patrick he is not going to play."

"What about the fact that Scotty Stirling gave away a first-round pick for Oldham, and now you've just traded him for a second?" he is asked.

"I'm not here to throw stones at anyone. I'm here to get this team in shape. Get us under the cap. Get Mark Jackson in camp. Get Trent Tucker in camp. Get everyone in camp and start showing progress."

This is also the first exhibition game for the star-crossed Nets, who have never recovered from losing Julius Erving to the 76ers. The Nets have tried in vain to create an identity in northern New Jersey, an area where all the old allegiances are with the Knicks. A month into the season they will have the worst record in the league, media star Pearl Washington will be the subject of trade rumors, and Dave Wohl will be the first NBA coach to be fired.

Rory Sparrow has a sore knee, and sits at the end of the bench with Louis Orr. The Knicks start Ewing, Cummings, Walker, Henderson, and Wilkins. The Nets counter with its veteran frontline of Mike Gminski, Buck Williams, and Orlando Woolwridge, with Pearl and rookie Dennis Hopson in the backcourt. From the outset the Knicks are in fullcourt pressure. In a gray suit and yellow tie, Pitino kneels on a towel in front of the bench. Early in the game Washington gets trapped and throws the ball away. "Did you see it?" yells Pitino, turning around and addressing his bench. "Did you see it? They can't make a pass."

He substitutes after a few minutes, the players entering and leaving in a revolving door. All the while Pitino paces the sideline, constantly coaching, criticizing, encouraging. "Deflection . . . deflection . . . deflection." "Get a hand on it . . . deflection." Ron Moore goes to the foul line and throws up two shots that miss badly. "Tomorrow, Ron Moore gets forty-five minutes of extra foul shooting," Pitino says to his assistants.

The game is ragged. The Knicks press constantly but miss numerous defensive assignments. Still, the pressure bothers the Nets, whose forwards have to come up near midcourt to receive the ball from the guards being pressured in the backcourt. The result is they quickly are out of their of offense; the game is being played at Pitino's pace. Early in the second quarter the Knicks are down four and he calls a timeout. "We have gotten every loose ball except one. Don't lose any. That's a pride thing. We should have every-one on the floor."

Two minutes later he takes Moore out. "This is the first time I'm pissed off in the NBA, and it's all because of you," he yells as Moore sits down on the bench, the game still going on. "If you don't start to hustle, you can get on a bus tomorrow and go home. I don't care if you miss free throws. I don't care if you miss shots. Hustle. Run. *Do something*. Make something happen. You're playing like you're a twenty-year veteran."

He says all this out of the side of his mouth while still watching the game. It is a tactic he often uses. Instead of chastising so that people can see, he gives the appearance of a coach clapping his hands and being positive.

The game is tied at the half, but the Knicks quickly start falling behind in the third quarter. "Got to hang tough," he says in another timeout. "Adversity. Here it is. Fight through it." But with three minutes to play, they are down 20. "They were ready to surrender," he says pointedly, "but you were the ones who surrendered. You surrendered to fatigue."

The arena is nearly empty as the clock runs out. A guy in the front row yells, "Hey, Rick, it's going to be a long year."

"That's right," Pitino yells back. "We're going right through to May and then right through to the playoffs."

But on this night in the Meadowlands the playoffs seem as far away as the dark side of the moon.

October 23

On Friday morning, St. John's coach, Lou Carnesecca, and assistant Brian Mahoney sit in one corner. They are here to see Mark Jackson, who signed quickly after Oldham's departure opened up some money. The Knicks have beaten the Washington Bullets in an exhibition in Richmond, beaten the Rockets in Houston, and lost to the world-champion Lakers by three in the Forum. In the Laker game, the Knicks substituted 14 times in the first quarter, committed 46 fouls, and pressed the entire game. Afterward, Laker coach Pat Riley told Pitino that he wasn't exactly sure what it was, but he had never before seen anything like it.

"I wasn't sure if it was a compliment or what," Pitino says.

A wire-service story reports, "It's a tossup which is a more effective way to get in shape: a week at Paris Island or a night against the New York Knicks." The Lakers' Mychal Thompson says, "The Knicks put more pressure on you than an IRS audit."

Pitino also isn't sure about his team. "I like their attitude and their effort, but we need a power forward, and Kenny Walker isn't ready at small forward. I hope Cartwright will be traded to give us the scoring forward we need. Originally, I didn't want to press during the exhibition season, but before the first game against the Nets I decided that to be competitive we had to press. Right now we're getting by on hard work, but to be competitive once the regular season starts, we're going to have to be much better."

Running up and down on the SUNY court again, the Knicks are working on the press. The whistle blows, a new team comes in. Ron Moore and several others start heading for the sidelines. "Ron, you don't rest anymore," shouts Pitino. "So no one comes in for Ron again. You're staying in the game until you get in shape."

The practice continues, as intense as ever. Pitino is constantly on top of things. "Our rule is to trap the dribbler." "We're fouling too much. The Lakers went to the line 66 times." "We don't want that kind of foul." "Pick it up, come on, come on." "Swing the ball." The players are in constant motion as the morning wears on, showing all the intensity of players in a college practice.

At one point Rory Sparrow, under pressure in the backcourt, floats a pass that goes out-of-bounds. "See?" says Pitino excitedly. "You had a lousy press and a lousy trap, which is fine because that's going to happen, but you had pressure on the ball and he threw it out-of-bounds." Then he turns to the offense, his voice lower, harder. "Everyone look at me. Especially Rory and Gerald. No more of those passes. Come hard with the dribble and throw a bounce pass."

It is nearing noon; they have been practicing hard since ten. The players are in two lines, one at one end of the court, one at the other. Malone stands near one foul line holding a ball, O'Brien at the other. The players collectively have to make 85 layups in two minutes. With their off hand. The whistle blows and they start, each player all out. By the second minute they all are struggling. They finish and bend over, hands on their knees, sucking for air.

"Ron Moore, don't slow up," yells Pitino. "Keep running. Faster. Faster." Moore roars in for a layup like a runaway truck, throws it up with his left hand, and misses.

Pitino blows his whistle, the players stop.

"How many?" he asks Malone and O'Brien. "Eighty four? You missed by one. Do it again."

You can almost hear the players groan.

It's a drill Pitino's been doing for years. Not only is it conditioning, it also is designed to promote team unity. Every player has a vested interest in his teammates' performance. Every player also has a responsibility to go all out on the drill, since he lets his teammates down if he doesn't.

The players start clapping rhythmically, urging each other on. Everyone is visibly tired now. Cummings looks exhausted.

"Faster," yells Pitino. "Faster. Don't let up. Faster . . . Faster." "Don't let up." "*Don't let up.*"

Again they fail to make 85 off-hand layups in two minutes.

"Do it again," says Pitino.

When they fail to make it again, he changes it to 45 in one minute. This time they make it.

Afterward Pitino talks to Fred Kerber of the *News*. Kerber asks about the Knicks' proclivity to foul. Pitino says it doesn't worry him. Although certainly he wants to avoid excessive fouls, fouling gets other teams out of their rhythm. He says he wished the Knicks were more "athletic" in certain areas.

"How about Cartwright to Atlanta?"

"The deal with Atlanta is dead, but Cartwright is playing fantastic basketball. His stock is rising. We might get two starters for him instead of one. Billy has a great deal of pride and wants to win, and when he's been healthy the team has always won. When Billy's gone down, the team always has lost. Right now the center position is the strength of our team, and what we should build upon. Next year's draft will provide us with the power forward and the small forward we need."

A few feet away Gerald Wilkins sits in a chair. He arrived in New York two years earlier virtually unknown, a second-round draft choice from Tennessee-Chatanooga. Not that he was any stranger to anonymity. Growing up in his brother Dominique's large and overpowering shadow, he was ignored even in his own family. Their world revolved around Dominique's games, Dominique's career.

The family lived in a Baltimore housing project when Gerald was a young child. He was the third of Gertrude Baker's eight children, nearly four years younger than Dominique. The summer before his sophomore year in high school, Dominique was visiting his father in Wilmington, North Carolina, when the local coach convinced Dominique to come play high school ball. The one hitch was his mother had to live there too. So Gertrude Baker moved everyone to North Carolina. Three years later, when "Nique" signed with Georgia, she moved everyone to Atlanta.

Through all of this, Gerald's fate was dependent on his older brother's talent. He didn't even like basketball. Instead he played ping pong. He didn't start playing in earnest until he got to Southwest Atlanta High School. By that time Dominique was starring at Georgia, and Gerald was playing high school ball in obscurity.

"Dominique was the number one guy," he told the *Sporting News*. "I was playing high school ball literally across the street from our house, and Mom and the family almost never came to see me. It was tough."

Having nowhere else to go when he got out of high school, he went to a small junior college in Missouri, then to Tennessee-Chatanooga, about one hundred miles from Atlanta. Two years later, the 48th player picked in the draft, he actually made the Knicks, sneaking up on everybody, including his family.

He is an exuberant person: talkative, easy with the media, with a proclivity for losing things. Tim Walsh, the assistant trainer, is forever trailing after him on the road, finding his wallet, his bracelet, whatever. Shortly into training camp Wilkins had asked Pitino if he would call him Dougie instead of Gerald, since one of his favorites was rap singer Doug E. Fresh. So Dougie it has become.

"The practices are harder than last year," he said, an ice pack on his left knee, "but we need it. Need every bit of it. I asked to come out three times against Houston, and I've never done that before. Believe me, at the end of these practices you are tired."

"Do you like it?"

Wilkins looks up, his eyes twinkling. "Last year we came down and ran power left and power right. Now everyone gets their shots."

It is a reference to Hubie Brown, the departed coach, who employed a structured offense, known in the game as a halfcourt offense. It's also a delicate subject. A couple of years ago Hubie was one of the coaching gurus, another obsessed coach in the macho mold, a basketball Patton; one of the coaches America loves, one part Marine, one part Vince Lombardi, one part genius, one part bluster. Put those overpaid, pampered athletes in their place, take the charge.

There long has been a certain mystique around Hubie Brown. It started in Atlanta, when he took a bunch of no-name Hawks and made them play defense as if someone was trying to steal their paychecks. Making it better was that he swore like a trooper, and talked as if he were a basketball version of Jonas Salk. After every game he would read the stat sheet to the media, and if you didn't pinch yourself you would have thought someone was explaining the Pythagorean theorem.

But when it started to go sour for Hubie in New York it unraveled in a hurry. He began being buried in the tabloids, for everything from his unimaginative offense to his decision to play Ewing and Cartwright together. Mostly, though, he got buried because he didn't win. So what if Cartwright and King had gotten hurt? So what if his team still was well prepared, still played as hard as anyone in the league? He once had been billed as a coaching king, and now he was just another coach of a bad team, trying to get blood out of a stone.

In one sense he was a victim of the incredibly high expectations that surrounded Ewing's arrival. He was supposed to have come in and wake up the echoes, turn the Garden back to the days when Willis was in the middle, Clyde was in the backcourt and Woody Allen was in the front row. That hadn't happened. Ewing had missed 54 games in two years, and as Hubie was quick to point out, "If he missed 54 games, how many practices do you think he missed?"

In another sense, Hubie became a victim of his own myth. Shortly into the 1986–87 season, the Knicks were 4–12. Rumors were swirling everywhere that he soon would be gone. Hubie was fired, kind of like having the body die after it had been on the respirator for months.

But he didn't leave without a certain legacy.

Pitino first had met Hubie at Five Star years before. "He was a guy I said hello to once a year for fifteen years. But I didn't really know him. And when he first offered me the job, I wasn't sure I wanted to leave college. I saw it not so much as a job change than as a career change. But Hubie convinced me the experience would make me a better coach. And it did. Hubie was extremely well organized and I learned a lot from him about game preparation and man-to-man defense.

"The first real staff meeting we had was on the beach near his house in South Carolina. It was early September, there was no one on the beach. It was me, Richie Adubato, the other assistant, and Hubie. He went down by the water where the sand was hard and drew the dimensions of a basketball court in the sand with sticks. Then, in our bathing suits, we walked through Hubie's offensive sets.

"Things were never dull with Hubie. About a hundred times a year you'd say to yourself, 'I can't believe this.' One night we're in the Boston Garden and Ron Cavenall, whose averaging something like 2.2 points a game, makes a nice move, misses the layup, slams his hand into the basket support in frustration, and then doesn't get back on defense. Hubie jumps up and turns to the bench. 'Why is he so surprised? He's averaging two points a game. Why is he so shocked?'

"Another time we're in the Garden and this guy is killing Hubie behind the bench. All over him. And this goes on the entire game. So finally Hubie gets up, turns to him behind the bench, and says in that booming, bellowing voice of his, 'I know what you're doing. I know you can go home and act like an asshole. But that wouldn't be any fun. Because there everyone knows you're an asshole.'

"Then one time we're in Indiana and this nice, jovial man comes in the locker room and introduces himself to Hubie. He says what a wonderful coach Hubie is, and what an honor it is to meet him, and on and on. After he leaves Hubie says to me, 'What a nice man. How nice of him to come in and say things like that.' So we play the game and we get beat in the final seconds and Hubie is beside himself. And the same jovial man comes in the locker room and tries to make light of the game, how it was just one game and all that. Hubie, who's not even looking at him, says, 'For openers I didn't think it was that funny, see you later.' I thought to myself, This relationship didn't last very long.

"But Hubie was at his best with the press. One night we get beat and Hubie goes into the interview room and gives twenty-five reasons why we lost. Among those reasons he gives six reasons why Bernard King was off his game. So some writer asks, 'Why do you think you lost the game?' Hubie says, 'Where have you been for the past fifteen minutes? I just did a whole thing on that.'

"'What did you think of Bernard's performance?' the writer then asked. Hubie gives him that look. 'What newspaper are you working for? Because if you don't get here on time you can wait out in the hall and not bother me with all these ridiculous questions.'

"With Hubie it always was an adventure, because you never knew what was coming next. But the one thing you always respected about Hubie is he told you exactly the way he felt to a fault. But I probably learned more basketball around him than anyone else I could have been around for two years."

October 27

Tonight is the first exhibition game in the Garden, and it doesn't take the New York crowd long to voice their displeasure at the new Knicks. Both Walker and Bob Thornton, starting for an injured Pat Cummings, are booed in the pregame introductions. Cartwright is roundly booed when he enters the game after a few minutes. The Knicks quickly throw up a couple of bricks, and the chants start: "We want Bernard . . . We want Bernard." They roll down across the court like a soundtrack to the game.

"Do you believe this?" says publicist John Cirillo one of the most positive people about the new Knick regime, a believer from the beginning. "Four minutes and they start booing. I was afraid of this. Everything has been going so well."

The night before the Knicks beat the Phoenix Suns in Miami by four, but again they had shot poorly, and afterward Pitino expressed the need for more outside shooting. "We can't go on like this." This is even more evident tonight when the Knicks continue to misfire from the perimeter, and fall behind the Rockets by 12. Pitino calls a timeout and a cacaphony of boos chase the Knicks to the bench.

"Bring back Bernard . . . We want Bernard."

The Knicks are down 20 at the half, and the boos chase them off the court and into the locker room.

"Where's Bernard? . . . We want Bernard."

"Nice crowd, huh," said Pitino before the third period begins.

Again, Pitino is nonstop motion on the sideline, exhorting his players, coaching every play, urging his players to keep the pressure on. Gradually, the Knicks begin cutting into the Rocket lead, spurred by Ewing, now down to 12. Referee Tom Woods runs by the Knick bench after missing a call. "You're a better official than that, Tom," says Pitino.

"I've had enough, Rick," says Woods on the way by.

"I've had enough too," yells Pitino, following him up the sideline. "You're killing us. You're goddamn killing us."

Woods gives him a technical and Pitino retreats back to the bench. The Knicks eventually lose by 16, but one thing is apparent: there is a lot of resentment against the Knicks. Bianchi and Pitino can talk all they want about being patient and building for the future, but to the Garden crowd that's all hollow words and empty promises. Their patience seems to last as long as it takes for the Knicks to fall behind. Tonight that took four minutes.

"At the end of the first quarter we knew we were going to get booed," says Wilkins. "It's tough on the younger guys, but I've been here before, so it really doesn't bother me. The fans are going to be the way they are. They are not going to be with us when we lose and I don't blame them. We have to come out and redeem ourselves. Prove we aren't the same old Knick players."

He is standing in the Knick locker room, a narrow aisle with orange lockers on both sides. The rug is blue. The walls are white. On one end are photographs: a large one of Trent Tucker jumping into the arms of Ewing, a freeze-frame of happier times. Smaller ones of Willis Reed in his white Knick uniform; Bill Bradley, complete with long sideburns, jumping into Reed's arms in 1973.

Nearby is Trent Tucker, no stranger to New York crowds. He had grown up in Flint, Michigan, where he learned to play indoors rather than learning the game in the playgrounds as most city kids do. The result is he played a "white" game, based on outside shooting, rather than a "black" game, based on jumping and taking the ball to the hoop with style. After starring at Minnesota he had been the sixth pick in the 1981 draft, but when he was introduced at the Felt Forum on draft day, on what was supposed to be the happiest day of his basketball life, he had been booed by Knick fans not happy with their team's choice.

Welcome to New York.

In front of Tucker is the shower room. To his left, through a door, is a larger lounge area with red plaid rugs, light blue walls, and brown leather couches. At a table in the corner the assistant coaches huddle over their charts, already starting to break the game down.

Pitino already has met with the press in a small room across the hall, "I told the team at halftime that there obviously was a lot of adversity and negatives surrounding the team, and the only way to alleviate them is to win. The fans have a right to feel this way because the Knicks have only won 24 games in each of the past three years, and that until we start to win we can expect to hear boos."

Pitino calls Glen Clem into a hallway, and tells him he is waived. Clem comes out and sits down on a couch, a far-away look in his eyes. He grew up in Alabama, the son of a coach, and with his blond hair and smooth features looks like he stepped out of the movie *Hoosiers*, as All-American as a kid shooting baskets in the backyard in the dying twilight. Not only had he been forced to play underneath at 6–5 at Vanderbilt, he also had played in a slow-down offense, only averaging five points a game. But he had impressed Pitino with his savvy. If he had come to New York as a fifth-round draft choice, in his heart knowing he was here on a wing and a prayer, he had stayed around for a while. Tomorrow he will go home to Alabama, maybe try and hook on with a CBA team. His time in camp has convinced him he can play in the league. It's too early to give up on the dream. Gerald Henderson comes over to say good-bye.

While Clem sits on the couch, Pitino calls Mike Morgan into the hallway. He too is being waived. Morgan comes out and sits down on a couch, his eyes rimmed with tears. He had been the surprise of the camp, maybe the best in the press, always had played as there were no tomorrow. All the coaches had loved his attitude, his desire, his athletic ability. Everyone had hoped he could somehow make it.

But he was another "tweener," too small to be a small forward, not a good enough handler or shooter to play in the backcourt. More than anything, he seemed to be a victim of a lack of basic fundamentals, a deficiency he had compensated for during rookie camp with his great desire, but didn't seem to be able to overcome in the exhibition games as the level of competition rose. He was an example of what Bianchi told the staff during rookie camp, that the things you like about a certain player in rookie camp are often nullified as the competition gets better. Still, Morgan had his moments, and now as he sits on the couch, the dream shattered, he seems lost, almost bewildered.

Malone and Dick McGuire come over to say good-bye and wish him well. All around him the players are getting ready to go outside to the bus. They are going to a hotel near LaGuardia Airport for the night. In the early morning they will fly to Houston, then bus for three hours to Lake Charles, Louisiana, where, according to the whims of the NBA preseason schedule, they will play an exhibition game against the Detroit Pistons. So what if the same Pistons had played the first game tonight in the Garden? Who ever said the NBA made any sense?

Clem and Morgan will not be going. Their schedule has just ended.

3 | The Sorrows of November

People think the NBA is glamorous, but it's not. Not at all. It's never getting enough sleep and looking at film half the night and then getting an early wakeup call. Then flying somewhere else and doing it all over again.

Baseball and football are heaven compared to the NBA. Any sport where you come into a town and spend a couple of days seems the life of Riley to me. In the NBA you aren't in town long enough to have a cup of coffee. You're always watching film. You have just enough time to set your VCR and TV up. You always look forward to coming home.

That was one of my biggest surprises when I first came into the league four years ago. I followed the New York Knickerbockers when they had Clyde Frazier and Earl Monroe. Those guys had great charisma. From the way they played to the clothes they wore, everything about them was larger than life. The Knicks were a study in contrast. Frazier and Monroe were flashy. Bradley and DeBusschere were the blue-collar guys. Reed was the stately guy in the middle. I was an avid Knick fan then, and my whole conception of the Knicks and the NBA was that it was glamorous.

In my first two years as an assistant with the Knicks, I found that it is work. Hard work. Hubie always gave his assistants as much responsibility as they could handle. Hubie's organizational skills are incredible. Even in midseason Hubie would distribute ten-twelve-page scouting reports to the players. He wanted his players to think they were the most prepared team in the league. Even if they only retained ten percent, we were in good shape. Also, Hubie had everything timed down to the second. At halftime I was allotted exactly two and a half minutes to go over my chart, and the other assistant, Richie Adubato, had equal time for things he had charted.

My experience as an assistant coach raised my respect for pro coaches about one hundred percent. Until I got in the league I was your typical college coach who had all the traditional stereotypes about the NBA. I really didn't like the pro game. I felt that the players were all spoiled athletes who played no defense. The only important part of the pro game was the last five minutes. But Hubie set me straight. He said I could learn game preparation in the NBA and the greatest man-to-man offenses I had ever seen.

NBA coaches have to coach under constant mental fatigue. They pick up a newspaper, and they are going to be knocked. They have to make so many moves in the course of a game. And they have little time to prepare for the next game.

People sometimes have a misconception that the players aren't putting out one hundred percent. But on any given night, fifty percent of the players are playing with nagging injuries. Either that, or they're tired from too much traveling. How much we press is determined on fatigue. If we feel we are the more rested team, we press a lot. If not, we play more halfcourt defense. That's the great X factor in the pros: who is tired.

With a college player you tell him to run through the wall, and he says how many seconds do I have to do it in? With professional players you sit them down and tell them why it's important to run through that wall, and, if they do it, how much money they can make doing it.

The glamour for me is in the games. That's my high: the games and walking into the different arenas. I love walking

into the Boston Garden and thinking about all the great
players and great games that have been played there. That
is glamorous to me.

But the life isn't.

✝✝✝✝✝✝✝✝✝✝

November 5–6

After practice at SUNY, Pitino drives over in his new
gray BMW to the nearby Arrowwood Hotel in Rye. A
dealer had delivered the car to him to use for the year. As
compensation, he had shot a BMW commercial a couple of
weeks before underneath the elevated tracks in Queens. It
was supposed to take a half hour to shoot, but every time
the camera began rolling, someone would drive by and yell,
"Bring back Bernard," or "Yo, Rick, I won money on you
at Providence," or "Go back to college." The commercial
took three hours to shoot. "That's New York," Pitino says.

It's become one of the overriding themes. A home team
that gets booed in the Garden? That's New York. A coach
on the phone for two hours a day with reporters? That's
New York. Everything is speeded up, like a record spinning
on 78? That's New York. This unique city has a life of its
own. Its tentacles are everywhere, changing everything.

In the locker room at the Arrowhead, where he's about to
play racquetball with Jim O'Brien, he describes the Garden
crowd at Saturday night's exhibition game against Indiana.
Starting with the national anthem, there had been the inevitable "We want Bernard" chants, complete with heckling of
both Bianchi and Pitino. "Go back to college, Pitino," one
guy directly behind the Knick bench kept yelling. His voice
seemed to resound through the Garden as if boomed through
a loudspeaker. "Go back to college, you bum."

"The players got booed in the introductions. Al got it. I
got it. If the market goes bad, come out and boo the
Knicks. If you hate your life, come out and boo the Knicks.

It's scary. I told the players the only way to teach people how to cheer is to get up and show them how. I couldn't believe the vulgarity. My kids wanted to come to the game, but that's out of the question until we start winning.

"My wife is really down. She thinks back to Providence and how positive it was there. How much fun it was to go to the Providence Civic Center to the games. How different the atmosphere was. I just tell her that things will get better, that winning will change all that."

The Knicks are due to fly back this afternoon to Detroit, where they will open the season the next day in the Silverdome against the Pistons, the team picked by many to unseat the Celtics in the Eastern Division. Training camp is officially over, the Knicks have finished 5–3 in the preseason, and an article in the *Daily News* says the Knicks could be one of the NBA's dark horses. "But I know the preseason record is a basketball version of fool's gold. We won games on hustle, not talent. There is too little margin for error. Still, I always try to be optimistic. We haven't had one bad practice yet, and that's unheard-of in the pros."

The Knicks finally have obtained Sidney Green, ending a three-week soap opera that included Green at one point saying he was going to take advantage of his no-cut contract and stay in Detroit just for spite. Green is happy to be with the Knicks. He says all the right things: the past is past, and he just wants to be a part of making the Knicks great again. As a kid from Brooklyn, he used to sit high in the Garden, in the section known as Blue Heaven, and watch the Knicks. "Coming back to play in New York is a dream come true." His price to Detroit was Ron Moore and a second-round draft choice.

Green also knows Pitino from the Five Star basketball camp. "I remember him as being real intense. He used to have this drill where you carried around wooden blocks. We used to go to sleep dreaming about that drill."

The signing of Green officially ends the Bernard King era

in New York, though even King said he knew it was over for him the day the Knicks made their original offer for Green. At the time King said that in his heart he always would be a Knick, but that he harbored no ill feelings.

If the Knicks were at the level of Boston or Atlanta and needed a proven scorer, they would have felt different about King. But now they were just trying to be respectable, trying to go young. King didn't fit into their long-range plans, not with his demands of a multiyear deal at his old salary base of $874,000. King also hadn't made too many friends in the upper levels of Gulf & Western when he essentially had been in seclusion in the two years he was rehabilitating his knee. There also is the feeling that King belongs to the past, is the most obvious symbol of it.

"It was the most difficult decision of my coaching career. The one great thing about Bernard is his competitiveness. He always comes to play, whether it's against the Celtics or the Kings. It was extra tough for me because I have such great memories of Bernard when I was an assistant here. Even if he comes back only eighty percent, he is still better than most of the players in the league. But I can't gamble on his knee holding up for 82 games in a pressing style. Dr. Scott, who operated on him, says there's no telling if he can come back. No one has ever had this kind of operation before, and Bernard is now in uncharted waters. We can't have that. We need consistency above all.

"The Knicks have been on a roller coaster the past few years. The most important stories have been the ones that took place off the court, not on it. The first thing we have to do is bring in some stability. Bernard is another ride on the roller coaster because you can't know what is going to happen to him.

"People don't understand that this style of play would be suicide for Bernard. He'd play one year and his career would be over. Going to Washington is the best thing for him and us. I would have had to change all my beliefs for one player."

King already has become the property of the Washington Bullets at $2.2 million for two years. He also had 33 points in his first exhibition game. The *Daily News* will periodically run a "Bernard Watch" throughout the season. All year Bernard King will be a ghost in an out-of-town box score.

Trent Tucker also has signed. To make room for him, the Knicks waive Geoff Huston. Leo Rautins also has been waived, and Bob Thornton placed on the injured list.

An hour later Bianchi snaps on his seat belt on the runway at the Westchester Airport. "I've learned one thing from the two games in the Garden. You better be tough to play in New York. If a guy's not tough, he can't play here."

On the flight Pitino and Stu Jackson lament the fact that if they had stayed at Providence, the Friars would have had a monster recruiting year. It is Jackson's third year with Pitino. When Pitino first got the Providence job, one of his first priorities was hiring an assistant coach, preferably a black assistant coach. At the time Jackson was an assistant at Washington State. His career had been an odyssey of a type not uncommon in the world of basketball. He had grown up in Reading, Pennsylvania, had been one of the most sought-after high school players in the East, in addition to being a good enough student to be recruited by Princeton. He went instead to Oregon and became one of Dick Harter's kamikaze kids in the mid-Seventies. After a knee injury curtailed his career, he transferred to Seattle University and graduated in 1979. He then went to work for IBM, based in Los Angeles.

While at IBM he helped out Oregon in Southern California in his spare time: made a phone call to a potential recruit, saw a kid play, picked up a kid at the airport when he returned from visiting Oregon. He was keeping his hand in, as if the game was a lover he couldn't forget.

Ironically, he was lured into this by none other than Jim O'Brien, now his colleague with the Knicks. Back then

O'Brien was an assistant at Oregon. They had known each other from when Jackson was being recruited by St. Joe's in Philadelphia and O'Brien was a player there. So throughout the two years Jackson was selling for IBM, O'Brien always was telling him he should get into coaching. In 1981 he finally decided to. He had made a big sale for IBM, had enough money to get by for a year, and went back to Oregon as the graduate assistant coach, a lowly paid, entry-level position on the Oregon coaching staff. The next year O'Brien left to become the head coach of Wheeling, a small West Virginia school, and Jackson became a full-fledged assistant coach. The next year he went to Washington State.

As fate would have it, Pitino and Jackson had a mutual acquaintance and one day Pitino called him back after Jackson had left five or six messages. "We talked for forty-five minutes," remembers Jackson, "and then he said, 'I like what I've heard, but I can't justify flying you in here for an interview because I've just spent too much money interviewing seven people I know. I can't justify spending more on someone I don't know.' I was going to Los Angeles to recruit anyway, and I found out I could fly East for something like $250. I called Rick back and told him I would pay my own way. He says fine. So I take the red-eye and meet him in the Penta Hotel in New York, across the street from the Garden. We talked for two hours, then we go to P.J. Clarke's. All through lunch Rick's on the phone. Now understand, I've been up all night. Rick finally gets off. He says, 'I've been on the road for weeks, and I have to take my wife to the theater or she'll never speak to me again. But I'm afraid you'll have to go up to Providence and speak to the athletic director.' I tell him that I'm still recruiting for Washington State, and I have to be back in Los Angeles the next day. He tells me not to worry about it, that I'll be there.

"I'm all set to go to Providence and Rick says, 'Wait, I'll drive you to Providence, but first I have to call Joanne and tell her. No, on second thought, I'll call her from the road because she won't be able to talk me out of it.' It takes us nearly four hours to get to Providence and meet Lou Lamoriello. Every time Lou asks me a question Rick answers for me, like he's assuring Lou not to worry about it. I don't know what's going on. I've been up all night, and now it's nine-thirty the next night, I know there are no flights out of Providence and how am I going to be in Los Angeles the next day? Rick says, 'I'll drive you to Newark; there's a People's Express at two-thirty.' So we start off and he drives ninety miles per hour down the Connecticut Turnpike and into New York, but he takes a wrong turn and we end up near Shea Stadium in Flushing Meadow. Here we are, stuck in this big parking lot and we can't find an exit. We keep riding around and around looking for a way to get out, and since I don't know him I can't say anything.

"Finally we get to Newark in the nick of time. He buys me a ticket, and says good luck. I'm walking onto the plane after twenty-six of the most grueling hours in my life, and thinking, Here's this guy telling me 'good luck.' I couldn't believe it.

"Two days later he called and said I had the job."

In the Detroit airport the players congregate near the entrance, large men who cannot walk anywhere without stares. The bus scheduled to take them to the Northfield Hilton an hour away hasn't arrived, so everyone waits. Forty-five minutes later the bus is still not there. Everyone gets into cabs.

"Welcome to the NBA," said Pitino.

"That's Rick Pitino?" a cabbie says to Stu Jackson. "He don't look like himself."

All along the way are constant reminders this is Detroit, Motor City: the Walter Reuther Highway, the General Motors building, a Goodyear tire billboard. The River Rouge plant seems to go on for miles, a monument to the Industrial Revolution. It all speaks of another America, blue-collar, second-shift, so different from the mobile world the players now belong to: contemporary hotels with glass elevators and new arenas off interstates.

The Silverdome is in Pontiac, an hour from downtown Detroit, off an exit seemingly in the middle of nowhere. From the outside it looks like a big milky-white balloon. Inside, under a Teflon sky, is a portable wooden floor stuck in one corner of the football field and expanses of blue empty seats. It is also drafty.

The morning of the game, the Knicks start up and down the floor in a simple drill, trying to get loose. This is known in the trade as a walk-through or a shoot-around. Pitino stands on the sidelines in a blue blazer and gray slacks, saying how different the Knick organization is from two years before.

After the Knicks made the playoffs his first year, Cartwright got hurt, the slide started, and by the end of the year the team was in disarray. It was a bad NBA team, its roster littered with the likes of Ken "The Animal" Bannister and Ron Cavenall, part of the lumpenprole of marginal talent who come and go in the NBA. Cavenall's route to the NBA was a bizarre one, and pointed out how far the Knicks had fallen in one year. Pitino had been giving a lecture in the Catskills the summer before, and picked a seven-foot kid in a Knick hat for one of his demonstrators. The kid had continually messed up all his drills.

"Afterward he came up to me and asked if he could get a tryout with the Knicks. I said, 'How can you want a tryout with the Knicks when you couldn't even do the drills without messing up every one of them?'"

Not that Cavenall was the first guy to ask for a tryout. Down through the years many guys have shown up at practice begging for tryouts. One, about 5–3, showed up in training camp at SUNY, saying the Knicks were "sorry in the backcourt" and he could instantly help. Another kept calling the Knick locker room saying he wanted a tryout. He did it so often that one night early in the season, trainer Mike Saunders said, "Will you stop calling this number?" Then he put down the phone, turned to Pitino, and said with a shrug, "Rick, the way we're going, what do you think?"

"We brought Cavenall into camp that fall, and he actually made the team. Then one night in the Boston Garden I look out on the court and there he is playing against Bird and the Celtics. That's when I knew we really were in trouble.

"But I really enjoyed my two years with the Knicks as an assistant. Joanne and I used to go out with Richie Adubato and his girlfriend, Carol, after a lot of the games, stay out until four-thirty, five in the morning. We loved it. Richie had coached against Hubie in high school at Our Lady of the Valley in Jersey. Then he had been Dick Vitale's assistant at Detroit, and later the interim coach. Now he's the top assistant with the Dallas Mavericks.

"Richie is one of the funniest guys in the world, so there always was a million laughs. Joanne and I were there the night Richie met Carol. It was hysterical. We all were in the bar at the Statler, where Richie was meeting his daughter Beth. She was there with two friends and Richie immediately tries to make a date with one of Beth's friends, striking out badly. So he turns to the friend's sister, Carol, who's in her twenties. Joanne and I can't believe this scene. A few minutes later Joanne and Carol go off to the ladies' room and Richie says to me, 'Don't tell Carol my age. I told her I was forty-four, not forty-nine." I said, 'What's the difference?' He said, 'Don't mention my age.' But as soon as Carol comes back she starts saying how Richie is so young to have a daughter Beth's age, only being forty-four. 'Forty-four?' says Joanne. At which point I kicked Joanne under the table. Only trouble is I kicked her too hard, and she yelled in pain and gave it away. But Richie started dating Carol and now they're about to get married.

"One of the first times he talked about getting married was in the backyard of Carol's mother's house. Hubie was there and he says, 'Richie, how can you be thinking of getting married. In fifteen years she'll be forty and you'll be almost sixty-five.' 'No big deal,' Richie says. 'The way I live, I'll probably be dead by then anyway.'

"It's strange, Richie has been a part of winning programs wherever he's coached, but he hasn't gotten the break in the NBA he so deserves. He not only is an intelligent basketball mind, he relates to the players as well as anyone I've worked with.

"But Richie always says, 'Although I've led a rocky life, having worked for both Dick Vitale and Hubie Brown gets me an automatic entrance to heaven.'

Even as he's laughing, he's watching his players do their drills. Watching them sobers him, and he adds, "No, seriously, back then there was no conditioning program, no extensive weight room. Everything is in place now to start building a franchise the right way.

"In five years Ewing and Akeem Olajuwon will be the best centers in the league. Mark Jackson is a good young player. Wilkins and Walker will be good players. We are not bad off, but the fans can't see that. They don't want Rome to be built in a day. They want it built in an hour."

"Are you nervous?" he is asked.

"No," he says. "I was more nervous at Providence, where I felt that if we didn't win right away we wouldn't be able to recruit."

For an hour the Knicks once again familiarize themselves with the Pistons' offensive sets. A week before, the Knicks beat the Pistons in an exhibition game in Lake Charles, Louisiana, what Pitino feels was an unfortunate bit of scheduling. Not only have the Pistons played against the Knick pressure defense, they've had a week to prepare.

Afterward, the players are boarding the bus as Isiah Thomas drives up in a red Porsche. Isiah has struggled in the preseason. He is constantly asked both about the errant pass that cost the Pistons the fifth game and probably their playoff series with the Celtics last year, and his ill-timed remark that Bird is given superstar status primarily because he's white. Now he smiles and hugs Ray Tolbert, who played with him at Indiana.

"Listen up, guys," says Saunders when the bus returns to the hotel. "The bus leaves at five-thirty. Get some rest and get some good food and meet in Rick's room at five."

The players file through the modern hotel lobby, basketball businessmen on a business trip. This scene will be reenacted many times throughout the year: wealthy, large men in brightly colored warmup suits walking through lobbies filled with short men in gray business suits and briefcases.

A few minutes before the game, both teams are on the floor. The energy level is starting to rise inside the Silverdome. There are 28,000 in attendance, the second largest opening-night crowd in NBA history. Pitino walks over to the bench in a dark suit. "Hey, Pitino, what's a white boy like you doing coaching all those niggers?" "Hey, Pitino what makes you any smarter than Hubie?" "Hey, Pitino, why don't you get some white boys who can play, like Laimbeer?" "Hey, Ewing, Pitino's messing with your game." "Hey, Cartwright, you should be working in a steel mill." On and on goes the abuse.

It's coming from an elderly black man known throughout the league as Leon the Barber. One of the NBA's constants, Leon always sits behind the visiting bench leveling a steady stream of insults. He's as much a part of the Superdome as Isiah's smile and Laimbeer's outside shot. Tonight he is quickly all over Pitino and the Knicks, a vocal reminder that even the good teams usually lose on the road in the NBA.

The Knicks start Henderson and Wilkins at the guards, Ewing in the middle, and Walker and Cummings at forward. Five minutes into the game all twelve players have been in the game. "I've never seen this before," says Dave

Twardzik, shaking his head. Twardzik, who once played for Bianchi with the old Virginia Squires in the ABA, is now an assistant coach with the Indiana Pacers. He is here to scout the Knicks for tomorrow night's game. "I hope I brought enough paper with me."

The Knicks are using constant fullcourt pressure, and are leading by two at the half. The Pistons already have 14 turnovers. A veteran team that came within a few points of going to the NBA finals the year before, tonight they look confused, frustrated. Isiah has had several turnovers. "It's not pretty, but its effective," says Twardzik. "They make you do things you're not used to doing."

The press continues to give the Pistons fits in the third quarter, but the Knicks struggle offensively, too. Cartwright in particular is awful. Everyone else seems out of synch. Still, the Knicks lead by one at the end of the quarter. Then Vinnie Johnson, nicknamed Microwave for his instant offense, comes off the bench and sticks some of his patented jumpers. The Pistons escape, pulling away in the last few minutes to win 110–99.

"I'm ecstatic with the win," says Detroit coach Chuck Daly, sitting outside the Detroit locker room. "With the Knicks it's an all-out scramble and gamble, and there's no way you can get a team ready to play that kind of style. They are a very, very tough team to play against, and will continue to be so. They are going to be successful. They are going to take everyone out of their offense, and you will not see a pretty game they play. You can't be pretty the way they scramble and gamble."

"Does anyone else play that way?"

Daly shakes his head. "Not even close."

Over in the hallway outside the Knick dressing room, Pitino talks to a group of reporters. His jacket is off, he looks drained. "I'm very pleased with my club's effort. They played well except for a couple of offensive droughts. They played a championship team on the road, and were ahead most of the way.

"I can't wait until January, until this team gets used to the press, because all my teams get better as the season goes on. This will be an effective system. It just will take time. Toward the middle of the year we will be a good basketball team. I saw a lot of great things out there tonight, but the experience showed the last five minutes of the game."

"You can't be happy with Bill Cartwright," he is asked.

"Bill Cartwright didn't lose this game," he says quickly.

Marv Albert, the longtime Knick broadcaster, comes over to Bianchi and says it's the most exciting Knick game he's seen in three years.

An hour later in Charlie's Crab, a restaurant adjoining the Northfield Hilton, Bianchi, Pitino, Stu Jackson, Mike Saunders, and Hal Childs, the Knicks' new administrative assistant who once worked with Bianchi at Seattle, have gathered. Like soldiers who have been to war together, the men at the table share a camaraderie of a club that has its own initiation rites, rules, and codes. Outsiders can look in, but they never really belong. In this world the talk is always of the game, past and present, the old stories intermingled in with the new.

It is a world Bianchi is made for. He has a million stories, from his Syracuse Nationals days back in the early days of the NBA to his many years as an assistant in Phoenix. They are NBA war stories, of old battles fought and old rivals who have now become friends. Like K. C. Jones.

"One time I go in for a layup and he pushes me. I go right into the basket support. So the next foul shot I line up next to him and say don't ever leave your feet when I'm around. Don't ever leave your feet." Then he laughed. "But you know what? He was so fast I could never catch him. Now when we see each other it's 'Hi, Case.' 'Hi, Al.' I like K. C. He's a good guy."

Bianchi grew up just over the 59th Street Bridge in Long

Island City. He grew up swimming in the East River and bunking school to go over into Manhattan to the movies. He played only two years of high school basketball, and felt his future was to be a "working guy like my dad." But Bruno Valvano, the uncle of North Carolina State coach Jim Valvano, intervened, and Bianchi went to play basketball at Bowling Green. Four years later he was a draft selection of the Minneapolis Lakers, later cut. But he got another chance with Syracuse, where he carved a reputation as a tough, blue-collar guard in a blue-collar town. He stayed in the league ten years. His first coaching job was as an assistant in Chicago with ex-pro teammate Johnny Kerr. Later he was the coach of Seattle for a short while, then coach and general manager of the Virginia Squires of the old ABA. When they folded, he went to Phoenix as an assistant to John McLeod. All along the way he's had a reputation as someone who has never backed down from anybody, a legacy from his playing days.

Like the time in 1968 when he was at Seattle and one of his players was punched out by Bob Ferry, now the Bullets' general manager. Bianchi bolted off the Seattle bench, only to be met by the Bullets' Gus Johnson, then one of the league's most feared players. "Johnson sees Al and knocks him down," recalls Childs, who was Seattle's PR guy then. "Al's stunned, but he gets right back up and Gus knocks him down again. Everyone's trying to break it up, trying to keep Al from getting up, but he pushes everyone off and he gets up to show Gus he's not afraid. So Gus knocked him down again."

Bianchi's unwillingness to back down is a personality trait he's never lost. The booing and heckling in the Garden during the exhibition season has bothered him. Beneath the expensive suits and the Phoenix tan beats the heart of an old New York street fighter. "They better not heckle us anymore when I'm around," he says, "because I'll go right in the stands after them."

"He will, too," laughs Childs.

Pitino starts talking about how Cartwright appears beaten down. "It's like he's been whipped too many times."

Bianchi snorts in disgust. "We're paying him a million dollars a year. I see the check every week. And it's big."

Someone brings up a failed alley-oop pass from Wilkins to Ewing with the score tied. "It shouldn't be that hard," says Bianchi. "We're not asking guys to do brain surgery. We're just asking them to pass the ball to people who are open. To play simple, fundamental basketball."

November 7–8

The wakeup call is at seven. After the hotel operator calls the players, trainer Mike Saunders gives them a backup call. It is just one of Saunders' many duties. He makes all the travel arrangements and books the hotels. At the hotel he must make sure that the head coach gets a suite, the players king-size beds. The staff must be on one floor, the players on another, and the media on still another. He deals with the airline tickets at the airport, passes out seat assignments, makes sure there are buses to transport the team from the airport to the hotel to the game. He brings extra uniforms and practice gear because the players invariably are forgetting theirs.

Bringing extra uniforms is a lesson he learned early in his career. One night in the Boston Garden, when Tommy Barker had just joined the Knicks, Saunders spent much of the game having to draw a number 6 in chalk on the back of a blank jersey.

Saunders grew up in Queens and used to watch the Knicks practice at Lost Battalion Hall in Rego Park, Queens, as a kid. He carried trainer Danny Whelan's black bag while his friends watched the players. Only thirty-five, he already is in his tenth year as the Knicks trainer. He is the only constant through all the years of turmoil, and has seen hundreds of players come and go.

"The past three years have been torture for me," he says. "We had all the injuries and I took it all very personally. Because I get close to the players. In this business you're here today and gone tomorrow. Sometimes you don't want to make friends to have to break friends, but I keep taking that chance. And we have some good people here, not like in the past. Last year I didn't look forward to coming to work because you never knew what was going to happen. Every phone call I was on edge. I stopped reading the papers. At the end of every practice it was if another day had passed and we had survived.

"This year is already night and day. I thought training camp was the best ever. I don't know how many we're going to win, but I know that already it's one hundred percent better than last year."

The bus Saunders has arranged is due to leave for the airport at eight. It's a dreary, overcast morning. It seems too early to be flying to Indianapolis. Ewing and Walker, traveling bags over their shoulders, emerge from the elevator, along with Knicks PR man John Cirillo. Walker says he's already used to the traveling, doesn't mind it. Ewing hates it. "This is all the NBA is," says Cirillo. "The bus to the airport, the bus to the hotel, the bus to the game, the bus back to the hotel, then the bus to the airport again. Arenas and airports and hotels. That's all we know."

It takes nearly an hour to get to Detroit's Metro Airport. The flight to Indianapolis is another hour. The plane lands in drizzle, the sky the color of slate. The local newspaper reports that the Pacers were blown out in Philadelphia the night before. Coach Jack Ramsey is so upset with his team's performance he has scheduled a practice at the Hoosier Dome this morning. Fred Kerber of the *Daily News,* Nat Gottlieb of the *Newark Star Ledger,* and Roy Johnson of the *Times* join the team at the baggage counter, adding to the entourage. The only person who hasn't checked his bags is Ewing. He has had his bags stolen so many times before in airports that he now always carries them with him.

"When we traveled with Phoenix there might be fourteen people total," says Bianchi. "Now there is a gang."

Pitino shrugs. That's New York.

Pitino was up until nearly three the night before with Stu Jackson, going over the Detroit film. It is a postgame ritual, breaking down the film, seeing what worked and what didn't, long nights looking at reel after reel. The week before, the Knicks blew out the Pacers in the Garden in the last exhibition game, the press causing 27 Indiana turnovers. But Pitino knows the Pacers will be better prepared tonight. He's also concerned about playing back-to-back. Will his team be too tired for the press to be effective?

Late in the afternoon Pitino meets with Cartwright in the hotel. "I told him he has to play better. 'It isn't a tragedy that you're still with the Knickerbockers. Management is paying you $1.2 million a year. Forget about the press and the fans and the boos. Your teammates like you, the coaching staff likes you, and these are the important things. If you start to feel better about your situation, you'll start playing better.' "

The Knicks take a short bus ride over from the Hyatt. Ray Tolbert sits on one side of the bus, staring over the darkened seats. A large man with a thick, blocky body, he seems more suited to be a defensive end. In a sense this game is his homecoming. He grew up in Anderson, thirty miles away. He started for four years at Indiana under Bobby Knight, and was the leading rebounder on the 1981 national championship team orchestrated by Isiah. The next year he was the first-round draft choice of the New Jersey Nets. But his NBA career was short-lived. Diligent, dedicated, he has always played hard, yet at 6–8 he is too small to be an effective power forward, and has neither the skills nor the speed to be a small forward. He is one of the many former college stars called 'tweeners,' who find themselves somehow stuck between two positions.

Tolbert spent the previous year in the CBA, and was visiting his girlfriend in Seattle when the Knicks invited him to training camp. He came East knowing this was his last chance. He brought only three days of clothes, thinking he probably was going to be nothing more than training camp fodder. But no one hustled any harder than Ray Tolbert. He survived the free agent camp, still with only three days' worth of clothes. After the first exhibition game against the Nets, a game in which he'd done little to help his cause, he told a writer afterward he already had a marketing job waiting for him back in Indianapolis.

Before the last exhibition game Pitino told Tolbert he was going to be placed on waivers after the game. "I also told him a lot of scouts would be at the game, and would showcase him. If Tolbert played well, he might latch on with someone else." Tolbert did just that, scoring 17 points. Pitino decided to keep him.

So Tolbert is back home in Indianapolis, the dream still alive. "I may not be the greatest player, or the fastest, but I'm going to work one hundred twenty percent all the time. The coaches know that and my teammates know that. And so far, so good." A month later he will be waived by the Knicks, then picked up by the Lakers, only to be waived by them later in the year.

Market Square Arena is downtown. Inside, yellow banners memorializing George McGinnis, Mel Daniels, and Roger Brown hang high on a far wall, a legacy of the Pacers' ABA days. Tonight is the Pacers' home opener, and everywhere you look are examples of Middle America. As part of the promotion, shiny blue glitter wigs have been given to all the fans. Before the game there are drill teams on the floor, a gang of cheerleaders, everything as wholesome as an Up with People convention. A local Star Search is scheduled for halftime.

"This is what Pitino left the small time to get into the NBA for," quips Nat Gottlieb. He is sitting on press row underneath a basket, looking as if there is no worse fate than being stuck in Indianapolis on a Saturday night watching the Knicks. He is the most outwardly cynical of the Knick beat writers, a wiry man in his late thirties who looks at all the new system and new era talk through the world-weary eyes of a New Yorker. Next to him is Roy Johnson, a short man who has spent three years covering the Nets and three years with the Knicks, all of which adds up to six years of pro basketball oblivion. Six years of Darryl Dawkins and Micheal Ray Richardson and the peregrinations of Larry Brown. Six years of Cartwright's broken foot and the travails of Bernard King. Six years of new coaches and rebuilding programs and September hopes that turn into November dust. "I've looked at more X rays than a medical student and more contracts than a junior partner," he says.

There are several connectors running through the game. One of the Pacers' assistant coaches is Dick Harter, who coached Stu Jackson at Oregon. Twardzik, the other Pacer assistant, once played for Bianchi for Virginia in the ABA. Jim O'Brien is married to Ramsey's daughter, Sharon. Basketball networking.

Pitino's pregame concerns quickly turn out to be legitimate. Without their pressure defenses the Knicks are not a good defensive team. They pose few problems for the Pacers, who after their ignominious opener of the night before have turned this into a redemption game. Chuck Person, last year's Rookie of the Year, comes out firing jumpers, and Indiana is up 13 at the end of the quarter. It soon gets worse. The Knicks are abysmal at both ends of the floor, throwing the ball away 16 times in the first half alone. At halftime they are down 28 and looking at 24 more minutes of garbage time. Sidney Green has had four turnovers in five minutes. No one except Mark Jackson seems to be able to get the ball into Ewing in the low post. Cartwright once again struggles. Wilkins has had 12 turnovers in the two games.

"I take the entire blame for this loss," says Pitino in the hallway afterward as the New York writers cluster around him. "I took the press off in the first quarter, thinking we'd be too tired, and that allowed them to get into their flow. But we aren't going to win with 16 turnovers in the first half, and unless we learn offensive fundamentals we aren't going to win."

"How about your poor shooting?"

Pitino shakes his head. "That's something we're going to have to live with for a while. Baskets don't come easy for us. We need more easy baskets off the offense. But it's a new system. It's like starting from scratch. This system will get stronger and stronger. My players get stronger as the season goes on."

"How long will it take?" asks Gary Binford of *Newsday*, a short, dumpy man the players call Body.

"Thirty games. I guarantee it."

A few of the writers look skeptical. They've heard guarantees with the Knicks before.

"If it doesn't happen, I'll buy you all a gold watch," laughs Pitino.

"Hubie used to say he'd buy us dinner."

All losing locker rooms are the same. Low, almost funereal voices: defeat hovers over everything. In one corner of the small locker room a former Indiana teammate now in a wheelchair visits with Tolbert. In another Trent Tucker says, "It's time for the veterans on the team to assume more leadership. Motivation can't always come from the coaching staff." Cummings says Pitino's system is "totally opposite of what we did last year." Back outside, Bianchi shrugs, assuming his role of the wizened NBA veteran who has seen it all. "I've been whipped before," he says, puffing on a cigar. "You get beat bad. Then you turn around and beat someone else bad. That's what this league's all about. I know this team and we have to keep things on an even keel."

A couple of writers are still with Pitino.

"Are there going to be any trades?" he is asked.

"I really can't control that. Al's looking out there. He knows his job. He knows we need players. I have to do what I have to do, and he has to do what he has to do."

"Al says it's going to take five years to get to the top," one writer says.

"Well, he's looking at it from a general manager's eyes, and I'm looking at it from a coach's eyes. It's easy to say yes, it's going to happen down the road. I want it to happen now."

The writers leave and Pitino walks into the locker room. He looks at the stat sheet, visions of turnovers running through his mind. "You take it for granted that professional players can do fundamental things," he grumbles. "But they can't."

The next morning the Knicks are on a nine-thirty flight back to LaGuardia. From there they take a bus back to SUNY for an afternoon practice. The only problem is the plane doesn't have any first-class section, so the players sit in small seats, their long legs with no place to go. "They're really going to feel like practicing," says Pitino. "After this they're going to be tin men needing oil for their knees."

As the plane comes in over New York, the spires of Manhattan glisten in the sun. In the New York papers the reviews of the Knicks' first two games are in. "KNICKS GO DOWN UGLY," says the *News*. Lyle Spencer of the *Post* says Bianchi should "stop the dreaming and get on the phone and conduct his private Cartwright auction." Kevin Kernan in the *Post* says, "Once again it takes only one peek at Bill Cartwright to realize the Knicks have committed a serious sin by not trading the million-dollar stiff for any warm body." Fred Kerber of the *News* writes, "a miracle occurred at Market Square Arena here last night. Twelve mummies dressed in Knickerbocker uniforms bumbled and stumbled around the basketball court." A *Newsday* headline says, "NO SKILLS, NO THRILLS, AND NO FUTURE WITH CURRENT KNICKS." Mike Lupica writes the Garden has become a basketball ghetto.

Broadway shows have closed overnight with more favorable reviews.

On the escalator to the baggage claim, Pitino says, "The first two games have re-emphasized the monumental task of rebuilding the Knicks. I can't wait to get to practice and get going." He is holding a present for his wife, one he came close to leaving behind on the plane. "I can't lose this," he says with a wry smile. "This is the only thing I got going for me this weekend."

November 9–10

Monday night is the Knicks' home opener in the Garden. The concourse outside the entrance to Penn Station is jammed with people. Vendors sell pretzels and chestnuts. Every few feet is another ticket scalper. The scene harks back to the days of the early Seventies, when the Knicks were good and the Garden hummed.

The big crowd inside is lured not only by the home opener, but by the Celtics, the only NBA team with a real mystique. If they long have been, along with the Lakers, the league's glamour team, the Celtics also are the only NBA team with a tangible sense of tradition. It started years ago with Red Auerbach, Bill Russell, and Bob Cousy, and continues with Larry Bird. The Celtics also have long been the Knicks' fiercest rival, the franchise that long has seemed the antithesis of the Knicks.

The year before, the Celtics lost to the Lakers in the sixth game of the NBA finals, limping to the finish line like a tired old warhorse. Bill Walton, who had been such an important cog in the Celtics' title of the year before, missed

most of the season with a foot injury. Kevin McHale limped
through the playoffs with his own foot problems that required surgery in the summer. They also were a mediocre
team outside of the Boston Garden, blown out twice in the
playoffs in the Silverdome, three times in the Forum against
the Lakers. At the end of the season it had appeared the
Celtics' glory days were about to end. Walton's career was
in doubt. McHale needed surgery. Robert Parish and Dennis Johnson were in their early thirties, as was Bird. Lenny
Bias, who was supposed to be the team's young legs in the
frontcourt, was dead of a cocaine overdose. Though the
Celtics had been a case study in heart through the playoffs,
at the end of the 1987 season they no longer seemed
invincible.

But strange things have happened since June. Second-
round draft choice Brad Lohaus, a 7-foot forward from
Iowa, has been impressive in the preseason, as has 6–10
Mark Acres, who spent the previous season in Israel. Mirabile
dictu, what had seemed like a team that needed Geritol now
seemed to have an infusion of young legs. Plus, Bird had
returned in the greatest shape of his career, after spending
the summer back home in French Lick, Indiana, lifting
weights for the first time in his life. Not only did he look
more streamlined, complete with a new haircut that made
him look like a Harvard MBA candidate, his physical transformation served as a visible symbol the Celtics were not
going to go gently into that good night.

A few minutes before seven-thirty, the Garden abuzz,
both teams are on the court warming up. Near the Celtics'
bench is their assistant coach Jimmy Rodgers. For a while
last spring, after Don Nelson had said he wasn't interested,
it appeared Rodgers was going to be the Knicks' coach. But
the Celtics wanted a second-round draft choice as compensation for allowing Rodgers out of his contract, the Knicks said
no, and turned to Pitino. Such are the vagaries of coaching.

It's hard to find anything positive about the Knicks' start.

Once again their poor perimeter shooting and inability to score easily puts them in an early hole. At the other end of the floor they are not pressing fullcourt because Pitino is fearful of the Celtics' passing ability. His strategy is for the Knicks' man-to-man defense to wear down the Celtics, and make them more vulnerable to the press in the second half. They are down 14 at the half, and chased off the court by some boos. Midway through the third quarter they are down by 25, and as the quarter ends, the game is already apparently headed for the garbage time. People start to put their coats on and head for the exits.

But the Knicks open the fourth quarter in an all-out press. The Celtics quickly get out of their offense, and the Knicks begin whittling away the Boston lead. This coincides with a brief skirmish between Ewing and Greg Kite, the Celtics' reserve center and resident hatchet man. Enraged, Ewing turns his game up a notch and continually scores on Parish inside. With just under four minutes left, the Celtics lead has been sliced to seven.

The other Knick having a great night is Mark Jackson. The day before, Pitino had approached him. "I asked him if he was ready to start, ready for the pressure. I wasn't sure. Not only had Jackson come to camp late, he had been quiet, low-key. When he said yes, I replied, 'I'm going to give it to you. But you are going to have to come out of your shell and lead this team.' "

" 'Coach, I'm not shy,' he told me. 'I just didn't want to appear cocky.' "

Later in the season Jackson will say how he made a conscious effort to keep a low profile when he first came to training camp. He was careful of the clothes he wore, careful of what he said, how he acted. He didn't even want to drive his new black BMW to camp for fear of being considered showy.

It's apparent by the frustration on the faces of coach K. C. Jones and Jimmy Rodgers that the Celtics are bothered by the Knick press. They call a timeout. The Knicks get a standing ovation, the Garden once again resounding with cheers. But the Celtics hang on and go off with a 96–87 victory.

A few minutes later Pitino stands in the small tiled room across the hall from the Knick locker room, surrounded by minicams. His jacket is off and he is standing in his white shirt. In his hands is a stat sheet.

"There is no offensive continuity as yet, but the offense will come. It's not the players' fault. The comeback, the work ethic was great, but we just fell too far behind. They never quit, never lay down."

This attempt to find something positive in a loss is a theme he will use often in postgame press conferences during the year. He believes a coach's negative reaction often causes dissension on his team.

"How about the boos in the beginning?" he is asked.

"That's New York. It's where I'm from and I'm proud of it, but you have to take the bad with the good. The crowd reaction changes with the quarter. I told the team at halftime, let's get all the boos and adversity out of the way, and let's not worry about it."

The center of attention in the locker room is Jackson. He has had 14 points and 10 assists. If once upon a time Pitino had envisioned him as the backup point guard, breaking into the pros gradually, that is now obsolete. After three professional games Jackson has unequivocally become the leader in the backcourt. The knock on him has been lack of quickness, but Jackson believes at this level you don't out-quick guys, you out-think them. "I always thought that scouts rated players like they do ice skaters," he says. "The pretty ones get 10's."

The next day in the newspapers he is lauded. Dennis Johnson says, "Jackson reminds me of Walt Frazier. Sometime in the future, when the Knicks become a championship contender, it will be Mark Jackson leading the pack." Ainge says, "If Jackson can prove he can hit the outside shot, that will be the difference between being an average guard and a great one."

The next morning's reviews from the Greek chrous: Peter May of the *Hartford Courant* calls them the New York Bricks. Harvey Araton of the *Daily News* writes, "It's time Mr. Bill was put on the block," and points out Greg Kite has more blocked shots than Cartwright and played 1,244 minutes less. "For all the enthusiasm filtering down from Rick Pitino, you can count on most runs turning to jelly as long as Chris McNealy, Ray Tolbert, Gerald Wilkins, Kenny Walker, Rory Sparrow—have we missed anyone?—are anywhere near the ball with the defense cracking down in the halfcourt."

In the *Post* Peter Vecsey writes, "Bianchi's non-moves are beginning to un-nerve me. He wouldn't be the Knick general manager if his predecessors hadn't lived on the edge of tragedy where he now presides." Vescey goes on to say, "The good thing about having the Knicks around is that anytime you're embarrassed about your game, all you have to do is turn on the TV."

On a cold, rainy, gray, and dreary November morning, the Knicks are at SUNY for practice. Wednesday they will play the Atlanta Hawks at home, then travel to Landover, Maryland, to play the Bullets Friday night, then back to the Garden for the Milwaukee Bucks on Saturday. Pitino stands at the foul line in his blue warmups, the team around him. It is time for some motivation.

"We went over the film twice and we were flabbergasted. Out of a possibility of over 100 screens in the game, we only had one good one. That's staggering. You've got to set a screen every time you pass the ball. In motion every time: we pass the ball, we screen. You've got to set a pick every time. It's not just because we're not shooting well, it's that we are not setting screens."

He pauses a beat.

"We aren't getting any offensive rebounds. Last night one in the first half. Cummings none. Ewing one. Walker none. Eleven offensive rebounds for the game. Sidney had nine rebounds in 19 minutes."

He turns to Cartwright. "I know there's no difference in ability between Bill Cartwright and Sidney Green. I know that. And I know you're trying. But he just wants it more. I wish there was a drill for it, but it's plain and simple desire."

He pauses another beat. When he speaks again, his voice is louder, more insistent. "I think we're ready to break out against Atlanta and win the next three games. Now, Atlanta runs the wings like Boston, and they pound the boards like no team does. But they don't shoot the ball like Boston, and they don't pass the ball like Boston. I want to play the next three games as if the NBA title is on the line. All of us. The offense will catch up with the defense. We're going to play the next three games the most ferocious we've ever played. We will be three and three, and we will have a different outlook on life come Monday. I knew Boston would be a tough team to press, but they turned the ball over. All these teams will turn it over big-time. Big-time."

The team goes off and starts their drills, the same drills that are starting to become familiar. "It starts here in practice," yells O'Brien. "Not in the middle of a game."

The halfcourt scrimmage emphasizes setting screens. Pitino constantly yells encouragement: "Screening and reading the defense is all it takes to be a great offensive team. As soon as you set effective screens, you will get better shots."

Thornton quickly makes a bad pass and punches the air in frustration.

"It's not the end of the world,'" Pitino says. "You and Ray Tolbert make a mistake, and I think you're going to commit suicide. *Relax.*"

Jackson seems to be nonchalant guarding Gerald Henderson. Pitino quickly jumps all over him. "Mark, we're never going to get any better if you don't start pressing the ball. That's Doc Rivers there. Get in his pants." It is Pitino's way of telling Jackson that simply because he had a good game the night before he can't relax.

On the sideline Dick McGuire talks about the intricacies of putting a team together. It's delicate, like fine-tuning the engine of an expensive car. A couple of bad decisions can turn out to be ghosts that haunt you for years. On the court are two of these ghosts, Cummings and Henderson. The recently departed Jawann Oldham was another. Hovering over the Knicks is the realization that if they hadn't given up first-round draft picks for Oldham and Henderson, they could have had the fifth and eighth picks in last year's draft. "No one takes credit for Henderson and Cummings," says McGuire, "but they're here."

Practice over, Pitino heads for the Arrowwood. A deal is close with Portland: Cummings for a second-round pick. Sparrow is close to being shipped to Chicago for another second-round pick. The Sparrow deal would free up a roster slot, and Pitino wants to bring in Johnny Newman, whom he once tried to recruit when he was at Boston University. Newman, a 6–6 shooter from Richmond, recently has been waived after spending his rookie year with the Cavaliers.

At the Arrowwood Pitino is scheduled to play racquetball with a sportswriter.

"How good are you?" Pitino asks.

"No good."

He thinks for a minute. "Okay, here's what we'll do. I have to get fifteen points and you only have to get six. And we'll play a dollar a game."

Pitino wins the first and third games. The sportswriter is tired.

"You only have to get four points now," he says.

"Double or nothing."

Pitino wins two more games. The sportswriter now owes him eight dollars. He's also exhausted and wants to quit.

"Two points," says Pitino. "Double or nothing, and you only have to get two points.

"Just two?" asks the writer, breathing heavy. "Serve."

Pitino wins the game. The writer can't believe it, slams his racquet down in disgust.

"Welcome to the hustle club," says Pitino with a sly smile. He goes over to the exercise bike and begins pedaling furiously. "This is when it pays off," he said, rivulets of sweat running down his face. "You have to push yourself."

At twilight a hard, cold rain continues to fall as Pitino drives home to Bedford. He turns onto a road that curls up a small wooded hill. Every once in a while you can see the lights of a house set back from the road. Sometimes at night deer cross the front lawn. He couldn't see a neighbor's house until the leaves fell off the trees. Ivan Boesky, former king of the Wall Street inside traders, lives two houses away. The actor Frank Langella lives in back. Michael Douglas supposedly has a house nearby. It all seems a long way from New York City.

He met his wife, Joanne, the summer after his sophomore year at St. Dominic's High School in Oyster Bay on Long Island. She was the first girl he ever went out with, the sister of classmate Bill Minardi. "Myself and a bunch of guys from St. Dominic's were in Hicksville fooling around with lacrosse sticks when the ball rolled up on a lawn," he recalls. "Joanne was sitting on the front steps, and said hello. I said hello back, but I was shy around girls, so I lowered my eyes. Then the guys behind me started saying hello to her. They knew her from grammar school.

"Many of our dates revolved around her watching me play pickup games at Prospect Park in East Meadow. Or else going to watch other high school games. The summer before my senior year in high school, we made a pact. We were going to the gym at C.W. Post, where I would work out and she would rebound for me. If I had a good workout,

I would take her to Jones Beach in the afternoon. A good workout was judged by how many shots I made from specific spots on the floor. That was the pact. The only problem for her was that I'm a perfectionist. I rarely thought I had a good workout, so she rarely got to the beach. I always concluded my workout by shooting free throws, at which point Joanne, so tired from retrieving all my shots, would sit in a chair underneath the basket and simply slap the ball back to me. Afterward, I took her to Carvel and bought her a butterscotch sundae."

"My mother loved Rick because she figured there was no way he was going to get me in trouble," Joanne says wryly. "My parents never had to worry about me coming home late. We didn't go to parties. But I knew that if I wanted to pursue the relationship, I had to go into the gym with him. Because that's where his life was."

Returning from the kitchen with a few beers, Rick says how his professional goal is to go back and coach in college some day. "I want to win the national championship," he says softly, "or at least get back to the Final Four. I couldn't appreciate it last year. I was numb."

His infant son, Daniel Paul Pitino, died four days before Providence College played its first NCAA tournament game in 1987. Daniel, born in September 1986, had been born with a congenital heart defect. For the first four months of his life he was shuttled from hospital to home. Many nights Joanne stayed in the hospital with him. A month before Daniel's death, Pitino said the season had been the most difficult he had ever gone through.

In early March the Providence basketball team was returning home from the Big East tournament in New York. Also on the bus was Joanne. "The NCAA seeding was to be announced at four o'clock, and we were on the team bus back to Providence conducting a team pool on what site we were headed for. We were all laughing, happy as can be. As we crossed the Connecticut state line and came into Rhode

Island, a state trooper suddenly pulled the bus over. I remember it was exactly 4:05. At first I thought our sports information director was big-timing it, but when I saw the trooper's hand shaking, I knew something was wrong. Joanne passed out when he told us Daniel had died. I went from euphoria to the lowest point in my life. I was numb. After we got home, I was afraid to sleep, so I watched game tapes all night.

"The Friars' magic carpet ride through the NCAA playoffs was a blur for me. I mean, I knew what we did. We went to Birmingham, and beat the University of Alabama at Birmingham and Austin Peay. The next week in Freedom Hall in Louisville, we beat Alabama and Georgetown. We went to New Orleans for the Final Four. In a sense the games became a sanctuary, a kind of personal life raft where, for a couple of hours at least, my mind could focus on something else."

Two days after the funeral, still visibly shaken, Pitino coached the Friars against UAB. He did not meet the media during the three days in Birmingham, sending Stu Jackson instead. At the start of the tournament one of the NCAA officials announced there would be no discussion of the Pitino tragedy at any of the press conferences.

"Joanne stayed back in Rhode Island with her mother. She didn't watch the UAB game, only saw the last couple of minutes of the game with Austin Peay. When I came home the next day, I told her that if she didn't come with me to the regionals, I wasn't going, either. So for the rest of the tournament I coached the team, then retreated back into a private world with Joanne.

"Both of us have religious faith, but even with faith the pain never goes away. I tried to get Joanne involved in the NCAA games, but then as soon as a game ended, our thoughts were back to our son."

It wasn't until the Southeast regionals at Louisville that he spoke publicly about his son, and that was impromptu. At the press conference before the game with Georgetown, Pitino was fielding all the predictable pregame questions when someone asked him if the success of the Friars helped him deal any easier with what had happened the week before. The room was quickly silent.

"That's a personal thing," he said softly. "That's something that takes a lifetime to get over. Something I have to handle for the rest of my life. A cross to bear." He paused for a second, then continued. "I think my son Daniel is looking down on all this and is a big part of all this." He paused, the room still silent. "I hope so."

If college coaches consider a trip to the Final Four as the basketball equivalent of the Holy Grail, Pitino's had come with an asterisk. "During the NCAAs I was concerned about my team. But I was worried about my wife."

4 | Back to the Roots

One of the main things I've had to learn as a coach is what not to do. Learning what not to do is probably more important than learning what to do. Because we all have failings as a coach. So what I've tried to do is take what is good from people I've worked for, and learn from the things that are not as good. When I was an assistant at Syracuse, I saw that Jim Boeheim was easy on his players. Now, don't misunderstand. Jim Boeheim is an excellent basketball coach who's been unbelievably successful. He is a very bright, articulate man and we are very friendly. Even now we still vacation together. But we are total opposites. It is his personality to be easy on his players.

When I got to Boston University and my own job, I knew I was going to be tougher on my players than he is at Syracuse. Some of that was because I was coming into a bad situation at BU. There were rumors of drug use, there were attitude problems, and I was trying to inject some discipline into their lives, not just on the basketball court. The other was that it was my personality to play hard, to be competitive, and I wanted my team to become an extension of my personality on the court.

At Boston University I pushed my players to just about the absolute level of human endurance. And I learned two things: there are very few limitations to what the human mind and body can do, and that you can be tough on players as long as they know you care about them. The key is not getting your players to work hard. The key is getting them to like working hard.

But by my fifth year at Boston University I was not as tough on the players as I had been in my first year. Some of that is the maturation any young coach goes through, and some of that is once the work ethic is established and has become a part of their lives, you don't have to be on them as much. It becomes internalized. The other thing I learned is not to reinforce negatively so much. This can work in the short run, but after a while your team gets beaten down emotionally and starts waiting for the season to end.

My two years as Knick assistant also made me a better coach. The main thing I learned there is your way of doing things is not the only way. Other people can be right even if they don't do things the way you do them. Professional coaching also reinforces that you are part of a team, much more so than in college when a coach's word is the only word. You learn that sometimes you have to stifle your own ego and do what's best for the team, because if you are not a communicator in the pros you can take all your offenses and defenses and throw them in the garbage can.

I also learned there that you have to vary your practices, make them interesting. Hubie had the same practices from day one, and great as they were, they became repetitive. We vary it. Make it competitive. For example, have a scrimmage and make the losing team run afterward. Not in any punitive sense, but to give everyone something to play for.

I think the key as a coach is to keep making adjustments. Don't get stereotyped and always be willing to adjust what you do. I've already discovered that's the best way to play defense in this league. Keep changing. Fullcourt pressure. Halfcourt pressure. Overplay man-to-man. Straight man. Always a different look.

But even though we haven't won yet, my primary concern is that we continue to get along as a team. We must pull for each other; the players can't go running to the media every time they're frustrated. Some people have called it having more of a college atmosphere, but there are people who feel that has a negative connotation. I like to think of it as more of a family atmosphere. But everyone says you can't have that in New York, that there are too many reporters looking to break things down and get a scoop. I'm betting you can. For if you can't create an atmosphere where everyone is pulling for one another, then what's any of this worth? I'd just as soon go back to college.

✝✝✝✝✝✝✝✝✝✝

November 11

Honesdale, Pennsylvania, calls itself the birthplace of the locomotive engine. It's a sleepy little town tucked away in the foothills of the Pocono Mountains in the northeast corner of the state. American flags fly in front of sturdy houses with front porches and by ten at night kids cruise Main Street looking for excitement that's as elusive as waiting for Godot. It's a strange locale for the center of college basketball recruiting. But at a camp on top of a hill, complete with a sparkling blue lake and pine trees, Howard Garfinkel runs the Five Star basketball camp. It is one of the three showcase camps around the country that changed college recruiting. Here are the best high school players in the country.

"Quite simply," says Garfinkel, "camps have become the places where at least fifty percent of the recruiting is done. And for the big schools it is ninety percent."

A list of Five Star alumni reads like an NBA roster: Patrick Ewing, Moses Malone, Dominique Wilkins, Mark Aguirre, Chris Mullin, Sidney Green, Mark Jackson. Plus a slew of other guys in the NBA. If you are a decent high school player in the eastern half of the country, a trip to Five Star becomes as much a part of your high school experience as the junior prom. Sink two straight jumpers at Five

Star, and undoubtedly you will have college coaches all but camped on your doorstep.

Five Star has also become a breeding ground of coaches: Hubie Brown, NBA head coaches Rick Pitino, Chuck Daly, Mike Fratello, Mike Schuler. NBA assistants Jimmy Lynam, Brendan Suhr, Ron Rothstein, Richie Adubato. Brendan Malone. All have coached at Five Star, all are part of a fraternity whose arms link across the game. Garfinkel, long one of the basketball kingmakers, knows many people in coaching who owe him a debt of gratitude. They started out working at Five Star and quickly became part of the fraternity. And since head coaches tend to hire people they know, they turned to the fraternity at Five Star.

"I first met Howard Garfinkel over twenty years ago when I went to Jack Donahue's basketball camp in the Catskills. I was fourteen and about to go to St. Dominic's. It was the early Sixties, the end of an era in New York City basketball, although no one really knew it then. It was the last years of the bird dogs."

Bird dogs were unofficial scouts who would scour the city for young talent, Damon Runyon characters with names like Walter November, the Scout, the Spook, Glider. They were guys as New York as an egg cream, who seemed to spend their lives hanging around schoolyards and knew every kid in the city who took it to the hoop with a little style. Several worked unofficially for schools in the South, schools that relied on the old underground railroad, from the boroughs of New York to Tobacco Road. Two of the best known were Harry Gotkin, the eyes and ears in New York for Frank McGuire at North Carolina, known affectionately by scores of New York kids as Uncle Harry, and Garfinkel, who performed the same services for Everett Case at North Carolina State.

Back then Garf was a theater afficionado and opera lover, famous for recruiting kids out of his parents' swank Park Avenue apartment. After graduating from Syracuse, he began coaching neighborhood teams in Queens, hanging around playgrounds, became known as an "outside coach." One day he was introduced to Vic Bubas, then the assistant coach at N.C. State. Bubas asked Farfinkel if he wanted to help out in the city. The Garf became an instant Wolfpack fan.

If the underground railroad seemed to run more than the A train, Gotkin and Garf were the conductors. It was a way of life in New York back then, before the showcase summer camps, before assistant coaches were all but traveling salesmen, before recruiting became as sophisticated as a computer printout. The bird dogs discovered the young talent, nurtured it, then delivered it, usually for a finder's fee. A competitive, internecine world full of guys hiding in the shadows. Then came the point-shaving scandals of the early Sixties, in which a number of college players were found to have taken money from gamblers for trying to influence the outcome of games, and after that Garfinkel says he never recruited another player.

Instead he became an enterpreneur.

Garf began publishing his comments on the best New York area high school kids and selling them to colleges. He soon branched out and included many of the best kids in the East. He rated them from one to five—a five being a big-timer and a one a cadaver—and soon every coach in the East knew fives took you to the Final Four and ones got you fired.

The first year Garfinkel began Five Star, Pitino became one of the campers. Forget the Poconos location. The cast at Five Star was New York as Broadway, all orchestrated by Garfinkel, whom Pitino describes as "Woody Allen with slicked-back hair." For a high school kid chasing the game, it was like a Who's Who of basketball. One summer the head counselor was Bobby Knight. The next it was Hubie Brown, who had endeared himself to Garf that first summer by bringing his entire New Jersey high school team to the camp. What better training ground for a future coach?

"Basketball truly was the City Game back then. The game long had been ingrained in the culture of New York, complete with an oral tradition that blended the past with the present. I learned it early. Every night at Five Star everyone would sit around and tell stories about these marvelous characters that comprised the rich basketball tradition of New York":

Like Freddie "The Spook" Stegman, whom everyone knew was the guy in the city for Al McGuire at Marquette. After McGuire quit coaching and became a color commentator on NBC's college basketball broadcasts, he did a halftime feature with The Spook while they walked through a schoolyard together. The word was it was a payback for all the years The Spook had bird-dogged in the city for McGuire. "See these teeth," Stegman said a few years ago, pointing to a new set of shiny white teeth. "Al bought them for me."

Like Rodney Parker, immortalized in *Heaven Is a Playground*, the book about the Brooklyn playground that produced Bernard and Albert King among others. An alleged ticket scalper by trade, Parker became infamous in the Early Seventies for being able to deliver certain New York players. At the 1977 Final Four in Atlanta, Parker was at the NCAA coaches' convention carrying a copy of *Heaven Is a Playground* under his arm.

"Did you like the book?" he was asked.

"I didn't read the whole thing. Just the parts about myself."

"It was all a wonderful subculture, a basketball carnival full of guys who seemed stranger than fiction. They all also coached their own all-star teams and would try to steal each other's players. To this day they brag about how they discovered this guy, that guy. Garf claims he was the one who discovered Larry Brown.

"That era is as bygone as a two-hand set now. Now there are NCAA rules prohibiting recruiting by people not employed by the school. Now many of the best kids in the city play for organized teams like Riverside Church or the Gauchos instead of hanging around schoolyards talking to guys who want to buy them a soda. These teams travel around the country to AAU tournaments and are closely monitored. Now everything is respectable. Garfinkel runs Five Star. Tom Konchalski, who began as Tennessee's guy in New York and was known as "The Glider" when he was Garfinkel's assistant, is now the guru of the high school talent evaluators. He's the most powerful man in college recruiting today, but he looks like a high school history teacher, not some shadowy bird dog lurking around a schoolyard.

"It's different now. You don't have the laughs anymore. The laughs are gone."

Nor is New York the talent pool it once was. Now the great players come from everywhere. No longer does a kid need a subway token in his pocket to be a great player anymore, nor do the Southern schools need the underground railroad the way they did when high school basketball in the South was just something to do until spring football started.

Nor is the scene the same in New York anymore. The Big East tournament held every March in the Garden still has the aura that a big doubleheader at the Garden once had, but it's not like the old NIT, when everyone used to sit in the lobby of the Manhattan Hotel and trade stories. Everything's more upscale now, more of a business. "I remember when all the college coaches used to go to P. J. Clarke's on the upper East Side. Invariably, one of the old bird dogs would stop by for beers late at night. The dust would come off stories passed from generation to generation like family heirlooms. Later, when I was an assistant with the Knicks, it was the Carnegie Deli. Someone always was arguing about who were the five greatest high school players, someone always was digging up the past and keeping it alive.

"It's all different now. Five Star is a business that competes with other camps for kids. There's really no coaching fraternity anymore. Everyone's coaching for their own reasons. Guys used to sit around P. J. Clarke's and push around the salt shakers on the tablecloth, demonstrating some new defense. Now when coaches get together, the talk is of sneaker contracts. And New York is different, too. The Spook is forgotten now. Garf doesn't rate high school kids anymore and the Glider has taken his legacy. All the Damon Runyons are gone."

But for a young Rick Pitino, summers at Five Star were like being an apprentice in a basketball workshop. "While a student at the University of Massachusetts, I worked a station at Five Star—a place where players work on a specific skill—and coached a team in both the younger and the older divisions. I was the youngest person ever to do so. More important, I became part of the network. I listened to Hubie Brown, Chuck Daly, and Jim Lynam give lectures, ingesting a little of this, a little of that. From Brown I learned the importance of using your voice to get control. From Daly I learned the value of commanding respect by the way you carry yourself. From Lynam I learned the importance of being able to do the drills yourself, of impressing kids with your own basketball ability. To this day when I lecture at camps on shooting, I'm always my own demonstrator, shooting the ball and making shots as I talk."

"He won more trophies than anyone in the history of the camp," says Garfinkel. "Even in high school he was as good as most high school coaches. People say I discovered him, but Rick really discovered himself. I gave him a stage as a teenager, but if he wasn't as insistent and confident as he is he would have become just another good counselor."

"Rick was born to coach," says Hubie Brown. "You could see it even then. The most notable aspect was that Rick got the most out of his players even though he was only a couple of years older than them. Rick was always upbeat and he always had great charisma."

So even in 1979, eight years before he would burst into

the national spotlight with Providence, Garfinkel believed in Pitino's future. One afternoon that summer at Five Star, Garfinkel had assembled the campers inside the oversized Quonset hut getting ready for the afternoon lecture. It was a year in which seventeen out of the top thirty college players in the country, according to *Basketball Weekly,* were Five Star alumni. Already forty-two men who had worked at Five Star were coaches in either college or the pros. Campers including Ewing, then about to be a senior at Cambridge Rindge and Latin outside of Boston and already being touted by Garfinkel as the next Lew Alcindor, and current pacer point guard Vern Fleming.

On this sunny afternoon Garfinkel came through a doorway holding a ball. On the floor in front of him were the campers. Passing the ball from hand to hand, he began to introduce the next lecturer. Raised in a show-biz-oriented family (Milton Berle, Eddie Cantor, and Jerry Lewis were frequent house guests), Garfinkel always has known the value of a little hype. His service always was aided by his ability to turn a phrase. One kid jumped so high he "talked to God three times a quarter." Another was the "greatest swing man since Benny Goodman." Another one "may not make your team picture, but he'll make your team." He also always takes pride in his introductions at the camp. "Let's have a big Five Star welcome for a wonderful friend of Five Star." "Let's say hello to a former counselor who's now an assistant at. . . ." The intros not only tell the campers they are part of a tradition, this extended family, but also reinforce the notion of the camp's prestige. Pitino says they "make you feel like you're Frank Sinatra."

Garfinkel turned to Pitino, waiting in the wings. "I spotted greatness in him right away," he said, his voice rising, "and he has not failed us. One of the five best coaches in America—Rick Pitino of Boston University."

In March 1985, shortly after Pitino had been named the coach at Providence at 32 years old, Garfinkel was asked if

Pitino's rapid ascension up the coaching ladder surprised him. "This was written in stone years ago," said Garfinkel, between drags on a cigarette. "This is just the beginning. One day Rick Pitino will be in the Basketball Hall of Fame."

"Has he changed since you first knew him?"

"Leopards don't change their spots. He will not accept defeat. He didn't accept it as a kid and he won't accept it now."

Mike Fratello, coach of the Atlanta Hawks, is watching a tape of the Knicks–Celtics game in the visitors' locker room in Madison Square Garden.

"Like a Five Star game, right, Mike?" someone says.

He laughs.

Fratello got his first chance to coach in the NBA because of his Five Star old-boy connections. In the summer of 1978, an assistant at Villanova, he was working Five Star when Hubie Brown asked him if he wanted to join him in Atlanta as his assistant coach. Five years later, after a year with Hubie in New York, he went back to Atlanta as the head coach. He was in his mid-thirties and had never been the head coach at any level. Not high school. Not college. Nowhere. There might be greater Cinderella stories in the NBA, but not many.

In keeping with the Five Star connection, he hired Ron Rothstein, who had been a scout with Hubie in both Atlanta and New York, as one assistant and Brendan Suhr as the other. Not only had Suhr played for Hubie in high school, he is a former Five Star camper. Atlanta became Five Star South.

"Did you and Pitino share some of the same coaching philosophies?" he is asked.

"I think we do. I think anyone who worked for Hubie stresses putting pressure on the shooter, and on rotations back in the defense after you start trapping."

"So is there a Five Star fraternity?"

"I like to think there is. Both Rick and I owe a lot of gratitude and thanks to a lot of people along the way."

The game is close. The Hawks might have the most athletic team in the NBA, and a superstar in Dominique Wilkins, but tonight, playing without point guard Doc Rivers, they are bothered by the Knicks' press. Once again, points don't come easy for the Knicks. Cartwright, struggling again, is vociferously booed every time he comes off the bench. Cummings, who keeps reading in the press he's ticketed for Portland for a draft choice, knows the Knicks consider him obsolete. Told about the imminent trade before the game, he had said, "Good. I can't wait."

During a timeout he tells Pitino, "I can't play this way. I can't run up and down like this. I can't get to the spots."

"Am I complaining?"

The Knicks are down two in the closing seconds when Ewing dribbles out-of-bounds trying to make a move along the right baseline.

The plus side is that the Knicks have held the high-flying Hawks to only 94 points. The other side? They are 0–4. For the fourth straight time they have failed to score 100 points, thanks primarily to 29 percent shooting in the first half.

"Any consolation in—" a writer tries to ask Pitino at the postgame press conference.

"Not ever," he says abruptly. "Don't even suggest that. Next question."

"Can you keep pressing the entire season?"

"I don't want to press 48 minutes. I didn't want to press all the time in college. Unfortunately, every time we take the press off, we get blown out. I'm probably going to go through the toughest time of my coaching life. I want it more than anyone to have better players. Everyone wants to get rid of this guy, that guy, make blockbuster trades. But the good teams won it with the draft. Look at Atlanta. All those players came through the draft. The Knicks have made mistakes by trading improperly. Panic sets in. Terrible things are done out of weakness, not strength. That's the reason the Knicks are where we are. Trade, trade, trade, panic. The biggest mistake right now is to trade Bill Cartwright and get nothing for him."

Someone asks about Walker, who has had another bad game, and is starting to hear boos. "He's down a little bit. My job is to pump him up. He didn't play this position in college, and he's had to alter his game. It might take him three or four years to settle down and be a good basketball player. I think in time he will be. But not everyone becomes great."

The minicams are gone now. Most of the writers are gone. Pitino looks exhausted.

"How are you doing?" asks Gary Binford of *Newsday*.

"I've been better."

November 13–14

Tonight it is the Washington Bullets at the Capital Centre in Landover, Maryland. The cavernous arena is typical of many of the newer arenas: in the middle of nowhere, cut off from the mainstream of the city. There is no public transportation, no bars or restaurants within walking distance. These modern arenas are built for the automobile; the key words are parking and easy access to the highway. Unlike Madison Square Garden or the Boston Garden, where the game can become part of an evening downtown, in these arenas the game must be the sole attraction. If the team doesn't win, nobody comes to watch. On this night nine thousand people will rattle around in the large building.

The seats in the Cap Centre are dark blue, and the overall effect is dark. The morning of the game the Knicks are coming in for their walk-through as the Bullets are finishing theirs. Trent Tucker shakes hands with Bernard King, who says, "We are ready for you guys." The Knicks start to loosen up as assistant coach Jim O'Brien starts giving Johnny Newman a crash course in the Knicks' offense.

"Is Newman in shape?" Pitino is asked.

"I don't know," he says wryly. "The last time I saw him play was in high school."

This year has not been Newman's. J. New, as he likes to be called, is a spindly legged shooter who grew up in the small Virginia town of Danville, and spent many hours shooting by himself in the dark on a local playground. During training camp, he totaled his black Corvette. He was waived by Cleveland shortly afterward.

Pitino watches O'Brien talking with Newman, literally pointing to spots on the floor. "The difficult thing about bringing in any new player is we have to teach him everything in about two hours."

Newman is in for Kenny Walker midway through the first quarter in a Knick version of sink or swim. Shortly before the half, the Knicks down 11, Pitino is ejected from the game by referee Billy Oakes for protesting an offensive foul call on Ewing. After the game he will say, "I got tossed on purpose. I was trying to do something, anything, to turn the momentum around."

For this is not a good Washington team. It's built around Moses Malone, once the most effective inside player in the league, but no longer able to dominate a game. At one forward is King, still able to score, but no longer the explosive offensive machine he was before the knee injury. He is bothered by the Knick press, forces numerous shots, and finishes 3–18 from the floor with nine turnovers. In the backcourt is Jeff Malone and Tyrone Bogues, the 5–3 first-round draft pick, the most controversial pick of the draft. He is from nearby Baltimore, part of the great Dunbar High school teams that produced two other first-round draft choices, Reggie Williams and Reggie Lewis. He also will struggle in the early season.

The second half is as sloppy as the NBA gets, a mishmash of turnovers and fouls. The Bullets shoot 69 foul shots and make 60, an NBA record. Moses, who long ago turned getting fouled into an art form, seems to spend the game on the foul line, always putting his goggles on his forehead as he shoots free throws. The Bullets score exactly one basket in the fourth quarter. But Jackson misses two free throws with the Knicks down only four with 55 seconds remaining, and the Bullets hang on to win 107–101.

"That might be the worst game I've ever seen," says Kevin Kernan of the *Post* as the five New York beat writers wait outside the Knicks' locker room for Pitino to come out. A few feet away Bianchi is puffing on his ever present postgame cigar.

"Bernard was awful," a reporter says to him.

"I'm glad you said it," Bianchi says. "I don't know which team was worse. But I'd rather be where we are than where they are. At least we're young."

Pintino comes out of the locker room a few minutes later. "The NBA needs three officials," he says, and hesitates a beat. "I'll probably get fined for that too." He looks down at his stat sheet and sees all the free throws Moses took. "Moses Malone is the Paul Newman of professional basketball. He's the greatest I've ever seen at getting to the line, and that's a tribute to Moses."

Pitino then launches into what has become a familiar postgame theme. "The little things that are causing the Knicks to lose close games are things that time will cure. But I'm pleased with the effort. That effort is going to make this team a big winner one day. I'm terribly disappointed at being 0–5, but I'm not disappointed with the way we are playing."

Over the public address system is the song, "Mama said there'd be days like this."

That night Pitino, Stu Jackson, and Jim O'Brien start breaking down the film at the hotel. "Our original intention was to splice together all the bad Knick plays, the flip side of a highlight film. It quickly became a twenty-minute Sidney Green highlight film of things not to do: Sidney in the wrong place in the press, Sidney missing an offensive assignment, Sidney looking lost. We finished at three-thirty, then grabbed a few hours' sleep before the wakeup call and the seven o'clock flight back to New York."

That night before the game against the Milwaukee Bucks Pitino shows Green the film. "Sidney, you're so much better than this."

"I know, Coach," Green said. "Coach, I want to make you proud of me."

"Just relax and play ball."

Green came to the Knicks, after failing with both Chicago and Detroit, with the baggage that he didn't play hard enough and was a head case. "I feel Green's been misunderstood. He is overly sensitive, and goes into a shell when criticized. Thus he must be encouraged to play harder, must be told the coaching staff believes in him. I also think Green will respond to being back home." Green grew up in an underbelly of the American Dream known as East New York. As a senior at Thomas Jefferson High School he was one of the most highly touted players in the country. Going to UNLV, he developed an extremely close relationship with Jerry Tarkanian, the controversial coach who's both hounded by the NCAA and adored by his players. "Sidney doesn't want to be traded. He wants to find a home here. But he has to be motivated differently. I can get on Chris McNealy and tell him to play harder, and he will respond. That won't work with Sidney. That's one of the differences between the NBA and college ball. Here you have to motivate each player differently. Like the film: I had to take a negative thing and make it positive. I had to show him what he was doing, and then tell him how he can improve."

The game is another that goes to the wire. The Bucks, playing without holdout Ricky Pierce and coached by Del Harris instead of Don Nelson, are bothered by the Knick pressure. They rarely are able to get into their offense, but still lead by two at the end of the third period. Pitino is again perpetual motion in front of the Knick bench. In only his sixth game he already is known as the most animated coach in the league, bringing a college style to a game in which coaches rarely leave the bench.

When Ewing rattles home a medium-range jumper from the left side in the game's dying seconds, the Knicks have their first win of the year, 93–89. Sidney Green has been a presence on the boards all night long. The Knicks have beaten one of the NBA's better clubs.

November 18

The Boston Garden is the NBA's hallowed building: the parquet floor, the white championship banners hanging from the rafters, and the smell of a thousand Red Auerbach victory cigars. It is located in an old part of the city, alongside the elevated subway tracks, and everything about it speaks of an era when basketball was played downtown, not in some antiseptic arena on an interstate.

The Garden also means the Celtics and their storied past, a conga line that stretches from Russell and Cousy to Parish and Ainge, from Heinsohn and Sanders to Bird and McHale, from Jones and Havlicek to Johnson. On nights when the Celtics are in a close game and the Garden is rocking, you almost can feel all those old ghosts coming down from those banners to help out.

The night before the Celtics have been slaughtered in Cleveland. Bird left in the third quarter, bothered by sore Achilles tendons on both feet. In his hotel room Pitino watched the Celtics get embarrassed in the second half. "Just my luck," he muttered as the game ended, "I get to play the Celtics in the Boston Garden on the night after they get blown out."

The Knicks have waived Gerald Henderson, who once played with the Celtics before being moved to Seattle for a first-round pick that later translated into Len Bias. "Henderson's bench behavior in the win over Milwaukee was reported to me. It seems he was less than thrilled being on the bench. This all started when he realized Jackson was going to get the majority of the minutes at point guard. I asked him afterward if he had a problem with playing behind Jackson. He said he did. In fact, he already had spoken to his agent about it. I told him if he had a problem, it could be rectified immediately." Henderson is the fourth of last year's Knicks to be jettisoned.

Henderson had come to the Knicks a year earlier in what might have been one of the worst trades in NBA history. Mortgaging the future, GM Scotty Stirling traded his number one pick to Seattle for the 31-year-old Henderson. Now on the waiver wire, Henderson can be claimed by anyone for $75,000, and the Knicks have to pick up the rest of his $375,000 contract. Three weeks later he latches on with the 76ers. Later he will say he never felt comfortable with the Knicks. There was all "that negativism toward the team from the fans, the media. It left a bad taste in my mouth."

Taking his place on the roster is Tony White, the thirty-third player selected in the draft and recently waived by the Chicago Bulls. The year before he had led the Southeastern Conference in scoring, Tennessee's all-time scoring leader behind ex-Knick Ernie Grunfeld. "I wanted to bring in Billy Donovan, who had been my star at Providence. If nothing else, Donovan knows my system and thus would be able to play right away. Bianchi advised against it, telling me I would get attacked in the press for waiving a veteran guard to bring in someone perceived as my pet." The Knicks can always bring in Donovan. Bianchi lobbied for White, whom Pitino has never seen play.

White is the second player in less than a week Pitino has to give a crash course to. One quick practice is all he gets. The Knicks can run only certain plays when he is in the game because he hasn't had time to assimilate the offense. And he has to play. With the exception of Jackson, he now becomes the only point guard on the roster.

On the bench in the Boston Garden, White looks up at the banners hanging in the ceiling and smiles. "After all the years of seeing games on TV, I can't believe how small,·how cramped this place is."

With McHale still recuperating from offseason surgery and Bird sidelined with his sore Achilles tendons, the Celtics start Darren Daye and Fred Roberts at the forwards along with Ainge, Johnson, and Parish. The Knicks counter with what is now their starting lineup: Ewing, Walker, Green, Wilkins, and Jackson.

In the *Daily News,* columnist Mike Lupica has written that with the exception of Ewing, the Knicks have become the NBA's newest expansion team, right there with the Charlotte Hornets and the Miami Heat. "Incidentally, what some people worry about—not me, I look for the very best in people—is that Rick Pitino might turn out to be Hubie, only cuter."

Vecsey counters in the *Post* that Bianchi has rejected a trade that would have sent Cartwright to the Bucks for Ricky Pierce, the best sixth man in the NBA last year, center Randy Breuer, and Jerry Reynolds. He says if Cartwright gets hurt, "Every jury I've ever served on would convict Bianchi, in a heartbeat, of public imprudence."

The Knicks get off to a quick start, are up seven in the quarter, courtesy of some good shooting. Pitino is perpetual motion on the sidelines. "Tip the ball, tip it, tip the ball," he screams when the Knicks are in their press. "Sidney, get a man or you're coming out of this game." "Deflection, deflection." He urges, pleads, cajoles, and yells encouragement. Pat Cummings throws a nice pass to Ewing. "Great pass, Pat. Great pass." A few minutes later Cartwright comes out of the game. "You're playing great, Billy," he says as Cartwright walks by.

Everything is going right. The Knicks' press has the Celtics in disarray. At the other end the Knicks are running more, getting out on the break, their offense fueled by their defense. The lead grows to 42–26 midway through the second quarter and continues to grow as the Celtics continue to be frazzled. It is an incredible 61–36 at the half. The Knicks' best half of the year has been played totally to Pitino's script. The Celtics rarely have looked so inept in the Garden, and leave to a smattering of boos. (This is a phenomenon similar to booing the pope in Vatican Square.) They have shot 26 percent for the first half.

Pitino tells his team during halftime, "There is no way the Celtics are going to lie down in the Boston Garden. They are going to come back. You have to go out and win the game, not wait for the clock to wind down."

The Celtics come out seething. They have been embarrassed in the Boston Garden, and if the past has shown anything, it's the Celtics do not like to be embarrassed at home. Their increased defensive pressure takes the Knicks out of their offense in the third quarter. Since the Knicks don't score very often, they don't get into their press as frequently as they did in the first half. The lead starts to dwindle, slowly at first, then more dramatically. It is down to 12 at the end of the third period after a marvelous comeback by the Celtics.

"Patrick, take over the game," yells Pitino as the fourth quarter begins. Ainge hits a three-point shot with Wilkins in his face, then another. The Garden crowd goes crazy. Ainge runs by the Knick bench and says "You better get Wilkins off me, because I'm going to bust him out." This is a tactic Bird used when Bernard King guarded him and Pitino had been a Knick assistant. (One time, sick of hearing Bird continually say he was going to bust out King, Pitino asked Bird why didn't he guard Bernard on the other end of the floor? Hubie got upset at Pitino. Seconds later, Bird inbounded the ball in front of the Knick bench, got the ball back, and fired in a three-point shot. Then he turned to

Hubie, winked, and ran back down the floor. Hubie turned to Pitino "See," he snapped, "you pissed him off.")

It is now 85–81. The crowd is in a frenzy. "Here we go, Celtics, here we go," reverberates through the old building. What had started as a typical NBA game in November has turned into a game being played at playoff intensity.

Referee Bernie Fryor runs by the Knick bench.

"Bernie, got to be tough now, Bernie," says Pitino, clapping his hands at him. Fryor just looks at him.

Ainge hits another three with Mark Jackson all over him, and the game is tied at 93 with 45 seconds left. Jackson, who had a superb first half, forces a jumper from the right side with 19 seconds remaining. Dennis Johnson misses a short jumper in the lane with six seconds left. The game is in overtime. A few minutes later it's in double overtime, both teams going back and forth, refusing to lose. Before this overtime period ends, Cartwright's fouled out, Walker's fouled out, Jackson's fouled out. Pitino is platooning McNealy and Cummings, putting the more athletic McNealy in for defense. Still, the game is tied at 109 with only a couple of seconds remaining. Dennis Johnson throws up a fallaway jumper from the baseline under pressure. He misses, but Darren Daye sneaks inside the Knick defense and taps it in at the buzzer.

Pitino is devastated. He knows how difficult it is to win in the Boston Garden, Bird or no Bird, McHale or no McHale. Beating the Celtics in the Boston Garden could have meant so much to his team. This team's searching for its identity, trying to find a way to win after so much frustration. He knows how crushing any defeat is when you've been up 28 points. But he also knows he must be positive for the media. He gives himself a silent pep talk in the locker room, then goes out into the narrow hallway where the press waits for him.

"Is this your toughest defeat?" he is asked.

"I don't rate defeats," he snaps.

Down the hall Bianchi is again trying to be philosophical. "I've seen this up here before," he says in a reference to the Garden. "They know how to win and our guys don't. But they will. This is what happens when you have a team in transition trying to get to the next level. We play this game anywhere else and we win by twenty."

Inside the New York locker room Ewing sits on a bench in a small corner. The visitors' locker room in the Garden is the worst in the league: cramped, dingy, always either too hot or too cold. For years there's been the suspicion that this is one of Auerbach's schemes to get an edge. It has become part of the Garden mystique. Ewing is still wearing his uniform, ice packs on both knees, when Kevin Kernan of the *Post* approaches him. "Patrick," Kernan says, "now that you are an expert on losing—"

"No," says Ewing.

"No, what?"

"I am not an expert on losing," says Ewing forcefully.

The irony is that Ewing grew up only a few miles away, across the Charles River in Cambridge. By the time he was a freshman at Cambridge Rindge and Latin High School, only blocks from Harvard Yard, he already was a gangly 6–9 and seen as one of the next great high school players. Born in Jamaica and raised in a culture where the games were soccer and cricket, Ewing came to America when he was twelve years old. He was immediately placed in Achievement School for kids who needed academic help, and there he met Mike Jarvis, an assistant coach at Harvard and also the gym teacher at Rindge. Ewing was 6–1 and all arms and legs. By the next year he had grown five inches, and the junior high coach kept asking Jarvis for advice on what to do with Ewing.

Jarvis became the coach at Rindge the following year, and immediately became the architect in the development of Patrick Ewing. Jarvis had grown up listening to Celtic games on the radio. His ideas of how the game should be played were shaped by the great Celtic teams of the Sixties that stressed defense, togetherness, and an intimidator in the middle. He modeled young Ewing not on Wilt Chamberlain, whose game centered around getting the ball, or on Kareem Abdul-Jabbar, an offensive virtuoso, but on Bill Russell, "who played the game the way it's supposed to be played."

Ewing's high school teams only lost five times in three years and won three state championships. By the time he was a senior he was the most celebrated high school player in the country, already being called the game's next dominant center.

He also was perceived in Cambridge as someone to be nurtured, taken care of. He wasn't pampered, he was sheltered. He had chores to do around the house. He wasn't allowed to hang out on the street. Summers in high school he attended an Upward Bound program at Wellesley College, the result of his mother's ardent wish that he one day graduate from college.

"Patrick did what normal teenagers are supposed to do," says Jarvis. "He went to dances, proms, parties. He wasn't treated like a superstar around here. He was allowed to have as normal a childhood as he could have, given the conditions. And he always understood what it takes to win. He never cared about individual statistics or getting all the glory. Sure, he liked the attention, everyone does, but he always was conscious of it coming at the expense of his teammates."

And he always was a winner. In his four years at Georgetown, they won one national championship and went to two other Final Fours. It also was, of course, supposed to have been the same way with the Knicks. Before he played his first game in October 1985 he already had been on the cover of *Business Week;* CBS hyped him as the author of a new era, the most celebrated rookie to enter the league since Bird and Magic. One tabloid called him the eighth wonder of the world. His first game was sold out. When he dunked a rebound for his first NBA hoop, you almost expected the Garden roof to lift off its moorings.

But beneath all the attention was the feeling no one knew who Ewing was. The entire Georgetown program, reflecting coach John Thompson's wariness, was guarded from the media. Player interviews were doled out infrequently and sometimes monitored: Hoya Paranoia. Thompson became infamous at NCAA tournaments for sequestering his team far away from the host city. Ewing was permitted in a sole halftime feature as he and Al McGuire walked through Washington and talked about his fondness for drawing, a look at a softer Ewing, a human Ewing. But those glimpses had been few. By the time he was a senior Ewing was a sports version of Howard Hughes.

Then he was cast into a media circus in the biggest media town in the world. His first year he refused to even make small talk with the Knick beat writers. He lived just over the George Washington Bridge in Fort Lee, New Jersey, as if he didn't exist off the court. He still got the biggest cheers of any Knick when introduced in the Garden, but by no means was he revered as Bird is in Boston, Magic in L.A., or Jordan in Chicago. Two years later on a night when Ewing posters were given out to the crowd as a promotional gimmick, many in the crowd ripped them up and threw them on the floor. Three years after coming to New York as the savior, Ewing is sitting in another losing locker room.

A while later the Knicks trudge out of the Garden and onto a bus that will take them back to New York and a game the next night with the Nets. That game they will lose in the final minutes after being up most of the fourth quarter. Afterward Pitino talks to the media. "Rush, rush, rush. If people want to rush, then go to the subway. No one can make us rush. In Boston they talk about Celtic pride. Well, someday they'll talk about Knick pride."

5 | God Rest Ye Merry Gentlemen?

It's been awhile since I faced basketball adversity. Every place I've been I've had it my way. Boston University, Providence—I won right away. I had coaching honors right away. I had players go into the pros. I had players who cared for me and I cared for them. Now here is adversity.

One of the reasons is you just don't have as much of an impact as a coach in the pros as you do in college. Not right away. You do have an impact over the long haul: who you draft, who you trade, who you pick off the waiver wire. A lot of things behind the scenes: motivating positively, game coaching.

But.

And it's a big but. The pros are a players' game, and college is a coach's game. I miss the teaching and motivational aspects of college basketball. Here you can't do a lot of the teaching because there is just not enough time. In college you have six weeks before you play a game. Here you start playing exhibition games a week into training camp. There is too little time between games. Right now we are not a good foul-shooting team and that kills me. At Providence we broke the foul shot down into fundamentals and had everyone shoot them early every morning. We were the best foul-shooting team in the Big East. Here you don't have the time. Every time we miss a foul shot I would like to bring everyone in here at six-thirty in the morning like we did at Providence, but you just can't.

I'm tired of hearing people say our style of play won't work. I'm going to do it exactly the way I want, and no one is going to influence me either way. If the Knicks hadn't won only twenty-four games last year, I wouldn't be here. Poor shot selections, turnovers, lack of offensive rebounding: those are the reasons we are losing. We are losing because we don't yet know how to win. We make the kind of stupid mistakes down the stretch that are caused by losing and cause more losing.

I have, though, learned a few things already. In college you can keep their level of intensity the entire game. In the pros they don't. So I am trying to channel my aggressiveness to make it count. When they see me mad they say, "Oh man, he's really mad now, we have to really put out." In college they accepted my personality and became extensions of it on the court. That's one thing I'm learning about the pros: they simply aren't going to do that.

But I also can't be too negative. My first couple of years at Boston University I motivated negatively, and I found that although it can work at first, by the end of the year everyone is dying for the year to end and you have lost them. The last two years at BU, I motivated positively and got much better results.

For example, the other night Gerald Wilkins took a three-point shot in the last couple of minutes that missed, a really bad shot to take at that time. Rather than get all over him, I asked him in a timeout why he took it.

"Because I had time and I thought I could make it."

"Dougie, what's your percentage from three-point range? In the thirties, right?"

He nodded.

"Well, don't you think that at that point in the game we want a better percentage shot? You're a good three-point shooter, understand. I just think that in that situation we want a better percentage shot."

That's what you have to do in the pros. In college you can get down on a guy and not play him. Here, you can't have any doghouses. You have to find a way to get the most value out of every player. Doghouses get you fired.

✝✝✝✝✝✝✝✝✝✝

November 21–28

Saturday night the Knicks are back in the Garden against the Golden State Warriors. They are now 1–7. "What hurts the most is that we have been blown out of only one game. Three games we've squandered in the final seconds, including the last two. With a little more luck, and a little better discretion at the end of three games, we'd be off to a good start." On the plus side, they have gone over 100 points in three out of their last four games, a sign their offense is improving.

According to the schedule, this is just a November game between two struggling NBA teams, a game that will pass into obscurity as soon as it's over. For a young team searching for its identity, though, it's imperative they beat the Golden States of the world at home.

The Warriors are coming in 1–8 overall, 0–6 on the road. This also is the New York homecoming for Chris Mullin, the former All-American who was all but deified at St. John's. In a sense Mullin, the ultimate gym rat, was a throwback to another era, when the great players in the city were white and often the product of the Catholic leagues. Some had speculated that he wasn't quick enough to be a successful pro, but Mullin has compensated with his great court awareness and instincts for the game. He is smart, plays within himself, and if left open, drills that great lefty jumper, the legacy of all those solitary hours in Alumni Hall that became part of New York folklore. Periodic stories in the tabloids float Mullin's name in a possible trade that would bring him back home. Other rumors say he has a problem with alcohol abuse, a problem that supposedly started when he was at St. John's. Two weeks later he will enter an alcohol rehabilitation center in Inglewood, California.

Tonight he gets a big ovation when introduced.

Seated courtside is Joe Namath. Public address announcer John Condon introduces him to the crowd, calling him one of the greatest athletes ever to represent New York. Broadway Joe gets an even louder ovation.

Pitino starts Trent Tucker instead of Gerald Wilkins. "Tucker is the best defensive player on the team and rarely turns the ball over." What is left unsaid is Wilkins often turns the ball over, and is shooting 39 percent.

The Knicks continue to struggle offensively, but go up 10 with just over four minutes left to play. Pitino tells them during a timeout, "Unless you play Killer Bee defense, this game is going to the wire."

"We are not going to lose this game," says Ewing forcefully. ("Ewing had a fever and probably shouldn't have played," Pitino says later. "The fact he did shows how much he wants to win.")

The Knicks hang on to win their second victory of the year, 99–91.

"How about starting Trent Tucker instead of Gerald?" Pitino asked afterward.

"Dougie came to me and said he didn't think he was playing well. I asked him if he was giving 110 percent. He said he was. I told him if he is giving 110 percent, he is playing great. Starting is irrelevant in our system."

"He feels he's not in the flow," says the reporter.

"We're not interested in whether *he* is in the flow. We're interested in whether *we* are in the flow. It's tough to tell people you're happy when you're losing, but we really are playing good basketball. I play every game like I'm never going to coach again, and that's what I want the players to do." He paused for a second, then smiled. "I'm running out of motivational techniques. I've got all the Vince Lombardi books, but I'm running out. They've got to write some more books about Vince."

Later that night he and Joanne go to Smith & Walensky's on Third Avenue. At the table, among others, is Herb Sendek, a Providence assistant coach who began his coaching career two years earlier with Pitino. Sendek first met Pitino at summer camps, first at a clinic in Pittsburgh and later at Five Star.

"It was like positive vibes ran off him," says Sendek. "You didn't have to be a genius to figure it out. He was without peer as a camp lecturer. He demonstrates when he lectures. He plays kids one-on-one. The first year I saw him at Five Star he played against Delray Brooks. Now, Delray Brooks was a great high school player. And Rick killed him. He scored every time on him. Delray couldn't get a shot off. All the while he is talking about individual offensive and defensive moves, and every kid's eyes are getting bigger and bigger. You know how it usually is at lectures during camp. It's summer, the kids come back from lunch, some coach is droning on, and the kids are falling asleep. It's not like that with Rick. He talks and they are riveted."

Sendek was hired as the graduate assistant coach before Pitino's first year at Providence. "We got beat by Richmond at home the second game of the season. I invited these friends I hadn't seen in a while to come. After the game we're all set to go, but I have to check with the coach. In the locker room Rick is beside himself. Out of control. Blaming everyone. I had never seen anything like it. I mean, I had been around basketball all my life—my father was a coach—but this was a new experience for me. But I'm only the grad assistant, so I figure I'm absolved a little bit.

"Gordie Chiesa, one of the assistants, comes up and says me and him have to go back to the office and start making out the scouting report for the next game. I tell him that I got friends to meet. He looks at me, he looks at Rick, and Rick says, 'Both of you, do the scouting report.' I have to tell my friends to forget it, and me and Gordie go back to the office and look at film all night. We must have worked to five in the morning, and all I want to do is go home and go to sleep. The minute I walk into my apartment, the phone is ringing. It's Gordie. He says Rick wants us back in the office. So I go back there. It's now about six-thirty. Rick has been up all night, and he starts in again. By this time I'm so tired I want to throw up. At the time I thought that Rick was new on the job and must be feeling incredible pressure, but in retrospect I think he was making a statement: losing wasn't going to be tolerated anymore.

"He was always doing things that made you think that it was all part of some game plan. For instance, our first game that year was against Assumption, a small school in Worcester that had upset Providence the year before. We didn't know how good we were, or even if we were any good at all, and if we ever lost to Assumption, what was going to happen once the Big East started? Right before the game, Rick turns around to the team and says, 'I just was talking to the Assumption coach, and do you know what that mother said to me? He said that he had a good team and thought he could beat us again. Who the fuck is he? Who the fuck is he to think he can beat us?' The team went out the door like it was going to war. It wasn't until afterward I realized that there never had been any conversation with the Assumption coach.

"He always knew how to play the team. The second year we beat the Russians in a preseason game, an incredible win for us. So the next day the team comes into practice, and you could tell they thought they were good. They were big-timing it in practice, and all of a sudden Rick stopped play. 'That's it,' he said. 'Everyone out. Come back at midnight and we'll start again.' We must have practiced until three in the morning. They got the message.

"He could be very tough on them and tear them down, but the couple of days before a game he would start building them up. His pregame talk was always positive, no matter how bad we had practiced, or how many injuries we had. By game time he would have them believing they could beat the Celtics.

"The other thing about him is that it was all orchestrated. Against Austin Peay in the tournament he was all over Marty Conlon at halftime. Just burying him. I'm watching and thinking that maybe this time he has gone too far. After all, Marty was just a freshman, he wasn't even a starter, and this was the NCAA tournament. Before the half started, I saw him go down the bench and say something to Marty, touch his leg, then Marty went out and played the best half of his life."

Also at the table are John Parisella, one of the most successful horse trainers in New York, Pitino's longtime secretary, Barbara Kobak, and Larry Pearlstein, a New York hoop junkie known as the "Scout."

Parisella, in his early forties, was New York's leading percentage trainer in 1985. During the early Seventies, lured to California by show-business friends, he became known as the trainer of the stars. James Caan, Jack Klugman, Don Rickles, and Don Adams all owned horses trained by Parisella.

Parisella and Pitino first met shortly after a Final Four. It was at a party hosted by former New Jersey owner Joe Taub, who offered last spring to buy back into the Nets if the current Net owners hired Pitino as their coach, in a sense offering himself and Pitino as a package deal. Parisella, who looks a little like a younger Jack Nicholson, told Pitino he and the people in his barn became big Providence fans during the NCAA tournament. Now he is a regular at Knicks' games, in the lounge before and after games, part of the Knicks' inner circle. He also has given some of his younger horses basketball names: Knick Press, Five Star Camp, Stolen Pass, Backcourt Magic, Al the GM. Another one is named Daniel Paul, for Pitino's son.

Kobak first went to work for Pitino at Boston University. She was a friend of one of Pitino's college teammates, and it was her first job out of school. In the beginning she had no idea what she was getting into, especially after she realized Pitino regularly was coming to work at 6 A.M. and leaving at midnight. Ten years later she is the glue in the office keeping everything together. When Pitino went to the Knicks the first time, she moved to New York for a year and ran his personal business. When he went to Providence she went with him. Now she is back with the Knicks. Pitino calls her as many as five times a day. She pays all his bills. She knows who he has to call back right away and who can be out on hold. She used to babysit his kids. She's been the one constant in his professional life.

"Everyone thinks we're having an affair," says Pitino.

The Scout is one of the links to Pitino's past, one of the guys deeply imbedded in the New York tradition. "He goes back some forty years in New York basketball; he and Garfinkel used to hang around the old Garden together. Once upon a time he was Maryland's man in the city. I first met him years ago through Garf. The Scout spends much of his time on the phone gathering information. When I was at Providence, the Scout called at least once a day, always collect. He called our house so many times that our nanny thought his name was Larry Collect."

In late August the clan—Pitino, Hubie Brown, Garfinkel, the Scout—had gathered at the Carnegie Deli for a tribal reunion. Pitino constantly inquired about players in the league, trying to reacclimate himself. In addition, it was a crash course in the Knick players as Hubie perceived them to be. That night Hubie was the acknowledged star, the center of attention, having an opinion on everything. Pitino mostly sat and listened, once again in the learning role he had as a kid at Five Star. The Scout kept calling him Wonder Boy. This is a lounge act that's been going on for years.

Two nights later in the Garden, the Knicks lose to the San Antonio Spurs. They come down the stretch with the Spurs, neck and neck. Green fails to box out on a foul shot with a minute left and the Knicks down four, allowing the Spurs to get the ball back. Jackson gets called for traveling on a drive to the basket. Despite that, the Knicks, down three with nine seconds to go, steal the ball and get it to Tucker for an open three-point shot. Tucker, the team's best three-point shooter, misses.

The game is one more indication that the Knicks can't beat anybody if they don't play well. Unlike the better clubs that at times play on cruise control and still manage to win, the Knicks don't yet have that luxury. Every game is a grind.

The Knicks are 2–7.

"Ewing has been great, much improved over the year before. He's playing as well as any center in the league. Jackson is off to the best start of any rookie in the league. But they are the only two pieces of the puzzle in place. The others? So far they're role players at best. That's why we're 2–7."

Gerald Wilkins is as off and on as a light switch. He's capable of scoring lots of points some nights, and looking as if he just came out of the CBA the next. He doesn't pass or handle the ball well; thus he is incapable of taking pressure off Jackson. Kenny Walker is a player who jumped over people in the low post in college, but at 6–8 he is now too small to do that in the NBA. He must learn to play facing the basket. Green seems to drift in and out of games. He appears frustrated, he's having trouble adjusting to the style of play. He told the reporters he wished he had been in training camp with the Knicks.

Cartwright wants to be traded. Cummings wants to be traded. Tucker missed most of training camp. McNealy, Tolbert, and Thornton are with the team because of their hustle, not their talent. Johnny Newman appears too small at 6–6 to play forward, a refugee from the waiver wire. Tony White is having all sorts of trouble trying to make the transformation from a scoring guard to a point guard. During one game, watching White high-dribble the ball against defensive pressure. Pitino, an anguished look on his face, yelled, "Tony, will you please dribble the ball lower."

"I'm sure White is a better player than he has shown. And I know it's probably unfair to judge him so quickly, but we need someone who can spell Jackson without the offense immediately stopping.

"This team needs a scoring forward, needs better outside shooting. We have been able to stay in every game except Indiana because of our hard work and defensive pressure, but we need some firepower off the bench, someone who can score on the second unit besides Cartwright."

The game has been over for about an hour now. The workmen in the Garden already are cleaning up, the big arena is drained of life. The locker room is nearly empty, most of the players already having left. Wilkins heads out the door, wearing a blue leather suit, the pants of which are tucked into white boots. Around his neck is a white scarf.

"Just the outfit to spend a quiet night at home in, huh, Dougie?" Pitino asks.

Wilkins laughs. His dark eyes dance with life. "No, man, tonight I'm stepping out," he says.

"I like your outfit."

Wilkins laughs, a little nervously, unsure if Pitino minds or not. "Someone bought it for me. And you know, when I first got it I didn't know whether I could wear it or not. Thought it might be too flashy. But I looked at myself in the mirror about ten times and said, yup, I can handle it."

Wilkins steps on the freight elevator that goes from the fifth floor, where the court is located, down to the employees' entrance on 33rd Street.

"You know, some coaches look at you a little funny when

you dress flashy after a loss," he says. "Like they think you should be dressed in mourning clothes."

Two nights later the Knicks beat the Cavaliers in Richfield, Ohio, then beat the Cavs again two days later in the Garden, their first back-to-back wins of the year. The second game is interesting for two reasons: for the first time Cartwright gets enthusiastically cheered in the Garden. Diving for the ball in the third period, Mr. Bill brings the Garden crowd to their feet. Second, a sequence early in the fourth quarter, when the game is still close, is a sneak preview of Pitino's vision of the future. In the space of 15 seconds Jackson steals the ball on the press, passes to Ewing, who dunks. Ewing then blocks a shot and runs the length of the court for another stuff. Jackson steals it again, passes it to Ewing, who misses a dunk, gets his own rebound, and dunks it again.

The Knicks have forced 30 turnovers, stole the ball 16 times, and their press dictated the game. The Knicks have forced an average of 21 turnovers a game, tops in the NBA. They have outrebounded opponents in five of their last seven games. The past two years they were the worst rebounding team in the league.

Pitino is also elated with the two wins because they follow an item in the *Daily News* that the Knicks had come to Pitino asking for some days off. Pitino essentially said, when you win, you get days off, not before.

"It made it seem like it was a big deal," he says two days later, "and it wasn't. The attitude's been great. A week ago I told them that we were a young team and we can't get down. And yesterday in practice the guys were so happy I had to remind them that all we did was win back-to-back games, not the world championship."

December 1–3

Rick Carlisle is the newest addition of the Knicks, replacing Trent Tucker, who goes on the injury list with a bad knee. After spending his first two years in college at the University of Maine, out of sight and out of mind as far as bit-time college basketball is concerned, Carlisle transferred to Virginia, where he played with Ralph Sampson one year and went to the Final Four the next. The past three years Carlisle had been on the Celtics, a mid-round draft choice who had made the Celtics against all odds, largely because of his work ethic and knowledge of the game. The last man cut by the Celtics before the year, he had joined the Albany Patroons of the CBA.

Pitino remembered Carlisle from Boston University's games with Maine. His team had always had trouble pressing Maine because Carlisle made good decisions with the ball.

The day before Carlisle had been in Topeka in the CBA, in a league where you tape your own ankles. Tonight he will score 21 points, more than double his career high, against Seattle. More than that, he will instantly adjust to Pitino's motion offense, passing the ball, screening away, doing many of the little things that sometimes seem as complicated as nuclear fission to many of the Knicks. "His performance highlighted how the game has changed in the past decade or so. The premium now is often on athletic ability at the expense of basketball skills. Someone like Carlisle, whose athletic ability is suspect in the NBA, is in many respects a better *basketball* player than many players who are more valued in the league." Although in the next three games he will shoot poorly and see his time dwindle after Tucker returns from the injured list, on this night at least, his ability to pass the ball to an open man, use an up-fake, and hit an open 15-foot jump shot makes him stand out on the Knicks.

Even with Carlisle's unexpected boost off the bench, it will not be enough. The Supersonics escape with a three-point win. They are up 16 early in the fourth period before the Knicks make one of their late-game charges. But Ewing misses two free throws in the final minutes, and Wilkins misses three, including two with 44 seconds left.

Jackson, who has been named the NBA's Rookie of the Month, tries to do too much, and has one of his worst games of the year. In the fourth quarter he is hounded by Kevin Williams, who had been a senior at St. John's when Jackson was being recruited, and knew him because Jackson used to come to St. John's with Pearl Washington. "He was always much more serious than Pearl, like he was trying to prove he was just as good," Williams says later. "Tonight I used some of the things Maurice Lucas taught me last year. Beat up on those rookie guards. Hold them. Shove them. Be all over them."

Two days later Vescey will write that somebody should "investigate the New York child-labor laws. Mark Jackson is playing too many minutes."

Ewing has 21 points in another fine game. He is averaging 20 a game, compared to 11 a year ago. He also has become the Knicks "go-to" guy, the new NBA term for the guy who gets the ball when you most need a basket. Trent Tucker says Ewing has matured: "He's the man and he knows it." Pitino's style has unleashed Ewing's game, enabling him to use his rebounding and shot-blocking athleticism more than in Hubie Brown's power game.

"I'm the same Patrick Ewing," he says. "The system is different. Running up the court, catching the defense moving: this is my type of game."

Pitino leaves quickly after the game to go to New York University Hospital. His father, Rosario, has been there for a couple of weeks, and is not expected to live through the night. "The day after we lost to the Celtics in Boston, I learned my father had bone cancer. I've spent the past two nights at the hospital, grabbing a couple of hours of sleep in a chair."

Tonight he will sit in the hospital for a third night, thinking of his father and all he has done for him.

It is part of the Pitino myth, spread that day in July when

he was announced as the new Knick coach, that he grew up only a few blocks away from the Garden. And it's true that he was born only a few blocks from the Garden and spent the first four years of his life on 26th Street between Second and Third Avenues. But most of his childhood was spent in Cambria Heights, Queens. He was the youngest of three boys; his brothers were seven and ten years older. His father was the manager of a building on 26th Street in Manhattan.

"My family had little interest in sports. My father played a little handball, but he was not a sports fan. My older brothers, Bob and Ron, played some football, but they were not really sports fans either. They were ten and seven years older than I, and grew up in the Fifties era with hot cars and rock 'n' roll. Although they raised hell, they always kept me in line. What is that expression? Do as I say, not as I do? That was them. They played hookey from school and played music all night, but I never could. They'd be in the park hanging out, but they made sure I was home for dinner on time. In the environment I grew up in, I never could get out of line because of them. They always were watching over me. I think that's where my self-discipline developed. They made me disciplined. Today Bob is a retired policeman living in Florida, and Ron is a bond broker on Wall Street and comes to all the games.

"My father had a soft touch in dealing with me. My mother was a different story. She was a very organized woman, the glue who kept our family together. Everyone feels their mother is special, and my brothers and I echo that a thousand times over. We got our work ethic from our father, but the rest we owe to her.

"My obsession with basketball, though, is something I did on my own. I remember my Uncle Joe always was telling me to put down the ball and get a job, that the ball never was going to take me anywhere.

"I first picked up a basketball when I was seven. My

cousin, Walter Bachman—he was a few years older—suggested I try out for the team at Sacred Heart school. 'All you have to be able to do is make a layup and they'll put you on the team.'

" 'What's a layup?' I asked.

"Walter showed me how to do it, how to go off my left foot and shoot the ball high off the backboard with my right hand. After he left, I stayed until I was able to make a layup. The next day I made the team. A few years later I was ready for the parks, ready to plunge into that long and glorious tradition of schoolyard basketball in New York. It was as much a part of my coming of age as taking the train into the city." It was about this time Pitino asked his mother, Charlotte, for money to go to his third basketball camp of the summer.

"But Ricky," she said. "These camps are expensive."

"Think of it as an investment in my future," Pitino supposedly said.

Whether he really said this is irrelevent. The point is that by a young age his world had become ruled by the lines of a basketball court.

"I didn't go out with girls. I didn't have a social life. Basketball was my cocoon. It was my life. I used to go every afternoon to Colin Field in Cambria Heights. Both my parents worked, getting up at five-thirty every morning and coming home at four-thirty every night. When I came home from school there was never anyone there, so I used to go and play ball.

"When I was fourteen we moved out to Long Island, to Bayville on Oyster Bay. Suburbia was a new world for me. Kids hitchhiked instead of hopping on the back of a bus. They went fishing and hung around shopping malls. Unlike Queens, where everyone went to the schoolyard and played ball, kids on Long Island were into other things. I hated it. I didn't like hanging around shopping malls. My only outlet was playing in pickup games at Prospect Park in East

Meadow. I hitchhiked to the park, played, and hitchhiked home.

"The local high school I was supposed to attend as a freshman was Locust Valley. But one day in the park an older kid told me about St. Dominic's in nearby Oyster Bay. There, basketball was more than just a game suburban kids played in the winter. I said I was interested. The next day a priest came to the park, the athletic moderator of St. Dominic's, Father Suave. 'Tell your parents we'd like to have you at St. Dominic's,' Father Suave said, though I never had taken this test that was supposedly required to get into St. Dominic's. 'Given the circumstances, and because you have one of the best jump shots for a kid I've ever seen, we probably can do something.'

"Hey, I had my first recruiting experience.

"St. Dominic's was old. It was red brick, built in something like 1928. The gym was small and cramped. The lockers were old, the locker room was like a closet. The balls were old. It was everything I was used to. I loved it.

"As a freshman me and the junior varsity coach—Pat McGunnigle—began playing one-on-one every Friday night. These were marathon sessions and they continued for all of my four years. This was the late Sixties, mind you, the height of the counterculture and all that baloney. Other kids went out on dates. Other kids went to parties, listened to Led Zeppelin, grew their hair long, and wore bellbottoms. They'd smoke dope and tell me sports was a remnant of a dying, competitive culture. And where was I? I was in the gym playing one-on-one with the coach. I didn't have anything to do with the drug culture, or the anti-Vietnam stuff. I kind of blocked everything out. Every once in a while some kids would break my shoes, and say basketball was not the only thing in the world. I'd say, 'Right, it's wearing your hair in a ponytail.' "

December 7

The back page of the *Daily News* tells the story: a full-page picture shows Pitino with his hands outstretched, mouth open, anguish all over his face. Over the picture in big, bold print reads: "MAD AS . . . ," a takeoff on Howard Beale in the movie *Network*. Underneath the picture in smaller print is the quote, "My patience is running out. We've got to stand up and be counted. I don't want to hear about a title in four years. We've got to win now."

In Memorial Coliseum in Portland the Knicks have been blown out by 18, ending a disastrous road trip west that also included losses at Phoenix and Utah. It also was their fourth straight loss, The Blazers, off to a fast start on the season, scored 42 fast-break points, running the Knicks out of the building in the second half.

Afterward Pitino had had enough. He kept the locker room closed for twenty minutes. "I don't want to hear any more excuses. None. You are beginning to feel sorry for yourselves, and that has got to stop. This is the first time the effort hasn't been there. And for us it has to be there. We don't have as much talent as the other teams, so we have to have the effort.

"There are no more excuses," he said to the press when he finally opened the locker room. "Youth, inexperience, the future. We can't feel sorry for ourselves. We've been trying to stay positive," he said, "but I'm at my breaking point. There are no more excuses. I don't want to hear what we don't have. We will perform. We won't use that excuse about next year. This is not fun. This is not the way the game should be played. It is collectively coaches and players doing a poor job. We've got to win now. Management can wait. Coaches can't."

He also told his team the next morning, after they had flown across the country that night, that they were going to practice later in the day at SUNY and if they did not impress him in practice, he will abandon his pressing style for a more conservative approach. "If worse comes to worse, we'll walk the ball upcourt and play seven people. No more press. If we don't come out and play hard for four quarters, then we're going to walk it up the court."

He knows losing can be contagious. Feeling sorry for yourself can be contagious. And he knows it must be stopped now.

Because of his father's condition, Pitino considered not going on the trip, but there had been a slight improvement. All the while he constantly called New York. "I haven't thought about basketball in the past week. Even at that, I don't go to sleep with a clear conscience."

The first game of the trip was against the Suns in Phoenix, a homecoming for Bianchi. Before the game a gorilla, the unofficial Phoenix mascot, pretends to be Bianchi, stalking the sidelines with a clipboard, then throwing the clipboard. He is as accurate as the Knicks will be once the game starts. Once again the Knicks are victims of their poor shooting, missing 27 of their first 37 shots. The bench shoots an unbelievably poor 20 percent. So what if the Suns turn the ball over 28 times?

Cummings plays only six minutes and is upset. He can clearly see he no longer is in Pitino's plans, and wants to be traded. The Knicks say no one wants him. "This is bull-shit," he says in the locker room afterward, throwing his hairbrush into his traveling bag. "I'm not putting up with this anymore."

Pitino would love to get rid of Cummings. "I've made concessions for him. I don't press when he's in the game. We'd give him away for a third-round pick, but he makes too much money."

In contrast, after the game Stu Jackson tells Pitino that Ewing, Walker, and Jackson are really down about losing. "I went into the locker room and sat down with them. I told them there are better times ahead. Our attitude is what will get us into the playoffs. I was glad they were down. It showed me they cared about winning."

In the loss to the Jazz in Salt Lake City, Pitino tries Ewing and Cartwright together for the first time. It's no accident that it's first unveiled on the road, for playing Ewing and Cartwright together is a sensitive issue. The same strategy contributed heavily to getting Hubie Brown fired the year before; Ewing made it known he didn't want to be a power forward. "This time," Pitino says, "when the two play together, Ewing will be the center, and I'll only do it when the matchups are good."

The other reason is to showcase Cartwright, in hopes of trading him for the scoring forward the Knicks so desperately need. Pitino feels Cartwright is playing great basketball, but his stats don't show it. Cartwright still wants to end his career somewhere else. The latest rumor is that three weeks ago Dallas approached the Knicks about a trade that would send Detlef Schrempf and Bill Wennington to New York for Cartwright.

Pitino is unhappy with his forwards, period. On Green he says, "Sidney is Sidney. You look at him and think you're getting a great athlete. But you're not. What you're getting is a guy who will rebound. That's about it. No more. No less.

"We're fighting for the eighth playoff spot, along with Washington and Cleveland. Eighth would be a great year for us. We're not going to be a championship team with these players. We have to build through the draft. But I am not down. I look at the other teams and see how old they are, and I look at us and see Ewing and Jackson learning, and I see great things for us. That's what keeps your sanity."

Home in New York once more, before the practice at SUNY Pitino discusses his outburst in Portland. "I blew up at the players for the first time. It was intentional. I don't know what to do. I have to substitute because they are working so hard, but it's like we go from an NBA team to a college team."

He wants to bring in Billy Donovan to replace Tony White. Not only did Donovan play for him at Providence, in a sense his surrogate son, but he is someone who knows the system. Donovan, a third-round draft pick by Utah, was waived shortly before the season started. He then joined Wyoming of the CBA, but quit before Thanksgiving when he wasn't seeing much playing time.

"I have a hell of a decision with Billy Donovan. I don't know if I can bring him in now since he quit the CBA. How can we announce it? That we are bringing him in from St. Agnes High School? If I bring him in and he can't do it, we're all in trouble.

"But I'm at the breaking point right now. I can't accept it. I have to get after them hard. Somehow, some way, that second unit has to play. Maybe one pressing team and one twin tower team until help comes. I said I would stop pressing and only play seven men to scare the players."

He pauses for a minute, considering. "With Wilkins it's feast or famine. I have to waive McNealy, he can't give us anything. I can't decide who is better, Thornton or Tolbert." He laughs ruefully. "Someone said that's all you have to know about the Knicks.

"I thought trades would be imminent, but there haven't been any. Al says to relax, enjoy yourself. We are direct opposites. He has a pro attitude, I have a college attitude. I don't want to hear about the draft lottery. New York doesn't want to hear about it. We get along fine together, but it's a difference in philosophies. We have to make a run right now. I got to make this game tomorrow night like a playoff game: we have to win."

December 8–12

A big day for the Greek chorus.

The New York *Post* headline says "PITINO HITS WIT'S END

WITH KNICKS." In the story Kevin Kernan says it took sixteen games for the "new, upbeat, optimistic Knicks to reach their first official crisis." Pitino is at the breaking point, frustrated with management for its inability to acquire some quality players. It's certainly not as serious as "those good ole back-stabbin' days of Hubie Brown and Dave DeBusschere, but it's a situation worth watching, and it's not a healthy one for the franchise." He writes that it's easy to sympathize with Pitino, who has been asked to "go to war with rookie point guards, including one who is learning by connecting the dots," a forward in Chris McNealy, who can't score, and a starting power forward in Sidney Green, who is playing as if he "just arrived from Pluto." He also quotes Bianchi, who says there will be better opportunities for Cartwright in the future. "I'm not interested in winning five or six more games this season, I'm interested about getting on the road to winning the championship."

Vecsey, under a headline that says "NO BUDDY SYSTEM IN THE GARDEN," writes that one veteran Knick watcher thinks Bianchi is not making the moves he's supposed to be making so that Pitino will be fired, and Pitino is going along with them so that Bianchi will be fired. "If you're keeping stats," continues Vescey, "Pitino's tonguelashing of his players was his first honest public opinion since the day he was hired."

Only 13,000 people turn out to see the Garden homecoming of Bernard King. If once the presence of King meant vendors selling St. Bernard hats outside on 33rd Street, now the vendors are gone. King has been slumping and is no longer in the starting lineup. The problem is not his knee, he says, but an offense revolving around Moses Malone. He's averaging 16, but only shooting 42 percent from the floor.

The Bullets are slumping as a team. The Knicks score the first nine points of the game. King comes off the bench midway through the quarter and gets a standing ovation. He has 12 by the end of the quarter, showing a slice of the old

Bernard. Cummings comes off the bench in the first quarter and is roundly booed.

The scouting report revealed the Bullets had the worst overall shooting percentage in the league. Pitino decides to press less than he did in our first game, and make Washington prove it from the perimeter. His strategy also called for doubling Malone whenever he got the ball, make him pass.

It works. Moses looks old and slow. Unlike the first game, when he spent the night on the foul line, he is never a factor. At the other end Ewing abuses him on offense. The Knicks are up 16 by the end of the third quarter and headed for a rare blowout victory. King ends up with 19, but only has five in the second half. Ewing has 29, Cartwright comes off the bench for 23 in 24 minutes, and the disgruntled Cummings comes off the bench and hits seven of nine shots.

Pitino is pleased. "They responded to what I said in Portland, and came out and played with pride. This was our best game of the season. It was more than just the Patrick Ewing Show or the Mark Jackson Show. And I'm happy Cartwright had a big game. If ever the day comes when we have to trade him, I will be one sad coach.

"I'm also glad I decided to play Cummings, because when I came in tonight I wasn't going to. I even told Al I wasn't going to play Cummings anymore. Fine, he said, but tell him that. That's the value of Al Bianchi. Although he coached for twenty years, he understands the thoughts of both coaches and players, and now management. Sometimes I see things strictly as a coach. Al can look at things with more perspective. What I also appreciate is he thinks coaches are grossly underpaid. He doesn't mind what the players get, but think coaches need to catch up. And he speaks about this with bitterness in his voice, from all his years as a player when he made $1,000 a month. You can hear the hurt in his voice. For he now negotiates million-dollar contracts, while he spent a career riding buses and trains and staying in second-class hotels.

"But after the walk-through I had a change of heart. I went up to Cummings and said that maybe we both could go back to . . . square one. I told him that I hadn't had a problem with him until the night against the Hawks when he told me he couldn't play our pressing style. I told him, 'I'm not going to change my style of play just because of you. I'll play you, but I want you to stop putting your hands on people's backs on defense and picking up cheap fouls. And stop thinking you have to score ten points in a minute.' " He pauses for a second. "Five years ago I would have gone to hell before I played him."

Before he leaves to see his father, Pitino talks with Vescey, who is in the hallway. Vecsey is a true hoop junkie who, in his early forties, still plays in pickup games. "I asked him where he got the stuff about me not getting along with Al Bianchi. And told him, for your information I do get along with Al Bianchi. If you can't get along with Al Bianchi, you can't get along with anyone on this planet."

Two days later Pitino calls Billy Donovan, who is at his parents' home in Long Island.

"What are you doing?"

"Trying to hook on with another CBA team," Donovan says.

"I think I have a better situation for you."

"What's that?" asks Donovan, having no idea what Pitino means.

"You're coming with us."

Donovan had been the most obvious symbol of Pitino's ability to transform college players into better athletes. When Pitino arrived, Donovan looked too small, too slow, and had a one-hand push shot instead of a jumper. He had been recruited by prior coach Joe Mullaney primarily because of the way he passed the ball. But in his first two years, he had looked like a good kid who had gone to the wrong school.

"The first thing I did was tell him to lose twenty pounds. The second thing I did was tell him to get a jump shot.

When Donovan returned to Providence the next fall, I started calling him Billy the Kid, had him pose for a picture in a cowboy suit to boost the image, and gave him the green light on offense. Two years later Donovan was the MVP of the Southeast regional."

"I felt weepy seeing Billy and Rick together," says Joanne Pitino. "It's the nicest thing that's happened to us in a long time. I always felt they would be together again. Just like Rick used to spend so much of his time in the gym when he was younger, I saw that all the time with Billy. I know Rick can see himself in Billy. What Rick admires most is dedication and the will to win, and Billy has that."

His father dies Thursday night. In ten months he has lost both a child and a parent.

"The doctors told me he was getting better. But I was stuck in traffic on the West Side Highway and called him on my car phone. I could barely hear him. I asked him what was wrong. 'I'm in horrible pain,' he said. I never saw him again. But those nights I spent with my father were some of the most meaningful times I had spent with him in five years."

That night the Knicks beat the Denver Nuggets in the Garden. Stu Jackson coaches the team. Earlier in the day the Knicks waived Tolbert, and activated Thornton from the injured list. The word now is that Dallas, badly burned the past year in the trade that sent Dale Ellis to Seattle, are hesitant to give up Schrempf for Cartwright.

The next morning Kevin Kernan writes in the *Post:* "Knick bashing is a popular pastime in this time. And it's oh so easy to do. But for the first time in this decade the Knicks are taking the right road to rebuilding. . . . The signs are there that this team is light-years head of the Hubie Brown era. To rip the Knicks now is to take a shotgun to the first robin of spring."

Kernan goes on to say the Knicks' future in the Atlantic Division is good. The Nets are "the sorriest team, from the top to bottom, in all of sports." The Bullets are a "collection of aging players and circus freaks, destined to land on the scrap heap." Philly is "only competitive because of Charles Barkley, and when Bird goes so go the Celtics." It is the first time a New York writer has come out so positively for the new Knick regime.

The Knicks fly to Detroit, where they play the Pistons the following night. Pitino remains in New York for his father's funeral. The Knicks get blown out for another road loss. The only thing out of the ordinary is that Green and Isiah Thomas get into a fight. As teammates there was no love lost between them, one of the supposed reasons that Green became lodged so deep in coach Chuck Daly's doghouse.

December 15–20

Ten days before Christmas, Tucker comes off the injured list; McNealy is waived. Louis Orr also comes off the injured list; Thornton is waived. (He is claimed the next day by Philadelphia, in another NBA version of musical chairs.) It is the Knicks' fourth roster move in eight days.

The *Daily News* carries the screaming headline, "BRING MULLIN HOME."

Concerned Kenny Walker is picking up too many early fouls, Pitino starts Johnny Newman at small forward against Milwaukee. But the Knicks lose to the Bucks in the Garden by five after being up 15 in the third quarter. "It is one of the most disappointing losses of the season because we played our best half of basketball this season in the first half."

Two nights later, also in the Garden, they lose to the Philadelphia 76ers by 10. Charles Barkley, one of the league's superstars, has 40 points, 27 in the first half. The Sixers sag constantly around both Ewing and Cartwright, holding Ewing to 14 points and Cartwright to six. Once again the need for a consistent perimeter game is about as subtle as a neon sign in the desert.

The next day Gary Binford dissects the Knicks in *Newsday*. When the game is on the line, the Knicks have no one to go to besides Ewing, and all the other teams know it. "Can you remember the last time Trent Tucker buried a big shot? How many free throws and jumpers has Gerald Wilkins missed with the game on the line, not to mention the times he's been stripped of the ball when he tries to drive to the hoop instead of taking the open 15-footer? Mark Jackson has failed at the free-throw line several times in the clutch, but he's just a rookie. Kenny Walker is having enough problems just trying to score, period."

On Sunday in the *Daily News* Mike Lupica asks, "Has anybody asked Knick fans what they think about another 24-win season? I've got news for everybody: Knick fans don't really care if sportswriters like Rick and Al better than Hubie and Scotty. Knick fans don't want to be told things are getting better. Knick fans want some basketball players and some wins."

'Tis the season to be jolly?

December 22–23

At first glance it's just another road loss. It's the fifth in a row, their tenth in eleven road games. This time it's at the Mecca in Milwaukee, the downtown building with the Art Deco facade that Al McGuire made famous when he was at Marquette. What distinguishes this game, however, is an incident in the third quarter.

After a close first half, the Knicks are trailing by 12 in the third quarter when Sidney Green, who lost his starting job to Cummings three games ago, first loses the ball in the lane, then misses a 16-foot jumper. Then he loses the ball on an ill-advised move down the middle, and compounds the error by not hustling back on defense. Pitino is livid. He calls a timeout, and comes halfway out on the court to confront Green.

"What was that?" he yells.

"That was a good move," Green says defensively. "I had the opening."

"If you had the opening, why didn't you score? It was a bad move."

"It wasn't a bad move," says Green. "It was a good move."

"That's your opinion. When you knock a guy down going ninety mph, it's a bad move. Pass the damn ball and you won't have a problem."

Pitino has yelled at him too many times. Too many nights Green has been ineffective. The frustration all over his face, Green angrily yells back. Pitino yells at him to be quiet. Green waves a towel at Pitino in disgust and sits at the end of the bench.

"When the game resumed, I went over and kneeled down in front of him. Green was still seething. He wouldn't look at me. Kenny Walker was sitting next to Green and kept patting him on the leg to calm him down. There is a time and place for everything, and yelling at Green when he came off the court wasn't it."

By the end of the quarter the Knicks are outscored by 18 and the game is history. Ewing, once again bothered by foul problems, only plays 18 minutes. Afterward, Pitino tells the beat writers that it's "just an isolated incident. Sid's been fine up to this point. If he wants to vent his frustration once in a while, that's healthy."

Green won't talk about the incident, but says he feels he's been phased out of the Knick offense. I can't talk about it. I'm just trying to do what's asked of me. Trying to play defense and play defense. And play defense."

The next morning the headlines are about the squabble. "RICK RAPS GREEN" crows the *Daily News*. "GREEN SEES RED AFTER PITINO TIRADE" trumpets the *Post*. Pitino tells Kevin

Kernan of the *Post* he will allow a player to blow up one time. "One time. That's it."

That night, before the Knicks are to play Michael Jordan and the Chicago Bulls, Pitino meets privately with Green. "It's over, okay? It takes two to tango, and I'm just as much at fault as you. You gave me a silly answer and that triggered me off. I wish that if the incident had to happen, it would have happened with someone I didn't like so much. But I like you, Sid. I think you're a hell of a person. I brought you to New York. But so far I've been disappointed in your intensity level."

"I'm having a tough time in this style," Green said.

"Stop it, Sid. Don't tell me what you're having a tough time with. Don't tell me what you can't do. Tell me what you can do, and I'll listen to you. I want you to play harder. I want you to do everything at 100 percent. Or one of us is going to fall by the wayside."

One of the things he learned in his two-year stint as a Knick assistant was that pros must be reasoned with. "They must be convinced that what you are telling them is in their best interest. You can criticize a college kid in a group situation, and they'll respond. In the NBA, though, a pro's ego is usually as fragile as a robin's egg.

"I learned that in one of my first games as Hubie's assistant. Hubie went after Truck Robinson at halftime, telling him he wasn't rebounding hard enough. I am, said Truck, glaring. You're not, said Hubie, returning the glare. Dueling glares. One look and I told myself, it's best to criticize a pro in private. Last night I didn't do that, and the price tag was an ugly incident that got blown up in the papers."

Before the Chicago game he tells Fred Kerber the incident is over. "We said some words, but now it's over. I have no doghouses. I like Sidney. My problems with him are on the court."

Tonight the Garden is sold out. The scalpers are doing a big business on Seventh Avenue, harking back to the days when the Knicks were the hottest ticket in town and the Garden was the game's Big Room. Darryl Strawberry sits in the celebrity section across from the Knicks' bench. John McEnroe and Tatum O'Neal are a few rows back, as is the Mets' Keith Hernandez.

Michael Jordan, of course, is the attraction, the game's newest superstar. He has become the legitimate heir to Julius Erving, taking basketball where it has never been before, transforming a game played on a wooden floor into some strange new aerial dance. Jordan is the future king in a line that stretches from Connie Hawkins to a young Doctor J. You watch Jordon and all you see are possibilities, complete with his Air Jordans, his baggy shorts, and his imprimatur of sticking his tongue out when he gets excited.

"We have to make sure the tongue doesn't come out," quips Pitino. "When the tongue comes out, it's time to go home."

People line up behind the press table with cameras as the Bulls warm up, as if communicants to view the pope. "Michael over here, Michael." "Yo, Michael, hook me up with some sneakers." "Michael, over here." "Yo, Mike!"

Pitino's strategy is to double-team Jordan whenever possible. Deny him the ball, make him take jump shots rather than solo flights to the hoop. Jordan is averaging 34 points a game, tops in the NBA, and unlike his first years in the league, the Bulls have become more than a one-trick pony. Charles Oakley is one of the top young power forwards. Rookie Scottie Pippin, who used postseason all-star games to rise from the anonymity of Central Arkansas to the fifth pick in the draft, already is being called one of the top rookies in the league. At 15–9 the Bulls are a strong challenger in the Central Division and one of the best young teams in the league. Still, Pitino knows if Jordan has a big game, he can beat the Knicks virtually by himself, as Barkley did the week before when he had 27 in the first half.

Once again Johnny Newman and Pat Cummings are the

starting forwards. Much of the time the Knicks are in a halfcourt trap. When they are in straight-man, Wilkins is on Jordon, constantly trying to deny him the ball. When he gets it, the closest Knick rushes over and joins Wilkins in trapping him. "Find Jordan," Pitino constantly shouts from the sideline. "Jordan . . . Jordon . . . Deny . . . Deny."

The defense works. Jordan has only seven at the end of the half and has yet to find any rhythm. The traps either make him get rid of the ball, or else force him into taking a rushed shot. With 2:33 left, the game is tied at 86; both teams have had trouble scoring. With 13 seconds left, Ewing scores on the left baseline, putting the Knicks up 90–89. He also is fouled. He misses the free throw, and Jordan gets one more chance. With the clock winding down, the large Garden crowd is going berserk, chanting "Dee-fense." He tries to squeeze a shot up in the lane. Ewing comes over and blocks the shot, but a jump ball is called with six seconds remaining. Ewing controls the tap, it goes off Pippin, and the Knicks have an early Christmas present.

Ewing has had 22 points. Jackson has had 17 assists, tying his career high. Wilkins, with some help from Tucker and a great team defense, has held Jordan to 16 points, matching his season low, 5–15 from the floor. Green has had his best game in a while, once even diving on the floor. The Bulls have scored only 35 points in the second half.

Pitino tells the team it was a great team win. Then he gives them the next day off. He comes out of the locker room into the narrow hallway with the blue floor and the blue and white walls. He is immediately engulfed by reporters and minicams.

"You have to be pleased with Mark Jackson, him being a rookie?"

"I would be pleased with him if he were an eight-year veteran. Mark Jackson is a basketball player. We underestimate basketball players. Everyone talks about athletes. Mark reminds me of a poor man's Walt Frazier. You've got to start putting him in that class. He's very smart and heady. He doesn't have the great speed, but he has what it takes to be very good."

"You've got to be pleased with Gerald Wilkins' defense."

"Last year Gerald Wilkins never thought about defense. It was a disease. Look at what he did tonight. He and Trent played against the best basketball player in America, and played him the best I've seen him played."

"You got to be pleased with the way things went tonight, the big crowd and all."

"Someday the building will be like that all the time, but right now we are taking our hearts and throwing them on the floor. When we get some scoring to go along with defense and hustle, we will be really good."

The hallway is crowded. In back of the impromptu press conference are his wife, Joanne, and two of his kids. Michael, the oldest who just turned ten, was all set to come tonight until he found out he couldn't be the ballboy, and said he wasn't going. Now Pitino turns to the two youngest.

"And you said we couldn't beat Michael Jordan," he says to his son Chris, who is wearing a blue Knicks hat and a gray Final Four T-shirt.

"Dad, can I still get Michael Jordan's autograph?" he asks.

Pitino turns to one of the Knick ballboys and whispers in his ear. "I know he's probably feeling down, but can you go ask Michael for three autographs?"

Also in the hallway are five of his former Providence College players. They beat Xavier by 20 the night before, a great win for them, and are here to see both Pitino and Donovan. Pitino breaks away from the press conference to greet them. In his mind they always will be his players, the bond forged in all the practice sessions, the death of his son, Providence's unbelievable Final Four season, all the long hours spent together. In a certain sense this will always be his team in ways the Knicks can never be. For he knows he never can get as close to pro players as he did to those Providence kids, there's just not enough time. Unlike college, where the players forever are hanging around the basketball office or in the locker room, pro players practice and go home. They have their own families, their own lives, not the communal lives college kids have. And Pitino knows, deep down, that for all his talk of recreating a college atmosphere with the Knicks, he never will be able to replicate the one he walked away from.

December 25–26

This has become the Cult Game: Christmas in the Garden. Deck the halls with boughs of holly and slam dunks. God rest ye merry gentlemen disguised as referees. This is the Knicks at noontime, courtesy of CBS. Come, all ye faithful.

Today nearly all of them do.

Two years ago the Knicks, down 25 points, rallied to beat the Celtics. Last year they beat the Bulls by one. Christmas magic, Knick style. The opponent today is Detroit, the same Pistons that blew the Knicks out in the second half two weeks ago. These same Pistons have won eight straight, and are sitting high atop the Central Division with the best record in basketball. But they come in on this foggy, unseasonably warm morning without Adrian Dantley, suspended for a game for bumping a referee, and Ricky Mahorn, out with an injury. In their place in the starting lineup are second-year guys John Salley and Dennis Rodman.

In the season opener the Knicks constantly fullcourt pressed the Pistons. Today they spend most of the game in their halfcourt trap. By the second quarter it is controlling the tempo, holding the Pistons to a mere 12 points in the second quarter. At one point Detroit misses 12 straight shots, plus seven free throws. Six of those, including two air balls, are by Rodman, the worst foul shooter in the league. Midway through the third quarter the Knicks are ahead by 14 points and appear in control of the game. They have taken the Pistons out of their set offense and stopped their transition game.

But as has happened so many times before in this young season, the Knicks' offense stops attacking. Detroit coach Chuck Daly goes with three guards, Vinnie Johnson joining Isiah Thomas and Joe Dumars, and the Pistons find some offense. The Knicks initially try to take advantage of the 6–1 Johnson guarding 6–8 Kenny Walker by posting Walker up inside. When this doesn't work, Pitino counters with three guards of his own, bringing in Trent Tucker and moving Wilkins to small forward. The Knicks lead by five going into the fourth quarter, but Detroit catches them and goes ahead with 3:16 left.

Ewing, who will finish with 28 points, misses two free throws, but the game is still tied with 1:34 to go. Then Walker steals a pass and gives it to Jackson on a two-on-one break. Instead of making the easy pass back to Walker, Jackson tries a spinning layup against Isiah Thomas, something out of a playground primer. Bill Laimbeer, hustling back into the play, blocks it. Isiah saves it in the far corner, and Dumars buries a jumper from the top of the key. Trailing by two, the Knicks come back downcourt. But Wilkins throws the ball inside for Green a split second after Green has left to screen for Ewing. The Knicks, now down two, foul Johnson with 11 seconds left. He misses the first foul shot. Then he misses the second, but Salley gets the offensive rebound over Green. His two free throws end it, 91–87.

A tough loss. Not only did the Knicks control the tempo the entire game, once again they failed to grab hold of a game they should have won. Ewing's free throws. Jackson's playground move at a decisive time. Wilkins' bad pass. The failure to rebound a missed free throw. Each mistake by itself is not crucial. The cumulative effect is.

"What happened on that play?" Sam Goldaper, the venerable sportswriter for the *New York Times*, asks Jackson on his way into the shower.

"I took the shot and it got blocked."

"But what happened?" Goldaper presses. "Should you have passed it?"

Jackson looks exasperated. "I took the shot and it got blocked."

"Isiah said you should have passed."

"That's his opinion," says Jackson, pausing a beat, turning to go to the shower. "And we all know what they are worth."

Pitino knows he needs something special for the following night. The Knicks have left SUNY at seven in the morning for a flight to Atlanta and a date with the high-flying Hawks. "You don't have to be *Red on Roundball* to see a potential blowout lurking ahead. A tough loss yesterday. The fourth game in five nights. Our team's tired. All the ingredients for one of those games you can all but mail in."

He knows he's going to need all his motivational skills tonight, the ones he was so good at in college. Like the time against Austin Peay. But that was college. In college he could motivate collectively, because he knew everyone's primary concern was the team winning. Now that's not always the case. For instance, he knows Cartwright was down after the win over Chicago because he didn't get enough minutes. Billy feels he must produce numbers if some other team is going to extricate him from New York. Cummings is in the last year of his contract, and he's more concerned with salvaging his sagging career than he is with winning. He doesn't own up to his liabilities, that he's not the same player he was before he was hurt two years ago. If he tries hard, as soon as he has adversity he looks for someone to blame. Louis Orr, returning from back surgery and in the last year of his contract, is concerned his career may be ending. These players must be motivated individually, persuaded to believe their careers can benefit if the team wins, that everyone's value escalates when the team wins. In the NBA it's more complicated than giving a fiery locker room speech and telling everybody to go out and win one for the Gipper.

Then, too, there are too many games for fiery pregame talks. In college he could point to big games. There was time to prepare. Here the games pile up on one another, begin blurring together. Isn't every game a big game? How do you differentiate? The last thing he wants is to have everyone think, here comes College Speech number 48.

Here he has to be more of a psychiatrist. He has to bolster sagging egos, fragile egos that often have been coddled since adolescence when their great talent began setting these players apart. He is forever sitting down individually with many of his players. He tells Gerald Wilkins to improve his defense and passing. The acquisition of these skills will not only prolong his career, but prevent him from one day becoming a role player. Sidney Green has to be more of a presence on the floor. Pitino tells him to model his game on Buck Williams, the New Jersey power forward who has made a reputation by rebounding. He tells Kenny Walker to block out the booing in the Garden. He has coaches and eleven teammates who think he's great, and that's the important thing. Walker is a sensitive young man who's frustrated by being booed for the first time in his life. In a recent game in the Garden, Kenny went through a horrible sequence, complete with throwing an airball on an open 15-footer. The boos rained down. Afterwards, Pitino saw him with tears in his eyes in the locker room.

He is forever reminded of how fragile their egos are. A player is often reluctant to admit a mistake because he feels it will be used against him in the future. That is one of the reasons he admires Ewing so much: he always owns up to his mistakes. Jackson is the same way, secure enough as a player to admit he made a mistake. That's a very special quality in the NBA.

So as Pitino sits in his Atlanta hotel room on this day after Christmas, he knows he needs something special. He is going to get them together in the locker room in the Omni before the game, and go over all the games they let slide away in the closing minutes. The one-point loss in the Garden to Atlanta when Ewing stepped out of bounds on the Knicks last possession. The blowing of the 28-point lead to Boston. The loss to the Nets in the Meadowlands after they were ahead in the closing minutes. The loss at home to Seattle where they missed five foul shots down the stretch. The recent one to the Bucks in the Garden. Yesterday's against the Pistons. If they had won those games, they would have been 14–11 instead of 8–17.

"I went over all of them, each bloody one, and then asked my players if we were capable of going 32–25 the rest of the year. I didn't hinge my talk on winning tonight's game, for I smelled blowout. No, I asked them if we could go 32–25 the rest of the year. That would get us 40 wins. Not that I think we can get 40 wins, but if we shoot for 40, maybe we can finish in the 30's."

For things already have become different than he thought in July when he was announced as the new Knick coach, and said he didn't leave the best college in America to suffer through a 24-win season with the Knicks.

At the time he thought there would be wholesale changes. That Cartwright would be gone. Cummings would be gone. That in their place would be a forward who could score, more athletic players better suited to his style of play. At the time he thought the Knicks would have begun turning things around by now.

But, of course, it hadn't worked out that way. Essentially, he is playing with the same team that won 24 games the year before. Bianchi keeps telling him to have patience, that if they wait there will be better offers for Cartwright in the future. Bianchi's philosophy is to err on the side of caution. He believes panic was what had buried the Knicks in the first place. They mortgaged the future for a few more wins. If Pitino believes that intellectually, in his heart he wants to make moves, do anything to get the team better now. He's caught in the middle. On one hand he knows building for the future is the right approach. On the other he wants to win now. For he has never lost before.

He also believes the Madison Square Garden hierarchy will react to the New York media. He suspects that if the Knicks don't win now, the media will push the panic button and MSG will react to it, like they've done in the past. The only thing that matters in New York is winning.

He knows he's going to have to resign himself to no new players, at least for the short-term. That resignation had begun shortly before the season when the Cartwright-to-Atlanta deal fell through. It had been reinforced recently when the Knicks shopped Cartwright to Portland for Kiki Vandeweghe. That too has fizzled.

"Now there is no interest in Cummings or Tucker. Nor does there seem to be any in Cartwright. People are backing off due to Cartwright's history of foot problems, his large salary, and his age. Billy will be here for the year, or at least until the trading deadline in mid-February, when contending teams may decide they need his offense to make a run at the NBA title. Bianchi already has said there are worse scenarios than having Cartwright around for the entire year: 'There's not a team in the league as strong at center as we are.' "

The other thing, of course, is the New York media. Not too many days go by when the Greek chorus doesn't take a shot at the Knicks, little body blows that constantly send Pitino the message that he always must keep his guard up and keep back-peddling. After the Sidney Green incident Vescey wrote that Chuck Daly has a Pitino quote hanging in his office that says, "I'm not going to be like the last two coaches and quit on Sidney Green." Filip Bondy in the *News* asked, "What happens the next time Sidney Green goes off, now that Rick Pitino says he won't tolerate it anymore?" The next day Lupica writes the Knicks "got a fine coach in Pitino, but the best man available was Larry Brown."

He has come to realize no coach can stay in New York too long because the writers will get him. He saw it happen to Hubie Brown. The same writers who saw him as God with statistics were the ones calling for him to be fired three years later. There are too many writers and they all compete with another. Every postgame press conference becomes a cat-and-mouse game. He tries to sugar-coat everything and stay positive; they're trying to get him to say something that can make headlines on the back of the tabloids. So he tries to weigh each sentence carefully, because he knows the wrong one will be headlines the next day.

Most of all, Rick Pitino has come to realize that coaching the New York Knickerbookers is no longer the dream job it was that afternoon in July. That summer afternoon now seems long ago.

6 | "Sometimes I Thought He Was a Maniac"

We're losing, but the more you lose, the more positive you have to become. When you're winning, you can ride them harder because their self-esteem is high. If you are losing and you try to be tough, you're asking for dissension. I learned this by trial and error.

I get on Mark. I tell him he's been great, but he has to be greater. I tell them how great the attitude of my Providence team was last year, but how theirs is greater. I can't tell you how proud I am of you. Some guys look at me like they don't know what to think. But I think they feel good about themselves, because in the pros nobody speaks to them like that.

I tell them you're low-key people. When we're in Atlanta or Los Angeles, you go back to your room after a game. You're low-key, and I want you to have that personality. That's special. My Providence team was like that, too, but on the court my Providence team changed. They became an extension of my personality. They became killers on the floor. So far you haven't done that. I can go two ways now. I can go the Vince Lombardi way and give fiery halftime speeches and locker room slogans. But it's 82 games and you aren't going to do that, because you think it's too corny. Or I can go the Tom Landry way. You're professionals and you're computerized. If you are not going to be enthusiastic, you have to be a professional.

There are guys here who don't know how to accept constructive criticism. Patrick Ewing and Billy Cartwright own up to everything. Billy doesn't always like it, but he'll own up to it. Sometimes I say that I have made a mistake, to show them that it's all right to make a mistake, but you have to own up to them. Trent Tucker's biggest problem is not that he's afraid to admit he's wrong, but that he's afraid to get better, afraid to try new things.

I had a run-in with Louis Orr in Atlanta. I like Louis. I've known him ever since I recruited him for Syracuse. But he suggested before the game that maybe we shouldn't press that much, that we had been playing good halfcourt defense and maybe we should stick with that against Atlanta instead of pressing. I stopped him right there. Louis, it's not that we don't want your opinions, I said, but you probably thought about this all of five minutes. We have three coaches here who have been up all night running film.

After the game on the bus he came up to me and said, "You and I got to have a truce." "Look, when you say something like that, something so insensitive, it hurts." "I was just trying to help." "Just play hard, be enthusiastic, and leave the coaching to us."

Not that I don't want suggestions from them, I do. We ask them all the time what they think is the best way to play Bird, or whether they should play the screen on the high side, or the low side, whatever. It gets them thinking. We even vote sometimes. And sometimes it's better that it comes from them because they feel that now it has to work.

But under losing conditions, this is a very close team. That's rare in the NBA. We are playing good basketball right now. The presses are bothering people. We are shooting a higher percentage, recognizing our defensive reads better. Gerald Wilkins is improving, Newman is improving, Billy Cartwright is playing good basketball. I really think we can have a good second half.

I keep telling them how much respect I have for their attitude. How admirable it is for a professional team. That

Every New York schoolboy's fantasy come true: Rick Pitino and Mark Jackson at Tavern on the Green after Jackson was named Rookie of the Year. (George Kalinsky)

Above: This is where the myth began: a young Rick at Hawaii in 1975.

New coach Pitino sweeps out the old, and brings in the new with a trim Jacek Duda at Providence. *(Providence Journal)*

Above: Pitino gives the play at the Providence Civic Center. Players to the left are Dave Kipfer, Jacek Duda, and Dave Snedeker. (Thomas F. Maguire, Jr.)

Rick and Joan Pitino in Louisville in March 1987 after Providence upset Georgetown to advance to the Final Four. *(Providence Journal)*

Like father, like son: Ball boy Christopher gives some pointers to the coach. Star Providence guard, Billy Donavan, is on left. (Thomas F. Maguire, Jr.)

Pitino shows longtime Knick fixture Dick McGuire some new wrinkles. (George Kalinsky)

The motivator tells Pat Cummings, Bill Cartwright, and Sidney Green to take over the game. *(Providence Journal)*

How many flat-footed Sonics do you see? Mark Jackson slices in to the hoop. (George Kalinsky)

Take that! Patrick Ewing takes a pass from Kenny Walker and stuffs it. (George Kalinsky)

Slippin', slidin' Sidney Green eludes Celtic guards Dennis Johnson and Danny Ainge for the hoop. (George Kalinsky)

Stylish Gerald Wilkins shows yet again his tremendous athletic ability.
(George Kalinsky)

Above: Showtime at the Garden. Point guard Jackson catches Pistons' Joe Dumars leaning right. (George Kalinsky)

What happens when no one's open? The playmaker roars in for the score. (George Kalinsky)

Two giants head skyward: Bill Cartwright floats one over Celts' Robert Parish. (George Kalinsky)

How do you spell l-e-a-d-e-r? Pitino congratulates Patrick Ewing after another spectacular play. *(Providence Journal)*

Take-charge Patrick Ewing shows why he has become a dominant force in the NBA today. (George Kalinsky)

Wheeling and dealing Patrick slides around Kareem Abdul-Jabbar. (George Kalinsky)

Explosive Johnny Newman shows just why he is instant firepower. (George Kalinsky)

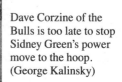

Dave Corzine of the Bulls is too late to stop Sidney Green's power move to the hoop. (George Kalinsky)

A rare pensive moment for the nonstop coach. Assistant Stu Jackson is at rear. (George Kalinsky)

Dad, Ricky, and Big Bird.

Happy youngsters Michael, Christopher, and Ricky.

The future and the past: Patrick Ewing slams one in against Kareem Abdul-Jabbar. (George Kalinsky)

there's no doubt in my mind that we're going to have a big second half of the year and make the playoffs.

In many ways it's like the first year at Providence when everything was for the future. It really didn't matter how well you ball-faked or how well you went over the screen, because there was a limit to how good you could be. There is just so much hard work can compensate for inferior talent. That first year they developed mental toughness, and that's what we're trying to do here. Work for the future. Practice is no different than at Providence. They work their ass off. No nonsense. We don't put up with it.

But we need some more points. I wish we could do something now to take a run for the playoffs. One guy who can score, that's all we need. I don't care if he can't do anything else.

✝✝✝✝✝✝✝✝✝

January 6–10

Although the Knicks are blown out by the Hawks the day after Christmas, Pitino believes his pep talk worked. "Guys were cheering for each other, but were just down physically." The big news is that Dominique Wilkins is quoted afterward saying that he wouldn't want to play in Pitino's system. Pitino thinks it's a plant by Gerald's agent, who is reacting to the rumors Gerald is ticketed to Golden State for Chris Mullin. Expectations that the prodigal son is coming home are all over the tabloids in big print, even if he's now in an alcohol rehabilitation center in Los Angeles. Bianchi wants Mullin, thinks it will be great for the perception that the Knicks are committed to change. Pitino is not so sure. "I'm afraid of Mullin's alcohol problem. This is not the right time to bring him to the Knicks."

Wilkins feels he's in limbo. "Last year I was the greatest. I was the light. This year, all I read in the papers is that I'm selfish, I don't want to play. I'm not a bad guy. There are no problems between Rick and me. Every day I see myself getting so much better as an all-around ball player under Rick."

"When he plays good, the system's great," says Pitino. "When the plays bad, the system's no good. But I have no problem with Gerald Wilkins. I feel sorry for the kid. His whole problem is thinking he's got to be like Dominique. I need to sit down and help him out, tell him to put family pressures aside. I also need to help him organize his life. He needs discipline and organization, someone to manage his life for him. But he could be traded in six weeks for Chris Mullin, and then you haven't been honest with him. In a sense we're all on borrowed time, players and coaches, and it affects the way you relate to each other. I feel badly I didn't get a chance to tell Rory Sparrow he'd been traded. I've known Rory for a long time. Al did it, but I feel badly about it."

Dominique's barb is not the only jab at Pitino. Bob Ryan, the respected basketball writer for the *Boston Globe*, writes, "Rick Pitino was a brilliant college coach, and I thought he'd be a brilliant pro coach because he knew what the NBA was all about. Instead, he's playing Mickey Mouse, ugly basketball, designed to steal an occasional W by virtue of this maniacal press. The Knicks aren't the worst team in the league, but they are, without question, the least entertaining. About the only good thing that's happened down there is that Patrick Ewing is playing his best NBA ball and Rick Carlisle has a job."

Underneath a headline in the *Daily News* that says "RICK PITINO—HUBIE CLONE?" Harvey Araton writes, "Sometimes, if you close your eyes while you listen to Rick Pitino at courtside, or talking to the press, you can almost make yourself believe it's really Hubie Brown. Sometimes, even with your eyes wide open, you're almost moved to say, 'Hubie, are you in there?' "

Dick Vitale says on WFAN that Pitino doesn't belong in

the professional game. He is the kind of coach who lives and dies with every play, and coaches like that belong in college. Araton says some members of the Knicks are complaining they are being forced to adapt to Pitino's style of play.

"I'd be the first to admit it," answered a beleaguered Pitino. "But I'm not going to adjust to them, because doing it their way won 24 games last year. Gulf & Western didn't hire me to do things the players' way. They hired me because I was a running and trapping coach."

On the first night of a homestand the Knicks beat Portland in the Garden, a game Pitino calls the best Knick performance of the year. They cruise by the Los Angeles Clippers New Year's night. Then they lose to Phoenix by five, after the game had been tied with 1:17 left. The Suns' Walter Davis scores seven of his 22 in the last three and a half minutes, pointing up the Knicks' lack of someone to go to in the closing minutes. The loss leaves the Knicks at 10–19.

"I would really be embarrassed if I made the kind of money you make and played like that," Pitino told the team after the game. "You didn't play hard. You played like you thought you were the Celtics or the Lakers, like you were going to let them hang around for a while, and then blow them out in the fourth quarter. It's like you forgot how to win. You have to scratch for every game. You have two choices. You can go out and play with all the enthusiasm of a college team. But I know you won't do that because that's too corny for you. Or you can go out and play like professionals. Give the team, the fans, everyone you represent a great effort. You did neither tonight. It's one thing to play poorly. We can live with that. But you should feel embarrassed. You didn't give a good effort, and that's what we promised the fans. I'm embarrassed being the head of this group."

Outside, it is a cold January night in Boston. Inside, the Boston Garden is preparing for another sellout that has become institutionalized in the Bird era. Organ music drifts through the Garden. Layers of smoke seem to hang over the baskets. Many of the players are casually shooting around, the Celtics in their white warmups, the Knicks in their blue. It is still about an hour away from game time. Pitino sits in the cramped visitors' locker room talking about the loss to Phoenix.

"I could see the lackadaisical effort the morning before the game at the shoot-around at SUNY. We got snowed out of practice the day before. Didn't practice the day before that. We had four games in five days coming up, the Suns had played the night before, and I'm sure everyone thought this was going to be the one. It's like we forgot how to win. Wilkins? A roller coaster would be a kind term for the way he played. The game was a disaster for us."

Minutes before the game, the team assembled in the locker room, he points to a blackboard. On one side are the shooting percentages from the night before. Wilkins: 3–15. Tucker: 1–7. Cummings: 1–5. The other side of the board has the names Newman, Wilkins, Walker, and Jackson. All have the number of minutes they played the night before. None of them had a defensive rebound, even though Wilkins, Walker, and Jackson each played at least 34 minutes.

"Now, there are some coaches in this league that would harp on your shooting percentages, but I never bring up to you what you shot. Rebounding stats are something else again. They're effort stats."

The Knicks go out on the court and lose. Afterward, Pitino stays behind. Ironically, the first successes of his coaching career took place only a few miles away. He was only twenty-five when he took the job at Boston University, and became the youngest head coach in the country. BU has a sprawling concrete campus and a student body with a high percentage of students from New York. It's known for its apathy toward sports. Hockey is the only sport that generates any interest, never mind success. There was no basketball tradition, no interest, and a legacy of bad teams. Pitino was an assistant coach at Syracuse when the Boston University job opened up. His boss, Jim Boeheim, told him the BU job was not for him. BU was a place where coaching reputations were broken, not made. Garfinkel told him the same thing. "It's a death trap. You can't win there."

But Pitino was itching for his own team, wanted to live in Boston, and in 1978 he arrived full of enthusiasm and energy. And his own imprint.

"From the first day he started changing everyone's attitude," says Glen Consor, who was a junior at BU at the time. "We had been 7–19 and 10–15 in the two years before Coach Pitino arrived. We didn't know how to win. I remember we had a team meeting, and he told us, 'If you do it my way, you're going to win. We're going to be the hardest-working team in the country.' We didn't know that to think.

"Then he met with everyone individually, and told us what he both liked and didn't like from what he had seen on film. He told me that I wouldn't play a minute, ever, if I didn't (a) gain twenty pounds over the summer, (b) become quicker, and (c) learn how to score. I was almost in shock. I had started at point guard for two years, and thought I had done all right. And here was the new coach telling me that if I didn't gain twenty pounds not to bother coming out for the team next year.

"I came from New York, and basketball was the most important thing in my life. I suppose, too, I was looking for someone to be a savior. So all that summer I lifted weights and worked out, and went from 160 to 178. I felt great, because at the beginning of the summer I didn't believe I could do it. But he told me he had said 20 pounds, not 18. So every morning for the first two weeks I had to get up at six in the morning and run two miles: a week of running for every pound I hadn't gained. You'd think that if I was two pounds short, he would have made me get up every morning and eat French toast or something, but what it did right away was develop mental toughness. All of us had certain

goals we were supposed to reach, and he held you account-
able if you didn't reach them."

The first year Pitino held an open practice, complete with
champagne, one minute after midnight on October 15, the
first day the NCAA allows practice. The idea was to hype
the program, a symbol of a new era. Four people showed
up. "One was my wife and two were guys who came for the
champagne," he says.

One of his assistant coaches that first year was Bill Burke,
who had coached at Nazareth High School in Brooklyn for
five years and knew Pitino from Five Star. "I thought I was
a bit of a lunatic, demanding with kids, up all the time,
calling out defenses. I thought I was intense and I was,"
says Burke, now a Wall Street stock trader. "But there was
no comparison. Rick was all these things and more. Right
from the start he created an atmosphere of incredible
hard work. Kids always are talking about how they want to
become great players. Rick gave them the vehicle. But they
had to do the work."

"I came to a practice one day when BU was recruiting
me," says Patrick Ewing with a smile, "and I thought he
was a maniac. I couldn't believe how hard he was working
those players."

One of the vehicles was an hour a day of individual
instruction, when each player worked with one of the coaches
on his individual game. Guards worked on shooting and ball
handling, inside people on post-up moves. "This evolved
from my time at Syracuse as an assistant coach, where I
often worked unofficially with some of the players on their
games, particularly Louis Orr and Marty Byrne. I took
many of the drills I had learned in camps and adopted them
to a college program. From the beginning I saw that it was
possible to make players better. The key was breaking down
the game, making sure the players were doing things that
were fundamentally sound, and then having them do constant repetition.

His philosophy at Boston University was twofold: get players in the best shape of their lives, and get them to play with all the intensity of Marines following Teddy Roosevelt up San Juan Hill. Then have them pass all over the court. In a sense it was a new way to play. If at first glance it looked helter-skelter, there was a method to his madness. "I learned early that if you play slow and control the tempo, that way you lose by four to six points and get a lot of moral victories."

"In other words, why let someone who is better than you come down the court every time and run their set offense? Isn't it better to do something that takes them out of their routine and forces them to improvise? So what if I didn't have great talent? We'd press anyway. We would apply fullcourt pressure whoever the opponent was, and make them play the full 94 feet. We would press and foul. We would dictate tempo. We would decide the way the game would be played, not the other way around."

An up-tempo style has always had practitioners. It's usually the staple of teams with great talent, the UNLVs of the world. Run and gun. But the corollary always seems to be that such teams either play questionable defense or are poorly coached. The purists shake their heads. Coaches from the old school, men raised on the bible of work for a good shot and fall back into a halfcourt defense, also shake their heads. They say it looks like a playground game.

"Constant pressure not only makes opponents physically tired, it makes them mentally tired also. The pressure of trying to get the ball up the court all the time is mentally draining. It's like walking down the street with a snarly terrier always nipping your ankles. The other thing pressure defense does is make opponents have to pass the ball. This is maybe the one phase of the game that's deteriorated in the past twenty years with all these sleek slama jamas taking it airborne.

"New philosophy or not, virtually no one came to the games. I learned early that I had to be the motivator because there sure was no one else. No crowd. No tradition. No student support. No community support. No TV. No media. Just me. I'd be giving a chalk talk about twenty minutes before the game, and through the windows I could see that there were only about forty people there. Throughout the game I had to pump them up because there was no one else to. My voice would echo throughout Case Center."

Right from the beginning he had a feel for motivating people. "We used to do a lot of good cop, bad cop stuff," says Burke. "We had this one kid from Brooklyn, Desmond Martin. He was 6–7 and had a lot of baby fat, so right away Rick did the weight thing with him. He was a great kid, but he really had to be pushed. He would go into a game and make a silly foul, and Rick would take him out. He would sit down between us, and as the game was going on, Rick and I would start talking about him like he wasn't there. Rick would say, 'It's too bad I can't play Desmond because he's just not getting after it.' I'd say, 'Yeh, I know, we should put a skirt on him.' 'I really want to play him, but he's just not doing it,' he'd say, and I'd counter with 'No, Rick, you shouldn't play him. He's a sissy.' We'd go back and forth like this, and you could see Desmond's fists start to clench and his legs start to shake. Then Rick would say to me, 'Maybe we should give him one more chance.' Three times out of four this would work with Desmond. He would go back in and play appreciably better.

"With someone else he would take a different approach. We had this kid, Johnny Ray Wall, who was a great athlete, someone who wanted to be a pro. So Rich wouldn't use the sissy stuff with him. Instead he would say things like 'Look at Johnny. I think he could be a great player. Am I wrong. Am I right?' 'I don't know. I think he could be great, but sometimes I'm not so sure.' Johnny would hear this and want to show Rick he was great.

"Rick also adapted in his years at BU. In the beginning he was so demanding at times that you thought he was going overboard, but he had this uncanny ability to pick up the players, too. A lot of coaches who are demanding can't pick their players up. Rick can do both. When I first came to BU with him I knew he was good. When I left after three years, I knew he was exceptional."

In retrospect, Boston University was the perfect basketball laboratory for a young coach. It's a time that seems bathed in the soft light of first love for him. Sure, he did take a struggling team and made it a winner. They averaged 18 victories in his five seasons there, complete with six kids who went on to become NBA draft choices. But it's more than that. At Boston University it was Pitino and his team against the world. After games they'd go to T. Anthony's, a pizza joint on Commonwealth Avenue near the campus. They'd rehash the game, talking it out over and over. The players often were over at his house. In a sense it was more pure at BU, college basketball without the trappings. He was closer to his players there. There was no outside pressure to win.

"We called him the Boy Coach," recalls John Simpson, the former Boston athletic director who hired Pitino. "I thought he was, one, a great teacher. He left nothing to chance. Two, he was a great motivator, especially when he convinced players what they had to do in the offseason. And he was a great recruiter. He was so driven by the game himself that he related this feeling to the people he recruited, particularly to their mothers and fathers."

He burned to transform BU into a first-class program. But it was never easy.

"One time my two assistant coaches and I went on a recruiting trip to Chicago. And we're not talking airplane here. No fly in, stay at a cushy hotel, and put everything on the tab. This was Boston University. This was driving twenty-seven hours in a Renault LeCar through a snowstorm, a deer running into the side of the car, then staying at some no-tell motel outside of the city, where the three of us stayed in the

same room to save money. To make matters worse, Joanne
was about to give birth, and the player we went to see was
in a high school tournament, which meant we couldn't talk
to him until his team lost. You guessed it. A week later the
kid's team was still winning, and the three of us had run out
of money. We spent the afternoons looking for happy hours
in bars so we could eat some free food. We ended up
having to change motels, ended up three in the same bed,
praying for the kid to lose."

It was at BU that Pitino's reputation as a crazy man
spread. Who was this wild man who had his teams practice
three times a day, had them running around the gym carrying bricks?

"It was called minute on the brick drill," says Consor.
"Every practice was monitored by the managers. If you
didn't take a charge, or made a stupid mistake, or didn't go
after a rebound hard enough, you were given a minute. At
the end of the practice you went into the lane in a defensive
stance holding bricks in each hand. Well, not really holding
them, balancing them on the tops of your palms, which is
hard, believe me. Then you had to go from one side of the
paint to another in a defensive slide. Had to do it something
like 18-20 times in one minute. And if you stood up or
dropped the bricks, you had to start all over again. It was a
killer. Your legs were humming.

"But you know what? It worked. Everyone hated the
minute on the brick drill so much that if you had a chance to
take a charge in practice, you stepped in and took it. If you
were coming down on the break out of control, instead of
throwing a lousy pass you stopped and pulled the ball back.
We were all so fearful of picking up minutes and having to
deal with those bricks that we played better."

Once, in his senior year against the University of Massachusetts, Consor was having a bad first half. Shortly before
it ended, he scored on a shot Pitino thought had been
forced.

"He chewed me out at the half, big-time," says Consor, "said I was playing selfishly. I went back and played the entire second half, and though I didn't think I'd played particularly well, I was happy we had won. But in the locker room he came up to me.

" 'Get your sweatpants on,' he said.

" 'Why?'

" 'Because you are going out on the track and run two miles.'

"Now, this was January and it was cold. But I went out and ran, and he had a manager time me. And not just around the track. Sprints and everything. So the next day in practice I'm all pissed off, but he calls me over and starts to talk, and after a while it was like nothing ever happened. Because the bottom line was that the love was there. We knew that he really cared about us. He wanted us to get better."

One time a few years later Pitino made two players run back to the hotel from the arena in Cincinnati. "It must have been ten below zero," laughs Pitino. "We had just played Cincinnati, and both Oscar Robertson and Jack Twyman were in the locker room afterward because Jack's son, Jay, played for me. I had these two players, Brett Brown and Danny Harwood, and they had been late for the bus before the game. So I went up to them in the locker room afterward and said quietly, because I didn't want Oscar and Twyman to hear, that they couldn't come back on the bus with us. And that they better beat the bus back to the hotel if they knew what was good for them. It was only a couple of miles back to the hotel, but it was cold. But they both did it. Harwood later said he felt like Rocky, running through the streets of the city."

"Sometimes you thought he was a maniac," says Consor. "One time we were playing Boston College in the NIT at BC, and right after the tap the ball is going out-of-bounds and me and John Bagley both go after it. The ref says the ball is off me. Then I hear the horn. Pitino has substituted for me. I run over to the bench—we always had to run—and he puts his arm around me, grabs about an inch of my skin, and says, 'If you don't get every loose ball in this game, you won't believe what is going to happen to you.' All the while he has a smile on his face so people will think this is a nice, friendly conversation. Then he puts me right back in the game. I remember thinking, What is it with this guy? Because it always was a mixture playing for him. Intimidation. Humor. Reality. All thrown together.

"But I can see now that everything was for a purpose," adds Consor, who spent two years playing in Europe and now is in commercial real estate in Northern Virginia. "The drill with the bricks helped your defensive stance. Even making me run those two miles that night. He instilled in our minds that for us to win we had to do this. And he was right. When we practiced poorly we played poorly. None of us were big names. We just came out of nowhere. Then in games we would put the press on, and you could see the look on the other team's faces in the last five minutes. It was the look of a guy in a fight who knew he was about ready to get knocked out.

"And you know, I have a very special feeling for all the people I played with at BU. We all worked so hard. There were times you thought he was crazy. There were times when you didn't want to do it anymore. But I left BU knowing I became the best player I could have been, and isn't that really what every player wants? Unlike a lot of guys who played in college and spend the rest of their lives saying, I could have been better if the coach had let me shoot more, or done this more. I am a happy guy, a fulfilled player. The bottom line is that I had a tremendous college basketball experience, and it was all because of Rick Pitino."

Despite all the work, people still didn't show up for the games. "I tried everything. I gave away free tickets. I labeled one of our more vocal cheering sections 'The Dog

Pound,' and made up hundreds of red shirts with that inscription. And still they didn't come. I was frustrated. What did the people want? I gave them a good team, an exciting team. I hyped the team everywhere there was an audience, and still the response was: So what?"

In 1983 he interviewed for the Penn State job. The choice came down to him and Bruce Parkhill, who had grown up in State College and whose brother, Barry, once had starred at the University of Virginia. Parkhill got it. "I was devastated. I couldn't understand it. I had been told by certain people that the job was mine. I was dejected for a month, and vowed never again to apply for a job where they had a search committee."

That June he went back to Five Star. In five years he had compiled a 91–51 record at BU. One day he got a call from Hubie Brown. Mike Fratello, who had been his assistant with the Knicks, had just become the coach of the Atlanta Hawks. Brown asked Pitino if he wanted to become his assistant coach.

"That's why we let him leave," Simpson said. "He was totally frustrated. He did everything he could to get the crowds, and he was bitterly disappointed. But, you know, he thirsted for the big time."

On this night in the Boston Garden eleven out of the eighteen players profiled in the Knick media guide are gone: Gerald Henderson, Rory Sparrow, Jawann Oldham, Bob Thornton, Chris McNealy, Ron Moore, Ray Tolbert, Leo Rautins, Mike Morgan, Glen Clem, Geoff Huston. Added to the roster since the media guide was printed are Sidney Green, Johnny Newman, Billy Donovan, Rick Carlisle. Then there is Tony White, who already has come and gone.

The Celtics win by nine. Bird goes for 41, McHale for 30. Pitino is not upset. The Knicks have given a good effort, and Johnny Newman has had his best game of the year, scoring 24 points off the bench. It's the first time he's shown the explosive scoring ability he had as a college player at Richmond. "I talked with him last week. I told him I didn't know if he could be great or not, but not to be afraid to fail. If he tried to be great and failed, he might end up being good. But if he tried to be mediocre and failed, he would be horseshit."

The next night the Knicks squander a 10-point lead against the lowly Nets in the Meadowlands and lose. Then they come back two nights later and beat the Celtics in New York. The hero is Sidney Green, who has 20 points, a season high. Afterward, he said how he went back to his scrapbook, reading about his glory days at Thomas Jefferson High School in Brooklyn. "I try not to listen to my critics. And the fans don't really bother me because I know what they're thinking. I used to be up there booing myself. I know what I can do, what's gotten me here. I know I'm not a flake. I study the game. I watch films. I work hard at my job."

"What Sidney has to do is learn how to play within himself, not try to do things he's not capable of doing," says Bianchi. "He can hit the jumper facing the basket, and he can rebound. He has a nose for the ball. And you know what? There aren't that many rebounders out there. And you know what? He's a good person. If he was a bad kid, I would have run his ass out of here already."

It's been a strange week. Lose to Phoenix at home. Play well in Boston. Play horribly in New Jersey. Beat the Celtics at home. Pitino feels like he's been in a Sybil movie.

"They're a strange team," says Kevin McHale. "They play hard and do a lot of things well, and one thing you can say is that they never give up. But they don't win. Maybe they don't know how to win. Maybe they're one big scorer away. I don't know."

"You figure out how a team can look so hopeful one night, so hopeless the next," writes Fred Kerber in the *Daily News.*

January 15

The Knicks have just lost to the 76ers in the Spectrum by 15 after leading by eight at the half. Barkley again has killed them, just as he had in the first game in New York. Several players trudge out of the locker room toward the bus that will take them back to New York. Pitino, trailed by his ten-year-old son, Michael, who has come down for the game to be a ballboy, comes through the locker room door. A man in a dark overcoat is waiting for him. His name is Ray Wilson.

In 1970, the summer before his senior year, Pitino was the MVP at Five Star. He was averaging 32 points a game and basketball was a full-time obsession. Rick Pitino had become one of the better high school players on Long Island.

"He was an unbelievable scorer," remembers Ralph Willard, who played at St. Dominic's several years ahead of Pitino. "You looked at him physically and said he couldn't be that good. But he was a fantastic ball handler and a very good shooter in high school. I saw him play one night against St. Agnes—the school Billy Donovan went to—and Rick had 45. He must have had the ball ninety percent of the time. Even then he was very combative. He never backed down from anybody."

Unlike now, when the NCAA says a high school kid only can visit six prospective colleges, back then it was open season. "I visited seventeen schools, but in the end decided on the University of Massachusetts. The main reason was Wilson, the assistant coach. He was Julius Erving's high school coach in Roosevelt, Long Island, and the reason why Erving ended up at UMass. [Wilson had been a college teammate of UMass coach Jackie Leaman.] He followed Erving to UMass a year later. His main role there was to take advantage of his strong ties on Long Island and greater New York City."

Not that this was an easy task. UMass is in rural Amherst,

a large concrete campus plunked down in the middle of rolling countryside in western Massachusetts. At the other end of the main street is Amherst College, one of the most prestigious small colleges in the country. Nearby are Mount Holyoke and Smith, two of the venerable Seven Sisters colleges.

"At the time UMass was in the Yankee Conference, one of the lower echelons of Division I conferences. The games were played in Curry Hicks Cage, a monument to the peach basket era, let me tell you. And as far as the Boston media was concerned, UMass sports might as well have been played on the far side of the moon. After Erving went on to the Virginia Squires and began being billed as the best young forward in the game, virtually no one in New England could believe he had spent three years at UMass. Who was this guy? Of course, even then no one could foresee what he would later become. Not only was dunking not allowed in college basketball then, but UMass played in a deliberate style not geared to showcase Erving. It was that style I would have problems with, too."

Pitino first met Wilson at the Long Island Coliseum. "I came down to see Rick play," says Wilson. "We were looking at him and some other kid on his team, and Rick went for 40-odd points that night."

Pitino ended up being the point guard for UMass, but not before a couple of incidents that changed him. After starting on the freshman team, he arrived on the varsity the following year, full of New York, wearing his cockiness like a new sports jacket, convinced he was going to start.

"At the beginning of practice I was playing behind two veteran guards, Mike Pagliaro and John Bettencourt, two guys I thought I was better than. My first instinct was to quit, to transfer. Ray Wilson talked me out of it. One day I got in a fight with Pagliaro. Pagliaro broke his finger in the fight. Now I'll start, I figure. The next day I'm playing behind Bettencourt. Eventually we get into a fight and wrestle to the ground. He also gets hurt. Now I'll definitely start, I tell myself. Leaman suspends me instead. I am devastated and want to transfer. Wilson again talked me out of it. 'You can't run away if you're a man,' he said to me. 'It is time to grow up. To learn how to sacrifice yourself.'

"When I came back to the team the next year I was the thirteenth man, a pariah. The others on the team would run together; I was told to run alone. Others would make mistakes and be ignored; I would make mistakes and be singled out. No practice went by that I didn't want to tell Leaman what he could do with his basketball team. But every day I vowed to stick it out, knowing that it had become a battle of wills. Four days before the first game, I broke into the starting lineup. I felt like I had survived boot camp. Then in the locker room, minutes before the first game, Leaman announced the starting lineup and I wasn't in it. I was crushed. I felt tears coming into my eyes. Would this ever end? Hadn't I already proved myself? What more was I expected to do?

"Thirty seconds into the game Leaman motioned for me to go into the game. 'It's over, Rick,' Wilson whispered as I walked by.

"What Jackie Leaman did was make me a man. He shaped my life.

"It's a lesson I use often in my own coaching: breaking a player's individual will, his selfishness, and then mold him into someone who will be able to sacrifice himself. It is what I did with my players at Boston University, what I did at Providence, and what I'm now attempting to do with the Knicks. I've stressed it from the first day of training camp."

Although Pitino went on to love the school and respect Leaman, and although he played on good teams, he never really was happy as a player at UMass. He always felt his talent had a harness on it. "Leaman's philosophy was based on patterned, control basketball. We rarely ran, and the point guard's job was to run the offense and pass the ball inside. I played good defense and I ran the team well, but I never really got better as an individual. It's so easy for college players to get locked into a coach's system. Because of my frustration as a player, when I began coaching I vowed early never to devise an offense that took a player's game away from him. My college team walked the ball up the court? My teams would run and play up-tempo. My college team played an intricate, patterned offense? My teams would be more improvisational. In the end I created an offensive style I would have been happy playing in as a player."

But if Pitino often felt stifled as a player, at UMass he exhibited many of the characteristics he has now. "When he was twenty," says Wilson, who now runs the Erving Group, Julius Erving's businesses, "he could make both his peers listen and my peers listen to him. That's unique. He was aggressive and could be demanding, but he was both streetwise and bright, and that's a powerful combination. You knew even then that you were in a chess match when you locked up with him. I would like to say that back then I knew Julius was going to turn into the type of player he became. I didn't. But I did think that Rick was going to be a great coach."

"We'd go to the gym to play pickup games, and it was Rick who always organized them," says former teammate Dave Dibble. "Guys would just be hanging around and before you knew it, he'd be choosing the teams, getting the game going. Then keeping score. As a sophomore he would be running the show."

Dibble, who was a year behind Pitino at UMass, first met him the summer before he went away to college. Pitino was visiting Pete Trow, a teammate, and they all began playing a pickup game. "Right from the beginning he was elbowing me, pushing me," remembers Dibble. "You could see he didn't want to lose. He would do anything not to lose. Since that day we've probably played a thousand one-on-one games.

I've probably won two or three games. I've played pool against him a thousand times, and have never won a game. He never just goes out to fool around. He plays a three-on-three game like it's the Final Four, and it's always been this way."

If Pitino struggled for a while at basketball at UMass, he loved the social life. "Rick was the social chairman of the fraternity," says Dibble. "We used to have Thursday night parties, and Rick was in charge of getting the girls. He was a master at it. He would call all the girls' schools in the area and tell them we were having a big party, buffet, champagne cocktails. Then they'd show up, and it would be keg beer and no food. Then the next week he would be on the phone again, talking about the champagne cocktails."

It is another part of the Pitino mystique that he always knew he wanted to be coach, that he came out of the Five Star environment burning to be a coach. But by the time he was a senior in college Pitino wasn't totally convinced. He often thought about law school, envisioning himself as Perry Mason fighting for the underdog. At the same time he wanted to keep playing. The plan was to go play professionally in Italy. But in March of his senior year, while UMass was at the NIT, he ran into Bruce O'Neil, the Hawaii coach, in the hotel lobby of the old Statler, across Seventh Avenue from the Garden.

"What are you going to do next year?" O'Neil asked him.

"I want to play in Europe, but you're at one place I would give up playing for."

"Send me a resume," O'Neil said. "I'm looking for a grad assistant."

"I had a group of people write letters for me. Then he wrote back and said he had hired someone else. But four days before I was supposed to go to Italy, he called me back, said the guy he'd hired decided to go to school instead, and the job was mine. I asked, When do I start? He said now. He wanted me to babysit Tommy Barker, a 7-foot recruit that North Carolina State supposedly was trying to steal away. So my first task in coaching was to hide a 7-foot black guy in Hawaii.

"One of my other tasks that first year was to coach the junior varsity team. I had a real hodgepodge: one Chinese kid, one Japanese, one black, one white, and one Polynesian. The Bad News Bears disguised as the United Nations. The team was so bad at one point that two of my roommates, Marty Keider and Ray Buck, temporarily out of school, re-enrolled and joined the team. I said, Fine, but you both have to cut your hair and stop drinking beer.

"Two months later I became a full-fledged assistant coach, in charge of organizing Hawaii's recruiting. It was a great opportunity for someone not yet a year out of college. I spent much of the year in the continental United States, searching for players, trying to sweet-talk them into coming to Hawaii. Oh, I was a regular Fuller Brush man, filling their heads with visions of alohas and Don Ho. I loved it. Loved the competition for players, the thrill of the chase, selling myself, everything. I loved living on airplanes and making thirty calls a day, doing the hundred and one things that go with being a college recruiter."

The next year O'Neil and the Hawaii athletic director were fired near the end of the season after four players were suspended by the NCAA for appearing in a TV commercial for an automobile dealership. Pitino became the interim coach for the last seven games of the season. He was twenty-three years old. For a while he thought he might get the job full-time. He didn't. That summer he came back to New York and married Joanne. On his wedding night in a Manhattan hotel, all set to leave on his honeymoon the next morning, he got a call from Jim Boeheim, the coach of Syracuse.

"As we entered the room the phone rang," says Pitino. "He said he was at La Guardia airport and he wanted to come in and talk with me. I said, 'Jim, you don't understand. I just got married three hours ago. This is my wedding night.' He said he understood but he had to talk to me now about being his assistant before he went out on a recruiting trip. 'But Jim,' I said, 'this is my wedding night.' He said it would only take a half hour. Joanne finally said okay, but only on the condition I never repeat the story to anyone that I took a job interview on our wedding night. But after a half hour I told Jim I had to get back upstairs. He mistook that to think I wanted more money, and raised the salary a thousand dollars. I keep calling Joanne and telling her I'll be back up in a few minutes. She keeps asking what's going on, what can possibly be going on, and I keep saying that I think Jim Boeheim is going to offer me the Syracuse assistant's job. She says 'that's great but this is our wedding night.' I tell Jim I definitely had to get back upstairs. He goes up another thousand. We met for four hours and in that time the salary went from twelve to sixteen thousand dollars. So I got a four thousand raise but an upset wife. Finally, I go back upstairs and tell Joanne not only are we going to Syracuse, but that instead of going on our honeymoon I have to go out to Cincinnati the next morning to recruit Louis Orr and she is supposed to go to Syracuse and start looking for a place to live."

"I was in Syracuse for three weeks by myself," laughs Joanne. "I stayed at Jim Boeheim's house, but the only problem was that Jim wasn't married at the time and had two other male roommates. So it was just me and the three guys. The place was a mess. The first day I went out and bought ammonia and Comet and cleaned the house. I ended up cooking meals for them. This was my introduction to married life. I couldn't even tell my mother where I was living because she wouldn't have believed it. Bad enough that my husband wasn't even in the room most of my wedding night. Here I was spending what was supposed to be my honeymoon cleaning house for three guys while my husband was recruiting."

Pitino was at Syracuse for two years.

"I all but lived on the road," he says, "and I loved recruiting. Some people say it's too cutthroat. But I loved the competitiveness of it. And I left no stone unturned. I didn't play golf. I didn't play tennis. I was a junkie for it. I liked calling people. I liked writing letters to recruits, trying to make each one different. And I knew every kid, even the ones we weren't recruiting. Other coaches used to call me up and ask me about kids. I loved all of it."

The bus waits outside the Spectrum to take the Knicks back to New York. In front is a box of grinders and potato chips, another box full of cans of soda. The players sit in the back in the darkened bus. Some are talking softly. Some sit silently, Walkmans on their heads. The engine drones softly. It's all timeless, a scene known to every high school team in the country. Take away all the money and nothing has changed.

On the New Jersey Turnpike an occasional neon sign pierces the darkness. Pat Cummings, a big man with a sleepy-eyed, hangdog face, sits in the middle of the bus. He grew up in western Pennsylvania in the middle of coal-mining country, and says he is a "basketball player in a coal miner's body."

If on one level he's proud he's lasted nine years in the NBA, especially since he came out of Cincinnati as a third-round pick with little fanfare, he also wants another contract in the NBA. He is in the last year of his contract with the Knicks. He knows that he doesn't figure in the team's future, and is hoping to be able to make a deal for himself as a free agent. To do this he needs the minutes in order to showcase himself. He has to prove he has come all the way back from torn ligaments in a finger on his shooting hand that caused him to miss the last 29 games the past year. "The whole thing in this league is minutes," he says. "If you don't get the minutes, you can't show what you can do."

The problem for Cummings is he no longer gets them.

Pitino is in the front of the bus looking at the stat sheet. "It just goes to reinforce how much this is a players' league," he says. "Barkley won the game by himself. Bird. Dominique. Barkley. It doesn't matter what offense you run, or how well anyone sets a screen, or how well you reverse the ball, or any of it. It doesn't matter how much film you break down, or how well you prepare, or how hard you work. They just get the ball and score."

Before the game Bob Thornton was telling some of the Knicks how different it is with the Sixers. They only practice about a half hour a day. The entire attitude is laissez-faire. It is just one more reminder that without the players, you can look at all the film in the world, have elaborate game plans, do all the coaching in the world, and it might not be enough. After all is said and done, a Charles Barkley will go one against the world and score, and there is not a whole lot anybody can do about it.

January 16

Pitino and Joanne are having breakfast at the Mount Kisco Diner, not far from their home. It's a beautiful Saturday morning, sunlight reflecting off the snow. He is wearing warmups and a blue Knicks jacket. The New York papers are on the table in front of him. The Scout had called Pitino earlier and told him he had to get out of New York. There is no way he can win with the team he has now.

"Everyone wants me to be patient, but Madison Square Garden never has been known for being patient. They're known for firing people. It's a chilling realization. Coaching is all present tense. No one wants to hear what you did last year. No one wants to hear excuses. Just win, baby. New Yorkers don't want to hear about patience, or working hard, or building for the future."

Pitino is down. Once again the Knicks have folded on the

road. On the bus he told his assistant coach, Jim O'Brien, that if the right college situation came up, he might have to take it. O'Brien said later how Pitino is always so positive, how it's a "constant thing, a daily thing. He makes his criticisms and gets to the positive. He said to me in the first interview for the job not to ever tell him what a player is not doing unless I could tell him what he can do to improve it. If you are going to coach that way, you have to be that way yourself. And that's not always easy. Who motivates the motivator?"

This morning is one of those times when the motivator needs a motivator. He goes out in the parking lot, gets into his car, and starts chauffering Joanne around for a few errands. When she goes into a store, he dials John Parisella on his car phone.

"I just talked to Al," said Parisella. "I told him he has to make a trade. He has to do something."

"He's trying, Big John."

"Right now, Rick, trying's not enough," Parisella says through the static. "He has to do something."

"I know, Big John."

He hangs the phone up, dials a number in Fall River, Massachusetts. Ken Ford is a 46-year-old teacher at Durfee High School in Fall River, whom everyone calls Jersey Red because he has red hair and grew up in Jersey City. He met Pitino years ago when he became the cook at Pitino's fraternity at the University of Massachusetts, known as one of the animal houses on campus. The first few weeks Jersey had prepared wonderful meals, and the fraternity members couldn't believe their good fortune.

"We'd be eating beef Stroganoff, gourmet meals, and we couldn't believe how lucky we were to find this wonderful chef. Then one night I come back to the house and say, 'Hey Jersey, what's for dinner?' 'Go order a pizza.' I think nothing about it, figured he had a tough day. The next night it's the same thing. And the night after that. Soon Jersey's telling us to fix our own meals, telling us not to bother him. He's also running a fraternity betting pool. Before long, there are football cards everywhere you look, and everyone owes a bookie. He's also drinking a quart of Jack Daniels a day and has become the campus character. So long, beef Stroganoff."

"Even then Rick could talk a dog down from a meat wagon," Jersey says. "He ran the fraternity. He had them all mesmerized. Every week we had something called Asshole of the Week, which all the brothers voted on. Someone would be nominated and just when everyone was in agreement, Rick would stand up and make this convincing argument that the guy was not the asshole of the week, that so-and-so should be. Every week he'd do this. Of course, he saved his best speeches for the weeks when everyone thought he should be the asshole of the week."

In a sense Jersey is as close to Pitino as anyone, a bond that became cemented when Pitino adopted Jersey as his "little brother" in the fraternity. "I was a stone drunk then," says Jersey, who quit drinking nine years ago. "But Rick saw something in me. He is unbelievably loyal. That's the side of him the public doesn't see. He takes care of his friends, and always has. The man can't say no."

Every day Jersey prepares a tape on his telephone answering machine, usually about the travails of Pitino and the Knicks, complete with music. They have become so popular that some seventy-five people call just to hear the tape. If at one level he is Pitino's court jester, he is also someone Pitino can talk to about things other than basketball. For Pitino knows two things about Jersey: he is as faithful as an old dog, and he always tells Pitino what he thinks, even when Pitino doesn't want to hear it.

Pitino calls to hear the tape every day. Today's is about a game show that Pitino will host. Pitino listens to the tape and makes a face. "It's a bad day for Jersey. He must have been watching us last night."

That afternoon he walks into Knickerbocker lounge, where trainer Mike Saunders is folding towels and O'Brien is watching a tape of last night's game. "We don't put a body on anybody," says O'Brien as he watches Barkley push Johnny Newman aside to get an offensive rebound. He plays it over and over as Pitino watches silently.

The tape continues. Hubie Brown, now a color commentator on the Sixers' games, is talking about the Knicks. They are a young team, capable of being good one minute, self-destructing the next. They may have a horrible road record, but have lost five road games by a total of eight points. Since they hustle and trap they are never out of a game, but they also have the propensity to have lapses that kill them, particularly on the road. It's an assessment Pitino agrees with, not like a lot of the negative analysis he feels Marv Albert and John Andariese, the Knicks' TV people, constantly give on the Madison Square Garden network.

"I'm always being told how negative they are," says Pitino. "Not that I agree with the Johnny Most school of broadcasting where he always looks at the Celtics through green-covered glasses, or like the Yankees where Phil Rizzuto is a cheerleader. But I'm constantly being told how Albert and Andariese always are finding fault with the team, to the point when I use a tape of their broadcast to show the team, it never has any sound on it. This is something I hope to change. I feel they have fallen into the same den of negative thinking."

A half hour later the Providence–UNLV game comes on national television. Pitino sits down at the couch to watch the game. It's the first time he has seen Providence play, and in a sense it's déjà vu. The Providence coach, Gordie Chiesa, was Pitino's assistant. Two of the Providence assistant coaches on the bench were on Pitino's staff the year before. All the players were either on the team the year before or had been recruited by Pitino. Plus, Providence still plays Pitino's style.

Providence immediately goes out in front. UNLV is bothered by the Providence fullcourt press and repeatedly make ball-handing errors.

"Sid, I see where you learned to pass," quips Pitino as Sidney Green, who played at UNLV, walks through the room. Green smiles.

The night before Green sat in the locker room in Philadelphia and said, "There are people on the team who really don't care whether we win or lose, and I'm tired of it. I was at Detroit, the Pistons expected to win, took it personally when they didn't. But some of the older players here almost take it for granted that they are going to lose. There are some guys here who are afraid of success, and if that doesn't change I'm going to get into their face."

The Friars are up 10 and playing well. By this time Donovan and Stu Jackson also are watching, a sort of Providence reunion in the Knicks' locker room. Also watching is Mark Jackson.

"Mark," Pitino says. "Just like last year against the Johnnies. When we beat you by thirty here in the Garden."

Jackson tries to battle back, but is quickly drowned out by Stu Jackson. It's all good-natured locker room stuff, the constant put-downs, the one upmanship. It's also part of the environment Pitino wants to create on the Knicks, more of a college atmosphere instead of the stereotype of the jaded pros.

A halftime feature shows last year's Providence team: images of a jubilant Pitino hugging players on the sideline, Donovan hitting a big jump shot. The same Donovan who's been struggling with his shooting in recent games.

"Hey, Billy," yells Pitino. "Come look and see yourself make one."

Before the game the Knicks have a team meeting. Bianchi, upset the night before when a few of the Sixers were laughing when Philly had put the game away, says, "Everyone has to protect one another. You can't have anyone laughing at you." Sidney Green and Louis Orr speak, the gist of which is the Knicks are close off the court, but not close on it. They hang their head too much, don't fight for one another.

"Dougie," says Pitino. "You went on WFAN last night. So did you, Patrick. And you didn't say anything negative. Both of you guys did nothing wrong. But I wished you would have protected me more. I wish when you were asked what your reaction was to being on the bench, you would have said that it was the coach's decision and you don't question that. Because I protect you. When writers ask me about trading Gerald Wilkins, I say I don't want to trade Gerald Wilkins. When people ask me about Patrick Ewing, I tell them that there is no one in basketball I would trade Patrick Ewing for. I stand up for you. I want you to stand up for me. We got to stand by each other. There are three tabloids in this town. We got to have the feeling that Patrick Ewing has for John Thompson. That Sidney Green has for Jerry Tarkanian. Don't tell me it can't be done in the pros.

"Dougie, you want minutes. So does Trent Tucker. He was the sixth pick in the draft. Patrick, you want minutes. So does Bill Cartwright. Sidney wants minutes. So does Pat Cummings."

He pauses for a moment.

"I don't know if it's going to happen this year for you guys. I don't know. But it's definitely not going to happen if we don't stick together."

That night they beat the Sixers by 14, Ewing getting a career-high 21 rebounds. Then they come back two days later and beat the Atlanta Hawks in the Garden on Martin Luther King Day. Then they go out West for three games, where they play well, even though they lose all three. The highlight is a close loss to the Lakers in the Forum, complete with a brawl. Cummings and A. C. Green square off, and end up with Cummings and Michael Cooper on the floor punching each other, Cummings' shirt ripped off his back. Afterward, Magic Johnson says this is the best Knick team he'd seen since he's been in the league.

The day of the game Kerber and Pitino were sitting around the pool at the Airport-Marriott. "This is heaven," Pitino said. "Here we are in L.A. Beautiful weather. Everything."

"The only thing missing is the New York papers," said Kerber.

"That's the best thing about it. That's the only good thing about being on the road."

January 26

An hour before the Kicks are to play the Nets, Fred Kerber of the *Daily News* is talking about the New York media war. A squabble has evolved over the Knicks. The beat writers think the Knicks are a much better team than they were a year ago. The columnists—specifically Mike Lupica and Filip Bondy—think it's the same old song. Kerber is in his fourteenth year at the *News*, his eighth in sports. He's covered the Nets, the Islanders, college basketball, baseball. "This is my first year on the Knicks, and I'm just not jaded yet," he says. "The other guys seem to judge them on what they've done the past three years."

Midway through January Filip Bondy has written, "Sorry, but the Knicks haven't improved since last season. Not by overall record, tough defeats, or big wins. Your move, Al Bianchi." Bondy points out that Bernard King is averaging 18.5 and shooting nearly 50 percent, while Kenny Walker is averaging 11 on 44 percent shooting.

Kevin Kernan gives his halftime report card in the *Post*. "Remember the note your teacher would send home with your grades. 'So-and-so is a lovely child who tries very hard.' Meanwhile you were flunking woodshop. The Knicks also are lovely people who are trying very hard. They are the youngest team in the NBA and despite their first-half failures, progress is being made. The only trouble is, they're flunking wood shop."

It is nearing the halfway point in the season and certain things are clearer than they were a month ago. First, Mark Jackson was the steal of the draft. Any adjustment the team had to make to a rookie on-court leader has easily been made. Ewing says it was comfortable playing with Jackson right from the beginning. Ewing is having the best year of his professional career. He still makes too many stupid fouls, fumbles too many passes that make you wonder about his hands, and sometimes passes poorly when double-teamed in the post. But he has moments when he dominates games. Benefiting from playing at a lighter weight and in Pitino's style, he is averaging nearly 20 points a game. Wilkins is much improved, sticking the outside shot more, playing better defense, cutting down on his foolish turnovers. His average is now 17 a game. Cartwright is among the league leaders in field-goal percentage. Green is playing with more intensity. Newman is starting to score off the bench, beginning to emerge from his cocoon.

On the flip side, Walker is still struggling, and there is strong sentiment within the organization that his psyche has never recovered from the high expectations and the booing. Cummings has seen his minutes slowly dwindle, but whereas he was actively discontent earlier in the season, now he is not, as if waiting for the next year to salvage his sagging career somewhere else. Tucker doesn't seem to fit into the team's future. Donovan has too many games where he appears to struggle; so far has not been able to take much pressure off Jackson. During one game he yelled, "Coach Pitino, Coach Pitino," trying to get Pitino's attention, and Kernan wrote in the *Post*, "Such choirboy politeness seems out of place in the NBA." Carlisle rarely plays. Neither does Orr, whose role seems to have become the team's elder statesman, a conduit between players and management.

In the game the Knicks blow out the Nets. Afterward

Gerald Wilkins, who was picked 48th in the draft, is asked if it surprised him that Mark Jackson, 18th in the draft, has been so good so soon. "In Mark's situation the scouts only had one eye," said Wilkins. "In my situation the scouts didn't have no eyes."

February 2

Knicks are 14–28, fourth in the Atlantic Division. Washington, whom they play tonight, is 17–23 in the standings and Philadelphia is 19–22. Boston is so far ahead the Knicks need a telescope to see them. That night the Knicks beat the Bullets by four for their fifth straight in the Garden. Pitino's team is on a roll.

7 | The First Signs of Spring

I've resigned myself to the fact that we weren't doing any trades. This is the team we're going to have the rest of the year.

I'm excited because our defense is really bothering people, but I don't know how much more we can take. On the road we have to pitch a shutout to win because we just can't score.

The other night we lost by one in overtime to the Bulls in Chicago. It was a great pro game. Chicago Stadium was bedlam, and we were really pumped: Mark had 18 assists. Down most of the night, we kept fighting back. We kept changing the presses and it bothered them. They couldn't get the ball inbounds. It was one of those nights that gets me excited about the future. We are only one scorer away from being a good team.

Right now we have a catch-22 with Bill Cartwright. He is making us better. Not only does he make Patrick better by playing against him, pushing him, in practice every day, his presence also allows Patrick to go all-out all the time. Billy also gives us the strongest center position in the NBA. On the other hand, he also is our most tradeable commodity. What we decide to do with him next year might well determine the future of the New York Knicks.

Next year we will have Pat Cummings' salary to play with,

and maybe we can do something in the free-agent market. There are a number of guys who probably won't be here next year: Billy Cartwright, Trent Tucker, Louis Orr, Billy the Kid. I think I'm going to have to waive Billy. Al wants to bring in another guard. Donovan is on the team because of favoritism, which is all right. But if we add another player, someone is going to have to go, and to cut another player just to keep Billy would be unethical. It will break my heart to tell him.

Deep down I still have a tough time figuring out why I left Providence. I keep trying to rationalize it. I had security. My family loved it there. I was a celebrity. Why did I leave? I keep trying not to admit that I only had forty-eight hours to make the decision, and that I made the wrong decision. I see Matty Guokas get fired and I say to myself, "What the hell did you do?" What did I do? If I had had a week to think about it, I wouldn't have done it. I changed my mind twice in that forty-eight hours as it was.

All through my coaching life I've strived to get to the top. That's where I was at Providence. Why did I need more? I keep asking myself. Do I have some insecurity that whatever I have is not enough? I had more of a life in Rhode Island. This is a gypsy's life. I've always been someone who has goals and keeps looking forward at those goals. This is the first time I've ever looked back.

What takes place in between the lines in the NBA is utopia: the practices, the preparation, the strategy, the games. What takes place outside of the lines is horseshit: the media, the way you're perceived, everything. The other night I'm watching Providence play Georgetown on ESPN. On the halftime feature there was some kid saying how much he hated me, how I was a traitor. I guess I now know more profoundly how my decision affected a lot of people: my wife, the kids at Providence I recruited, the fans.

It's not that I feel guilty, I feel selfish. I'm enjoying this so much from a coaching standpoint, and here is my wife and the kids I coached being negatively affected by it. I can't escape the consequences of my decision. It's a stigma everywhere I go. Everyone keeps bringing up that clipping in which I said I was going to stay at Providence for five years, and I keep looking like a bigger turncoat.

✝✝✝✝✝✝✝✝✝

From the moment he got the job Pitino promised a return to the glory days. He even had a five-year plan that ultimately would land the Friars in the NCAA tournament. The goal of the first year was to be the hardest-working team in America, the same thing he had promised his Boston University team seven years earlier.

"And what if you fail?" he was asked.

"I won't fail."

"And you have no doubts whatsoever?"

"None."

Pitino always had wanted the Providence job. In college he had played the team with Ernie DiGregorio, Marvin Barnes, and Kevin Stacom that went to the Final Four, one of the few Eastern teams to do so. This was back before the Big East, when the East was in many respects a college basketball wilderness overshadowed by the more prestigious ACC. Providence had been one of the rare exceptions, a school whose basketball roots went back to the Joe Mullaney era in the late Fifties and Sixties and players like Lenny Wilkens, Johnny Egan, Vinnie Ernst, Ray Flynn, Jimmy Walker, Mike Riordan. This legacy coach Dave Gavitt had enlarged upon in the early Seventies. Pitino knew of the tradition. He used to think of Providence as an Eastern version of Lexington, Kentucky.

When Mullaney, who had come back for a second stint as the Providence College coach, retired in 1985, Pitino was the first person contacted by Providence athletic director Lou Lamoriello.

"At the end of my second year with the Knicks, Hubie wasn't sure about his future in New York. He thought the front office was disorganized and the team was disintegrating. One day near the tail end of the season we were on a bus in Atlanta when he said, 'I see where your dream job opened up.'

" 'Where's that?'

" 'Providence,' he said. 'I see Joe Mullaney resigned yesterday. Are you interested?'

" 'No. I want to be a pro head coach. I didn't just make a coaching change when I left Boston University. I made a career change.'

"When I got to the hotel room I got a call from this guy saying he was Lou Lamoriello. I thought it was Mike Saunders fooling around. But it was Lou. He asked me if I was interested. I said I was. I eventually met with him in the Sheraton in Attleboro, Massachusetts, about a half hour from Providence on the way to Boston. We talked from eleven to four in the morning. For the first few hours I didn't talk about winning or recruiting or really anything about basketball. I talked about how the discipline from basketball will make the players better students. When I left that night I thought I had the job.

"But I had second thoughts when I saw Providence play in the first round of the Big East Tournament a while later. I was sitting between Sonny Werblin and Jack Krumpe, who ran the Garden, and at one point Krumpe said to me, 'Rick, you aren't seriously thinking about going to Providence? They're getting beat by forty to St. John's, and their three best players are all seniors. As a matter of fact, there's not one player on this team averaging in double figures.' I was supposed to meet Lou in the Abbey Tavern on Twenty-Sixth and 3rd after the game, and in the cab going over there I was all set to tell Lou I no longer was interested."

Providence is the capital of Rhode Island, a blue-collar town once described as a place where the Old World shadows are heavy. In the late Fifties the town fell in love with

Providence College, a small school from their small state that came out of nowhere to become a national name. People lined the highway from the Connecticut border to welcome the Friars back from their first NIT trip in 1958. In a sense Providence College basketball has been Rhode Island's pro team, unlike the nearby Boston teams that Rhode Islanders can lease but never really own. And for nearly twenty years it was an unbelievable story, the little Cinderella school where the clock never seemed to strike midnight. Good teams, enthusiastic fans, a succession of 20-win seasons that all but became part of the schedule.

Then the tide turned. The victim of a few poor recruiting years, Providence had been in a down cycle when the Big East started in 1978. As the seasons came and went, Providence seemed forever locked in a battle with Seton Hall to escape the Big East cellar. There was increasing sentiment that the school's basketball success had been a marvelous fluke that had run its course. Providence College was never going to be able to compete with the top echelon schools of the Big East Conference.

Into this, in the spring of 1985, came Rick Pitino. "I didn't expect to win right away. I was looking at three or four years of getting my ass kicked."

His secretary, Barbara Kobak, remembers the first time she met the Providence players. "I thought we were going to fail. One by one they came into the office and each one seemed heavier. I felt that Rick was totally over his head, that we couldn't win here. That entire summer I had my doubts."

At his first team meeting, when he essentially told his team that they were failures in all the important things that composed their lives, Pitino made clear that things were going to be done his way. He told Billy Donovan to lose twenty pounds. He told Jacek Duda to lose thirty. Donnie Brown twelve.

One of the players he inherited was Harold Starks, a

6-foot guard from New York City. Starks knew Pitino from
Five Star.

"At the first meeting he broke everyone's individual game
down, like someone had told him everything about us. He
had really done his homework. He told certain guys to lose
weight. He told us we were going to work out at six in the
morning. Everyone was in shock. You could feel it in the
room. This was night and day from what we were used to.
Even so, I think a lot of guys thought he was just talk.

"We had another meeting two weeks later, and he had
told everyone to be on time. Well, Dick Pennyfather walks
in a few minutes late. 'Where have you been?' he asked. 'I
was just outside,' Dick said. 'Well, you were six minutes
late. So you owe me six miles at six in the morning.' That's
when everyone's face dropped. I was never late for anything after that.

"Before we left he told us that we had to write him a
letter every week. Tell him how work was going, how our
family was, how things were going. After a few weeks I said
the same thing every week. But I told myself, I'm writing
this guy a letter every week even if I have to make things
up. That was the kind of impression he left."

One day that first spring Pitino called Dave Kipfer into
his office. Also there was Suzanne Fournier, the school's
academic adviser, who was aware of Pitino's plan. A Cana-
dian, Kipfer was a sophomore who seemed to epitomize the
Providence players: a nice kid over his head in the Big East.
He had arrived with the reputation of being a 6–7 banger,
but had spent his first two years showing a propensity for
shooting perimeter jumpers. What was worse, his attitude
suggested basketball was not his first priority.

"I think you should transfer," Pitino told Kipfer. "You
can't play for me."

"Why not?"

"Because you don't go to class and you don't work hard."
Kipfer tried to defend himself, but Pitino stopped him in

midsentence. "I don't want to hear any excuses. You don't work hard and you aren't going to be able to play for me. So bring me a list of five schools you want to transfer to, and I'll get you into one of them."

"But Coach, I like it here."

"It's not going to work out between you and me. Bring me your five schools."

Kipfer looked down in shock, his world suddenly wrenched apart.

"Rick, maybe you should give him one more chance," said Fournier, playing her role of good cop.

"No more chances," Pitino snapped.

"Please, Coach," said Kipfer, almost in tears. "Please give me another chance."

Pitino hesitated. "Okay," he said slowly. "One more chance."

For two years Kipfer was a tiger for Pitino, the embodiment of the Providence work ethic.

When the players came back to school that fall, Pitino suggested that they might benefit from getting up every morning and working out. He also suggested it might be beneficial to be in the gym playing every afternoon. Suggest might be too gentle a word. "In the fall we got another shock," says Starks. "We got back to school and had to lift weights early in the morning. Then in the afternoon we had to run for time. The first day we had to run three miles in eighteen minutes. If you didn't make the time, you had to run at 6:45 the next morning.

"I couldn't believe what was going on. But you know what? It made us closer as a team. We would run for time in groups of five and six, and the other guys always were there on the sidelines giving encouragement to the guys running. Or else telling them in the locker room afterward that they could make it.

"Every day after we ran, we played in the gym. We were awful. Your legs would feel like jelly. We busted our ass playing defense, but we were still terrible, even when we started practice. We worked on the press all the time, but it was a tough time. We weren't playing any games. We really couldn't understand what was happening. We knew we were in great shape, but we had no idea if it was going to help us or not.

"People often ask me how he got away with being so tough. But he was never there when we were running. He was never the guy yelling at us. The assistants were the ones yelling at us to run faster when we were killing ourselves. The assistants were the ones we'd be pissed at. He would show up once a week and offer encouragement, and because he was the head coach we would all try to impress him. I didn't realize it at the time, but it was very smart. We got mad at the assistants, not him. 'Cause he wasn't the guy yelling.

"He made up for it in practice, though, and it took some getting used to. But eventually the guys realized it wasn't a personal thing, that he only wanted us to get better."

The first public unveiling was a champagne toast one minute after midnight on October 15, the first day college teams can practice. One thousand people showed up to see Pitino prod Duda to rebound with a broom, as a symbol of ushering in a new era. It also gave him a chance to show off his players, all of whom looked as if they had just come back from basic training.

"Everyone lost weight," Pitino joked. "Jacek lost a person."

Jacek Duda was the most visible physical reclamation project. He had grown up in Poland, but defected to this country as a high school senior while playing for the Polish junior national team on a tour of the United States. He joined his parents, who had left Poland several years earlier and settled in Central Falls, an old mill town a few miles from Providence. Although Duda had arrived in Rhode Island knowing little English, he immediately became the center of a recruiting battle. So what if Duda was going through the trauma of leaving Poland and trying to find a new life? So what if Duda kept telling people he was not that good a player? He was 6–10, wasn't he?

When he arrived at Providence College the following year, it was apparent Duda had been right after all. He was slow, overweight, and didn't jump well. He was overmatched in a league as competitive as the Big East. If he was bright, friendly, and always hustled, his first two years he had been little more than a cult figure appearing at the end of games.

"I immediately told him his days of being a joke were over. Lose thirty pounds or forget it. I gave him a time he had to run the mile in, and every time he didn't do it, he was out on the track the next morning doing more running. 'If you don't start playing better, we are going to send you back to Poland,' I told him. Duda would look at me as if he didn't know whether I was kidding or not. Then he would work harder."

Soon a story circulated that Duda ran wind sprints with a bucket around his neck so if he threw up it would not get on the court: a new addition to the Pitino legend.

By the Friars' first night in the Providence Civic Center, everyone knew it was a new era. What better proof than this new version of Duda, now the starting center, still somewhat limited, but having no apparent regard for his body, taking the charge, boxing out, playing on heart instead of ability?

The Friars pressed all over the court, diving on the floor, playing with an unbelievable frenzy the entire game. Pitino was perpetual motion in front of the bench, screaming "Deflection" every time the opposition had the ball. It was all a wonderful show, and though the Friars started out the Big East season by losing their first six games, they upset Boston College by a point on the road and began turning the corner.

"Guys on the other team would say in the middle of a game, 'What is it with you guys? Don't you ever stop running?' " says Starks. "But there were some incredibly funny times too. We got blown out at Syracuse, and everyone knew he would be really pissed because he had been an assistant there and wanted to play well. So we're on the bus afterward and no one is saying a word. Not a word. And the tension is building. All at once the bus driver says something and he snaps, 'Why don't you just shut up and drive the bus?' Gets all over his case. We loved it. To this day we tell the story of how Coach got all over the bus driver too."

By the end of the year Providence was 17–9, and was invited to the NIT, the school's first postseason appearance in nine years. The Friars also had served notice in the Big East that they no longer were going to roll over and play dead against the top teams. They eventually lost in the NIT quarterfinals, but as they left the Providence Civic Center court that night, they were given a standing ovation.

So the 1986–87 season began with high expectations. In their college basketball issue, *Sports Illustrated* wrote about Pitino's War Room, where the walls were covered with the names, color-coded and listed by both class and position, of the best high school players in the country. He had the players write letters to prospective recruits. No detail was too small. "Rick is more organized than crime," said John Marinatto, the school's sports-information director.

Donovan was back. So was Kipfer. In the middle were Duda and Steve Wright. Ernie "Pop" Lewis, a good long-range shooter, was the other forward. Delray Brooks was the other guard. Once the number one high school player, he had disintegrated at Indiana. By his sophomore year his playing time had dwindled and he wanted out. He knew Pitino from Five Star.

"I used to get excited when I knew he was going to lecture," remembers Brooks. "He had the ability to motivate the entire camp. The summer before my senior year, he picked me as his demonstrator and told everyone how much I had improved from the summer before. I really appreciated that. He was the sole reason I came to Providence."

There also were three freshman, the result of Pitino's first full recruiting year at Providence: Marty Conlon, Carlton Screen, Abdul Shamsid-deen. Plus there was Daryll Wright, the first player Pitino had recruited from the year before.

Shamsid-deen was a 6–10 kid from Staten Island who had shown up for his recruiting visit at Providence the previous year wearing a St. John's hat. He made so many references to St. John's that finally Dave Kipfer, sick of hearing about St. John's, said, "If you like St. John's so much, why don't you go there?"

Sendek remembers Shamsid-deen's first team meeting as a freshman. "While Rick was talking, Abdul was looking at the floor, looking off into space. Finally Rick exploded: 'When I am fucking talking, you better be fucking listening. You were a pain in the ass to recruit, and we aren't going to put up with any more of it. This isn't fucking high school.' Believe me, that got Abdul's attention. Rick can strike the fear of God in you."

In a league as competitive as the Big East, this was not considered great talent. But it was a team that had learned how to win the year before, a team that pressed and scrapped for forty minutes, a team no one in the Big East wanted to play. It also was the first year of the three-point shot. Whereas many coaches first opposed it and later tried to ignore it, Pitino embraced it, constantly telling Donovan, Brooks, and Lewis to take the three. Symbolically, the first shot Providence took that season was a three, and from their very first game it sometimes seemed as if they all were playing H-O-R-S-E. By the end of the year they had used the three-point shot more effectively than any other team in the country.

The Friars broke into the Top Twenty in January for the first time in nearly a decade, largely the result of beating Georgetown in the Providence Civic Center. If nothing else, the game served notice that the Friars had moved uptown. Kipfer seemed to intimidate the Hoyas inside. Pitino got involved in a midcourt shouting match with John Thompson. Thompson called Pitino, "Young punk" and Pitino said, "Fuck you." The message? No more being intimidated by Georgetown. No more playing patsy for the top Big East teams.

They finished fourth in the league, then beat St. John's by 29 in the first round of the Big East tournament, one of the biggest losses in their long and storied history in the Garden.

"The amazing thing about that game is that Carlton Screen, our freshman backup point guard, hurt his knee. When he did, I called for Dr. Norman Scott to come down from the stands and take a look at him. Dr. Scott is the Knicks' doctor and a close personal friend. He said Carlton needed arthroscopic surgery. 'How long will he be out?' I asked, because I knew we needed Carlton in the tournament. 'About two weeks if he has good pain tolerance. Three to four weeks if he doesn't. If he has a really high pain threshold maybe only one week.' I knew Carlton was a great kid who would do anything to help us win, but he didn't have a very high pain threshold. But I wanted Dr. Scott to do the operation as quickly as possible. It was done the next day and Carlton played five minutes against Austin Peay a week later. Two weeks later he had 21 points in the national semifinals." Two days later, after losing to Georgetown in the Big East semifinals, the Friars were invited to the NCAA tournament.

The same day Daniel Paul Pitino died.

Their first-round opponent was the University of Alabama at Birmingham. The site was the Birmingham Coliseum. It seemed Providence was a patsy being thrown to the wolves. Instead, they won, 90–68. Two days later they played Austin Peay, a small school from Clarksville, Tennessee. At the half the Friars were getting beat, and Pitino pulled out all the stops.

"Jacek had had a bad half," remembers Stu Jackson, "and Rick started on him: 'The NCAA tournament is shown all over world. Even in Poland. And Jacek, in Poland they are trying to make you a hero. They would love for you to be a hero. But you won't let them. You won't run. You won't rebound. You won't use any of the moves we've taught you for two years now. If Lech Walesa is watching, he's shaking his head.' "

The second half was uphill all the way to the wire. Down 10 with five minutes left, Providence pressed all over the court, playing with an unbelievable fervor. With a few seconds left, Bob Thomas, an Austin Peay forward, had two foul shots. Make one and the game is over. He missed both. Providence won in overtime.

The next Thursday they journeyed to Freedom Hall in Louisville for the Southeast regionals. Their opponent, Alabama, had also been in Birmingham and Pitino thought they were awesome: Derrick McKey, Jim Farmer, Terry Conor. But they too disintegrated against the Providence press. Once again the Friars came out shooting three-pointers as if it were gym class. In the final minutes, the Friars up about a dozen and about to be one of the eight teams still in contention for the national title, Pitino kneeled on the sidelines, and screamed, "Final eight! Final eight!"

He screamed it over and over.

Providence won by 21.

The finals of the Southeast regionals matched Providence against Georgetown. This same Georgetown had beaten the Frairs fairly comfortably near the end of the season and again two weeks earlier in the Big East semifinals. Revolving around Reggie Williams, the last link to the Patrick Ewing era, this team scrapped and played pressure defense in the best Georgetown tradition. In the two previous games the Hoyas had put tremendous defensive pressure on Billy Donovan and Delray Brooks, holding the two Friar guards in check, taking away the three-pointers. So Pitino's strategy was to get the ball inside to Kipfer and Steve Wright, where the Georgetown defense wasn't so overpowering.

"I think the Georgetown game was Rick's greatest coaching job," says Jackson. "They had beaten us two consecutive times, but in the day and a half before the game he was able to convince all of us—the coaching staff included—that we were actually the better team. He changed our entire offensive philosophy and got them to believe it could work. He was telling them they had become America's team, all the Cinderella stuff, and by game time they all believed it, including me."

The rest is one of the biggest college basketball stories of the year.

The Friars went inside early, got off to a big lead, and cruised to a 88–73 win and a berth in the Final Four. When the game was over, Pitino cut down the nets in Freedom Hall amid the jubilation. Less than two years earlier he had stood before the Providence booster club and told them, "When you go to bed at night, don't worry about how much you owe on your Visa and your Mastercard, but dream instead about cutting down the nets." Everyone had called him an impossible dreamer, a basketball version of a tent evangelist. Now he sat on his players' shoulders cutting down the nets, all the promises delivered.

Then he retreated to his hotel and Joanne.

The next weekend the Friars played Syracuse in the Final Four in the Superdome in New Orleans. The bubble burst. Playing a Big East rival they already had lost to twice, they got down early, were really never in the game, and lost by 14. The next day Pitino was named Coach of the Year.

February 4–10

The Knicks beat Detroit for their sixth straight win in the Garden on their last game before the All-Star break. It's their first victory over the Pistons in thirteen tries. Green gets 18 and 13 rebounds, and shuts down Laimbeer, whom he hates. Wilkins and Ewing have big nights, and afterward Wilkins says, "It's taken awhile, but now I know Rick has confidence in me."

It is the weekend All-Star break, the symbolic halfpoint of the NBA season. Ewing is on the East team, named as a backup center by East coach Mike Fratello. From the Knick perspective the big news from the All-Star game is a Filip Bondy column in the *Daily News*. It reports that Ewing was uncooperative with the media, forgot the pictures of his youth the players were supposed to bring, and spent much of his time in the locker room with his Walkman on. For the highest-paid player in the league he stirs little fan interest outside New York. Bondy also quotes Bob Ryan of the *Boston Globe* saying Ewing is one of the worst interviews in the league because he doesn't do "hypotheticals and comparisons."

Vecsey wastes little time jumping all over Bondy in the *Post*. "When King Kong Bondy leaves Manhattan and drives through the Holland Tunnel, I get the distinct feeling he thinks he winds up in the Netherlands. One of us is disoriented, that's for sure." He also goes after the Ryan quote. "Funny, I thought players were paid to play, and reporters were paid to do hypotheticals and comparisons . . . Two things I've learned about Ewing is that he aims to please and he's fair."

Pitino couldn't care less if Ewing walks around the locker room with his Walkman on, or that he's not considered a great interview. His concern is Patrick will be bothered by the Bondy article, even though he says he's not. He talks to John Cirillo to see if the Knicks can do something to improve Ewing's image.

What concerns Pitino more is that the Knicks have two bad practices at SUNY coming off the All-Star break. Though the weekend was a welcome respite, it hasn't come at a good time for the Knicks, who had been playing their best ball of the season.

He is not surprised when they go into the Silverdome and lose to the Pistons by 11. It's the sixteenth straight road loss. In the *Daily News* Fred Kerber calls it their "most boring performance of the season."

It's also another night of abuse from Leon the Barber sitting behind the Knicks' bench. "Pitino, stop putting in your college backcourt." "Pitino, you got the ugliest white boy in the league in Cummings. You hurt the TV ratings if you put him in." "You keep telling all these things to your players. I've got something to tell you. Take your team on the bus and get the hell out of here."

"I knew we weren't ready to play," Pitino says afterward. "We can't handle success. We win a couple of games and we start thinking we're good. It's immaturity. These guys never have been winners before in the pros. But it doesn't do any good to bury them. Because they never own up to anything. You've got to be like a school teacher explaining a lesson."

He pauses.

"I should have listened to Leon."

February 13

A few hours before the Knicks are to play the Cleveland Cavaliers in the Garden, Pitino, Mark Jackson, and Donovan are in the Knicks' lounge watching Providence play St. John's.

"Mark," says Pitino. "Did you know that St. John's has one of the lowest graduation rates of its players in the country?"

"Marvin Barnes," retorts Jackson, a reference to the former Providence player who was charged with hitting a teammate with a tire iron while still in college and later became the archetype of potential in the pros squandered by drugs and flamboyance.

"How do you know about that?" asks Pitino, perplexed. "You're too young to know that."

"I know," says Jackson, a knowing look on his face.

Providence falls behind quickly and is down 20 in the first half. It has not been a good year for them. When Pitino left for the Knicks in July, he believed everything was in place. The Friars were coming off the Final Four, the sophomore class was considered one of the best in the Big East, interest was sky-high. "All that's needed now is for someone to push the buttons," Pitino said at the time, "and Gordie Chiesa can push the buttons as well as anyone."

But the season was already turning sour. Providence had yet to win on the road, getting beaten badly at Utah, Pittsburgh and Syracuse. Marty Conlon, the most promising sophomore, had quit the team in early January, saying he was tired of the constant verbal abuse from Chiesa. Other players were rumored to be unhappy. Chiesa was being bombarded on the talk shows in Providence. Everything seemed to be unraveling. Now on national television, they are getting blown out in the first half by St. John's.

"I thought there was a real game on TV today," says Jackson. It's already apparent he has won his dinner bet with Pitino. It's been a good week for Jackson. A few days earlier he had been profiled in *Sports Illustrated* as the NBA's top rookie. The story reported that Jackson still lives at home, still shares a room with his fifteen-year-old brother, Troy. Jackson thinks his family is one of the keys to his success. Another source of strength contributing to the confidence Jackson has played with since the season started is he believes this is all part of some higher game plan. Jackson also knows he's benefited from the confidence the coaches and his teammates had in him, especially the unloading of veteran guards Henderson and Sparrow that gave him the opportunity to play right away. "At the time it was a big shock. A lot of teams would have thought twice about having a rookie point guard. A veteran coach might have stayed with the veterans. But a rookie coach was more willing to give me a shot."

He's been profiled recently in the *Sporting News* and featured on ABC's *World News Tonight*. Kevin Kernan of the *Post* has written, "Jackson alone is reason enought to come back to the Garden."

Now Pitino also owes him a dinner. "Mark, since you started wearing those white pants and those white boots you showed up in the other night, I can't afford you anymore. You used to be the kind of guy you could take to the deli, with your blazers and khaki pants. Now with the jump suits you probably want to go to the River Café."

Jackson laughs and shakes his head. "Coach, you know I'm not like that."

The Knicks beat the Cavs by 17. Cartwright has 20 points in 36 minutes. Afterward, Cartwright is getting dressed in the locker room when Vescey and Fred Kerber approach.

"How are things progressing on the trade front?" asks Kerber.

"Everyone knows what I want," says Cartwright, who speaks softly. "Now it comes down to them."

"Are you willing to take a pay cut to get back to California?" Vecsey asks. Cartwright gives him a long look. "What's that look mean?" laughs Vescey. "Get serious. I know you're not going to take one to get to Indiana. But I figured you might if it was California."

"You know, I'm going to miss you guys once I'm traded." He pauses and puts on a brown suede jacket. "What are you guys going to write about when I'm gone?"

"We will lose a lot of space," says Vescey, who consistently calls Cartwright "Billy Idle" in his column. "No doubt about it."

Cartwright just shakes his head slowly.

"What's the difference between this year and last year?" he is asked.

"We play harder now. I watched the Nets play Milwaukee and it was a joke. The Bucks just kind of stood around. But they know they can't do that against us. Everyone is ready to play us, because they have to be."

The next morning a *Newsday* headline says, "PITINO'S PROMISES WERE NOT IN VAIN." Gary Binford writes, "The fans, and even some of the Knicks, were doubters when Rick Pitino made a series of promises prior to the start of the season. The Knicks, their new coach said, would get stronger as the season went on because of their pressing defense. . . . People were skeptical early, particularly considering the Knicks' dismal start. But Pitino's predictions are becoming a reality early in the season's fourth month."

For something is beginning to happen.

They now have won seven straight in the Garden.

February 15

This Monday night the Knicks are due to play the Nets at home. Suzyn Waldman, a reporter from WFAN, is in the press room at the Garden talking about how Vescey and Bondy had gone at each other in the press room the week before. "The media in this town take it all personally. It's their Mets. Their Yankees. Their Knicks. It's unbelievable. And they can ruin people in this town. Right now they are killing Kenny Walker. They killed Pat Cummings, with all that Pat Shortcummings stuff. The ugliest man in basketball stuff. What kind of human being can function with all that harassment?"

The Knicks are down 12 to the Nets at the half, and are chased off by some boos. Pitino is irate. From the beginning of the game he knew the Knicks were flat. He knows the Knicks are very capable of losing a home game they are supposed to win.

"My only wish would be to take away your salaries for one game," he yells. "Give them to the fans. I'm glad you're being booed. There's only one word for this: disgraceful. I'm so upset I'm shaking. If we don't come out and play a good second half, my head is going to completely come apart."

They catch the Nets in the closing minutes. Up one with seven seconds left, Ewing goes to the foul line for two shots. He misses both, but the Nets' John Bagley misses a shot at the buzzer from the deep right corner. The Knicks have won their eighth straight game at home, their 18th win of the season.

"I was bad with them at halftime," says Pitino. "Worse than a college halftime speech. For one of the few times this year I felt they needed a good ass-kicking." He slumps more on the couch, looking exhausted. "I'm a nervous wreck. I don't think I've ever coached this hard in my life. I felt like I did my first year at BU and Providence, back when I could never relax. If I didn't coach every play, there was no way we could win. That's what it was like tonight, and that's the most grueling kind of game there is in the pros."

Dick McGuire walks over on his way out. "That's the kind of game that can turn a season around," he tells Pitino. "You win one you don't deserve to win."

A few minutes later Pitino catches the bus taking the team to the late-night flight to Indianapolis for tomorrow's game with the Pacers, where they will lost by 13. Brendan Malone, the only holdover from last year's staff, watches Pitino leave the room. "We won tonight because he went in at halftime and jacked them up. He gave them one of his Rick Pitino speeches and it worked."

"What's the biggest difference between this year and last year?"

Malone ponders for a minute. "Rick is making them play hard and demanding they play defense. That's what a pro coach has to do: make his team play hard. We lost a lot of games early in the year that we win now. Early in the year there's no way we win this game."

In his mid-forties, Malone grew up in nearby Astoria, went to Iona, and later became the coach at Power Memorial, the Manhattan high school that produced Kareem Abdul-Jabbar. He became one of the most respected and well-known high school coaches in the city. Then one day he decided to jump on the college coaching carousel that goes around and around and where it stops nobody knows. He became an assistant coach at Fordham for a year. Then the coach got axed and he went to Yale. Then on to Syracuse. He was the chief recruiter there, securing the likes of Pearl Washington, Rafael Addison, and Eddie Moss. He spent so much time in the Newark ghetto chasing Addison the brothers called him "Syracuse." All the while he was looking for head jobs and not getting them. When he finally got the job at Rhode Island, "I had tears in my eyes." He was there two years before Hubie Brown called one summer and asked him to be his assistant coach with the Knicks.

"The first time I heard on the radio that I was the new assistant coach of the Knicks, I wanted to slap myself and say, "Wow." Who says playground dreams don't come true?

Nineteen games into the season Hubie got fired.

"I'm seeing Rick learn the pro game. He's gone from using the press almost all the time to using it strategically. He paces himself more than he did earlier. He's come to realize it's a long season. In this league you're only as good as your players, but he's done a great job with this team. He's like Patton, he's a tank commander. He's going to go up the hill and he's going to attack. He really wants to attack people defensively."

Malone gets up to leave. The next day he is scheduled to go out West to scout college players. "Rick was funny after the game. He went in and told them, 'I'm losing my hair, I'm gaining weight. You guys are going to kill me.' "

"How did the players respond?"

"They laughed."

February 18

The Sacramento Kings are at the Garden tonight. They are coached by Bill Russell, the former Celtic center who won ten championships in his career, one of the greatest accomplishments in sports history. As a coach he's become more controversial. After winning a championship as a player-coach in 1969, he coached in Seattle in the mid-Seventies, where he acquired the reputation as someone who didn't like practice and was aloof with his players and distant with the press. This year the Kings are going nowhere, and Russell already has been asked by several of his players if they could have more "professional practices." Peter Vescey quotes one anonymous King player saying, "Bill Russell calls timeouts to stretch his legs."

An intriguing matchup in the backcourt is Mark Jackson and Kenny Smith, the Kings' rookie point guard. Smith is from Jamaica and played at Archbishop Molloy High School. Jackson is from St. Albans and played at Bishop Loughlin. Though they were high school rivals, they also were friends, spending a lot of time together in summers, playing on different all-star teams. On the day of the draft in the Felt Forum, it had been Smith that helped Jackson through the emotional minutes before the Knicks chose him.

"Next to graduating from St. John's, those five minutes between the time the Portland Trail Blazers picked seventeenth until the Knicks picked me were the hardest five minutes of my life," says Jackson. "I felt like Dorothy from the *Wizard of Oz*. I was sitting there clicking my heels, saying there's no place like home. The fans are screaming and chanting, and I'm getting ready to cry. All of a sudden Kenny Smith walks up and sits next to me. That's the only thing that saved me."

Now they are the two leading candidates for Rookie of the Year.

On this night the dueling rookie point guards go head-to-

head the entire game, playing almost to a statistical stand-
still. But the Knicks win by four, and Gerald Wilkins goes
for 39.

Pitino goes to Bravo Gianni's on the upper East Side, his
favorite Italian restaurant in the city. Also there is John
Parisella, Jersey Red, and Bob Dempsey, who played at
UMass a couple of years ahead of him. The talk is of
Saratoga in August. There are drinks, laughs, and stories
old and new. Pitino is happy. These people he can totally
relax with. There are no questions to ask, no appearances to
keep up. And even if he is tired, says he hasn't been
sleeping well, he is starting to relax. The Kings have been
beaten. The Knicks don't play again for four days. There is
time, at least for a few hours, to put the Knicks and the
pressures of the job behind him. When he comes out of the
restaurant, though, someone has put a brick through his
side window and stolen his radio. Fragments of glass are
scattered all over the front seat.

New York, New York.

February 22

A Monday night in the Hartford Civic Center. The Knicks
are due to play the Celtics, who play a few games a year
here. Joanne Pitino sits in the front row about an hour
before the game as a few players warm up on the court.
Joanne is petite and wears a stylish pink outfit, her dark hair
pulled back. She is talking the changes her husband has
been through in his first year in the pros. "The only thing he
had left to learn as a coach was how to lose. Not that you
ever get used to losing. But I don't know if he could have
dealt with it before Daniel. Rick never again will look at
basketball in the same way as he did before Daniel died.
Never again will it be the be-all and end-all.

"I remember the first year at BU. If he lost he wouldn't
talk to me. Eventually I started telling him that you can't

stay in this profession if you are going to act this way after a loss. After that he got better." She smiles. "But not much.

"One thing hadn't changed since I first met him. He's always been super organized: the different boxes for the different days of the week, the colored pencils, the lists he's always writing to himself. I don't know where he gets the energy. But he's always had it."

Over the weekend Pitino went back to UMass for a ceremony honoring Julius Erving. One of the biggest disappointments of his college career had been he didn't get a chance to play with Erving, because the Doctor went hardship the year Pitino would have joined him as the point guard. Before the ceremony Pitino, accompanied by Jersey Red and Dave Dibble, went back to Lambda Chi Alpha, his old fraternity.

"We must have been there for two hours," remembered Jersey, "and when we were leaving the kids told Rick they were going to have a keg party that night. He reached in his wallet and gave them $200. The kids couldn't believe it. Then we went to the game and when we walked in, the entire student section started chanting, "Let's go, Knicks.""

"I was touched," Pitino says, "because I have such great memories of UMass. I loved going to school there."

The Knicks get off quickly, go up 12–3. "Be big, Mark," Pitino yells as Mark Jackson guards the Celtics' Dennis Johnson. It is part of the Knicks' strategy to get in Johnson's face, not give him the room to be able to make the good entry pass into the big men. "Stay down, Kenny," he yells at Walker as Bird gets the ball. Bird is infamous for his ball fakes that make defenders leave their feet. Bird gets the ball and makes a fall-away with Walker in his face. Pitino shakes his head in amazement. "It's like he's playing H-O-R-S-E out there."

The Celtics get the ball again, and Jim O'Brien peers down the sideline to hear Celtic coach K. C. Jones call out a play. "Post-up for DJ," he yells at Mark Jackson. "Post-up

for DJ." It's all a game within a game, basketball's version
of intelligence gathering. The Knicks steal the Celtics' signs
and try to react defensively. On the other end of the floor
the Celtics do the same.

The Knicks lead by three at halftime, a margin that would
be more except Bird already has 18 points, has Walker in
foul trouble, and has abused Johnny Newman with three
quick scores. Pitino quickly pulls Newman and doesn't play
him again. He instead goes with the seldom used Louis Orr,
who is experienced in guarding Bird. Only a week before
Bianchi wanted to put him on the injured list, a suggestion
nixed by Orr. He believes if he goes on the injured list the
perception around the league will be that he's never recovered from his back surgery, and his career essentially will be
over.

The Celtics go ahead in the third period, but the Knicks
tie the game at 91 with 52 seconds remaining. Bird then
makes two foul shots, Mark Jackson misses an outside jumper,
and the Celtics win 95–93. It's their 18th straight road loss,
but Pitino is pleased with his team's performance. "For the
first time I thought we got back to where we were at the
All-Star break. We fought back. Everyone played hard. We
didn't press because we have to play again tomorrow night,
but I was pleased with the way we played."

"So the difference was Larry Bird?" a TV reporter asks.

Pitino shrugs. "I think if you had him switch sides, things
would have been different."

The next night the Knicks beat the Bucks by two when
Gerald Wilkins scores on a three-point play with 44 seconds
left. Pitino plays Ewing and Cartwright together down the
stretch on offense, while putting in Green for defense, a
strategy that proves successful. Kenny Walker chips in 21,
his best outing in a while. Their tenth consecutive win in the
Garden is the most since the Knicks won 20 straight in 1973,
when there was nothing more chic in New York than having
two on the floor for the Knicks.

The trading deadline is forty-eight hours away and Pitino is asked afterward if Cartwright is going anywhere. "The only place he's going is on a three-day road trip," he quips. "It's more likely I'll be traded."

Since January 15 the Knicks have trimmed four games off the Sixers' lead. They haven't lost in the Garden since the loss to Phoenix in early January. Even though they have not won more than two games in a row all season and are 1–22 on the road, the Knicks have not been this close to a playoff spot since 1984.

8 | A Team Grows in the Garden

I have a problem with Sidney Green. Off the court he's the nicest person in the world, but he's totally disorganized. He's been late to practice three or four times, and he claims it's never his fault. I tell him, "Stu Jackson and Jim O'Brien both come to practice from the same direction you do and from farther away, yet they are never late. For an eleven o'clock practice I am here by ten o'clock. I make allowances for traffic. But you're operating like you live in Idaho, not New York." He is going to have problems later on in life if he doesn't learn to be more organized. Someday the fact that he can rebound isn't going to help him with his employer.

He tells me I'm always picking on him. His problem is that he doesn't own up to anything. It's what I call the pro attitude. For instance, we put a soda machine in the locker room at SUNY, and the first thing he says is that the Pistons cared about their players more because they put a juice machine in the locker room.

The other day in Denver we're all on the bus waiting to go to the arena, and Sid comes running out of the hotel about thirty seconds before the bus is due to leave. The first thing he does is ask Mike Saunders where his coat is. "How do I know?" says Saunders. So Sid turns to me and says, "I'll take a cab. I have to go back into the hotel and get my coat." I tell him we'll wait for him. Then when he finally gets on the bus, the bellhop comes running out of the hotel holding Sid's sneakers. Talk about being totally disorganized.

Then in the beginning of the game he throws a pass to Patrick that gets intercepted, and he starts having a discussion with Patrick instead of getting back on defense. I call a timeout and get all over him. I tell him that I don't care if he misses a shot or throws the ball away, but he's got to get back and play defense. He says I'm always picking on him. So I take him out and I can hear him swearing down the other end of the bench.

"That's it," I said.

"I'm mad at myself."

"Then keep it to yourself. Any more and I'm going to suspend you for two games. Considering how much money you make, you're not going to like that."

I came very close to suspending him.

Wilkins is just as disorganized, but he has made a 180-degree turnaround. About a month ago I had a long talk with him about being more disciplined—making lists of things to do, for example—and it seems to have helped. Maybe part of it is a con. He knows how to play me. He'll take a bad shot and I'll say, "Dougie, that's a bad shot," "I know, Rick," he'll say and then take three more just like it. But he knows the right things to say, and Sid doesn't. Sid fights you. All of his shortcomings come out when he's playing badly. That's when he's a time bomb, when he's irrational. So if I take him out and he starts to say something, I say, "Not now, Sid. We'll talk later."

It's taken half the year to get to know some of these guys better. I know Johnny Newman like a book now. For a while he had a sour attitude in practice. So one day I told Jimmy O'Brien to tell him that he had two days to change his attitude. Two days. If he didn't change it 180 degrees, I was going to waive him. In those two days in practice he was great. So I told him, "You take both life and basketball too seriously. You get too down on yourself when you miss a shot or you make a mistake. It's no fun being a pro that way, Johnny. When you're that way there are too many roller-coaster nights. These are fleeting years. Be more like Gerald Wilkins. Nothing bothers him. He's having fun with his life."

I know Kenny Walker. When he needs to have his confidence boosted, I tell him to keep shooting, because he has a tendency to go into a shell. I tell him that if he doesn't shoot, I will take him out. He also has a tendency to get down on himself. For instance, after we beat Golden State I could see he was down because he hadn't played much and Newman had had a great game. "Kenny, there have been a lot of nights Johnny Newman has sat and cheered you, so maybe it's nice that every once in a while you sit and cheer him a little bit."

"That's not it, Coach. I'm upset because I didn't play well."

"Kenny, after a victory the question of whether you played good or bad is irrelevant. Think about your performance after a loss."

Mark has to be handled delicately. You can't get on him, because he feels he's giving one-hundred percent. What you can do is appeal to his pride. I tell him, "You're great, but you need to be greater. You have to have better defensive technique. What bothers me is not that your man is scoring a lot of points on you, but your technique is bad."

My biggest fear coming into this job was that Patrick Ewing was not going to work hard in practice and was not going to rebound and block shots. My fears were alleviated right from the first day of practice. Patrick has worked hard every day in practice, and has blocked shots all year. He also is improving as a rebounder. But the best thing about him is what a good person he is. Last year this was a team that lacked leadership. But Patrick is becoming a leader, both through his work ethic and his attitude.

The players know me better, too. The younger players are receptive. Some of the others don't know where I'm coming

from. They probably think I'm too rah, rah college. I'm sure
Cartwright thinks that. Cummings. Probably Louis Orr. I
pump up the younger guys and I stay away from the older
ones. Billy Cartwright is a cynical guy. Not in a bad way
really, but he seems to feel the whole world is against him.
Pat Cummings is just trying to get as many minutes as he
can get. I understand that. I think I've reached Trent Tucker
in subtle ways, but he's not someone who puts a priority on
getting better.

But I avoid confrontations in public because I want to
stay positive at all times. The only one I've had all year was
the one with Sid in Milwaukee. If I have a problem with
someone, I have breakfast with them on the road, in private. Because they don't want to be embarrassed in front of
their peers. You can't yell at these guys, not in a volatile
situation like a game, or at halftime. In the NBA you're
wasting your time if you do it then.

✝✝✝✝✝✝✝✝✝✝

March 1–4

The Knicks have their most successful road trip of the
year, a three-game Western swing in which they beat the
Clippers and the Golden State Warriors on successive nights
before losing to the Nuggets in Denver. The victory over the
Clippers breaks an 18-game drought on the road. "Finally,
we got the monkey off our backs. Now I don't have to keep
reading about this damned streak."

The Knicks have had their first winning month since March
1984. They also have won six out of their last nine games,
and eight out of their last twelve.

Johnny Newman has 26 off the bench against the Warriors, tying a career high. He also goes 13–13 from the foul
line, including several key ones in the closing minutes. Not
bad for someone claimed off the waiver wire for a thousand
bucks. "If Red Auerbach had picked up Newman, everyone
would be calling him a genius," says Bianchi.

Wilkins has 34, including back-to-back drives in the fourth quarter to give the Knicks the lead. Ironically, he is matched against the same Chris Mullin he came very close to being traded for a few weeks earlier. "I'm not going to lie to you," said Wilkins. "I had something to prove. He probably did, too. We didn't even speak to each other before the game. I was mad because there was talk of trading me, and he probably was mad because he wasn't traded to New York. And all in all, we as a team have something to prove. We're checking the scores. We want the playoffs bad. If we get there this year, we'll feel we can get there next year and the one after that."

Cartwright has not been traded, ending for this year at least the ongoing drama of where and when he is going to go. By some estimates Cartwright's been rumored this year going to ten different teams. "I guess I just have to worry about where I'm going for another summer," he says simply, no visible emotion in his voice.

"I think he could be standing in the middle of an earthquake and be blasé about it," Pitino comments. "That's just the way Billy is."

They return to the Garden for a Tuesday night game against the Pacers. They played poorly at Denver on Sunday, what Stu Jackson calls a pro day. "There are certain days that no matter what you say or do, pros are just going to go through the motions. Denver was a game we could have mailed in."

After flying home Sunday night, they experience the inevitable day-after lethargy in practice. "They were throwing the ball away, not playing good defense, and I was getting more and more agitated. So I walked out. Told Jim O'Brien to take over, walked out of the building, and got into my car. At the time I figured it was a statement, a sort of grand gesture: no yelling, no lectures, just walk out in the middle of practice. The only trouble was the team failed to get the message.

"I asked Jimmy O'Brien the next day how we practiced after I left, and he said, 'Worse.' 'You mean they actually got worse after I left?' I couldn't believe it. He said, 'Rick, because you didn't say anything, they didn't think you were mad. Everyone was looking around to see where you were. They just figured you had to go somewhere.' Here I was trying to use it as a motivational tool, and they think I'm off making a phone call.

"So this morning we had a walk-through at the Garden. I told them they are professional athletes and I'm not going to yell at them. I told them that they didn't know me. Billy Donovan knew me, and Mark and Sid and Patrick knew me a little bit as a lecturer at a camp.

" 'You people don't understand me. Some of you think I've got problems just with Sidney Green, but it's with quite a few of you. When you face adversity, you fight back like killer bees. But every time you get a little success, you start to think you're better than you are. You practice poorly, You don't perform. And you know why? All you people are content. I want to make the playoffs so we can go far in them. You want to make them so you can breathe a sigh of relief. Our intentions are altogether different.

" 'The other thing you have to understand is how much I want you all to get better. To work hard. Gerald Wilkins has done that, and he's gone to the next level. When some of you are criticized, you act like you are fifth graders in front of the principal. But have you ever read even one sentence in the papers that we lost because the guards shot 5–28, or the forwards were 4–16? Did you ever read one thing about what another player did to one of you? Did you ever hear me pinpoint an individual? That's not the way I coach. But I can't want it more than you. I'm used to giving speeches about handling adversity. But you guys don't know how to handle success.' "

Against the Indiana Pacers that night, the Knicks are down big at the half.

"You play the way you practice," Pitino tells the team at halftime, "and this is just another indication of that. You think you've gotten the worst of it, but you haven't. They are tired, and their legs are going to go. You aren't. It's like a boxer who spends the early rounds working on the body. You've already worked on the body. Now go to the head and take them out."

The Knicks are down by as many as 20 in the third quarter before their press starts taking its toll. In the fourth quarter the Knicks hold Indiana to just 12 points. Up three with just 10 seconds left, they appear to have the game won when John Long hits a desperation three-point heave from the out-of-bounds line on the left wing. Mark Jackson responds with a leaning 10-footer at the buzzer for the Knicks' 11th straight win at the Garden.

"I've been waiting all my life to make that shot," says Jackson. "It was a dream shot. So many times on a court I've counted off the final seconds in my head and made a shot like that." He pauses, a slight smile on his face, "But when it went in, I didn't know who to turn to, who to hug, so I just ran in here."

Jackson credits the confidence shown by coaches and teammates as keys to his success. He can play his game without having to worry about missing a shot. This is another part of Pitino's coaching philosophy. "I never get on a player for missing a shot. In fact, it's just the opposite. Times at Providence when Donovan wasn't shooting well and seemed hesitant to take more shots, I often called a timeout just to tell Billy that if he didn't take more shots he was coming out. Part of it is that I believe you shoot better when you are loose; you can't be loose if you are worried about missing. Part of it, I guess, is that my coaching philosophy stems from my college career. My fantasy envisioned a world where you don't have to worry if you miss a shot. Shots aren't parceled out like pieces of some diminishing pie. And, of course, part of it is my belief that players must know that you as a coach have complete confidence in them."

Mark Jackson points out a game, one of the many losses early in the season, that in retrospect seems to have started turning the team around. "There were 15 seconds remaining, we were down seven, and Rick called a timeout. Everybody pretty much knew it was over, and here he is in the huddle going over a pressing defense where we can get two steals, score, then get a third steal and hit a three-pointer. We all kind of looked at each other. I think we realized right there how much confidence he has in us. That attitude began to spill over."

In what has become the standard postgame scene, Pitino is holding a cup of soda, his jacket is off. His face is drained of color, a pasty white. Immediately he is surrounded by a dozen reporters, who stick microphones in his face from all three sides.

"What you saw tonight is rare in the pros. It's rare even in college. That was one of the most fun games I was ever involved in. I don't think I've ever been more proud of a team since Austin Peay last year when we were down 10 with five minutes to play. This tonight took sheer guts. Our press tonight was as good as I had at Providence, and at Providence we had the best. This was a character win. We went to another level tonight, the most intensity we've played with all year. I haven't been this pumped up in a long time."

He pauses and shakes his head in admiration. "How about Mark? Mark should have been exhausted. I don't see how he was standing up in the end. He had pressed the whole second half, and he's the point man in the press so he does a lot of running. I wanted to give him tomorrow off, but I couldn't just let him rest, so I gave the whole team off."

The next day the Knicks place Carlisle on the injured list with a strained groin muscle, and sign Carey Scurry, a 6–7 forward waived by the Utah Jazz in January. Scurry grew up in Brooklyn, played in college at Long Island, and joins Pitino, Bianchi, Mark Jackson, Sidney Green, and Billy Donovan as guys who grew up in the New York area. You can't go home again? Who said so? Thomas Wolfe never could stick the jumper anyway.

Scurry has a reputation as an excellent defensive player. He also arrives with the reputation of being difficult to get along with. In addition to a DWI charge in Utah, he had questioned his playing time with coach Frank Layden, and supposedly had punched out teammate Mel Turpin on a team bus. "I don't ever care what other people say about a player," Pitino says. "I make my own opinion. When I first got this job, people swore to me that Patrick Ewing was going to dog it every day. That couldn't be more wrong. He couldn't be better. When I came to Providence, everyone told me that the kids were losers, that you couldn't get them to play hard. Nothing was further than the truth. So I never listen to anyone's judgments of character. I find out for myself."

The next day is a rainy, gloomy Friday in New York. Tonight is Philly, a game touted as the biggest Knick basketball game in four years. "KNICKS HOST A BIGGIE" screams a headline in the *Daily News*. The eighth playoff spot is at stake.

An hour and a half before the game many of the Knicks already are on the floor warming up. Among them are Cartwright, Cummings, Tucker, and Orr. All the veterans, the guys you wouldn't think would be out there early. "It's starting to happen," says John Cirillo, the Knicks publicist. "You can just feel it."

Cirillo grew up in Brooklyn, a typical Knick fan. He came to the Knicks from Roosevelt Raceway the year following the Knicks' last appearance in the playoffs, the year Cartwright got hurt and Bernard King led the NBA in scoring. He saw it start to sour after that. The injuries got so bad he once sent out a press release with a big Band-Aid on it. The finger-pointing came next.

"The problem with injuries is that they first become a reason why you lose, and then they become a crutch. A lot of guys become comfortable with losing. That's what Rick changed, and he changed that long before we started winning. Gerald Wilkins' transformation has been unbelievable. Now Kenny Walker is upset when we lose. So is Mark. And no one's madder than Patrick when we lose. I'm going to do a few more things for Patrick to help his image. The Bondy article is totally untrue. That guy never comes into the locker room. He's like those other authorities writing about us who never show up. Patrick never refuses an interview after a game. If people knew the real Patrick Ewing, they would love him. He doesn't want to be in the spotlight, and he doesn't want to do any call-in talk shows. He's a private kid, no doubt about it. About three or four times a year he'll bring his young son in here, but his private life is just that: private. I've never met a nicer kid than Patrick Ewing, and I'm not just saying that to create an image for him. I get him tickets and he must thank me about ten times."

The Knicks trail by seven at the half, but outscore the Sixers by 18 in the third quarter. It is a great quarter for the Knicks, highlighted by Barkley being knocked out at the end of the third quarter, the victim of an inadvertent Cartwright elbow. "Barkley sucks . . . Barkley sucks" chants the large Garden crowd as he is led through the tunnel into the locker room holding a towel to his head. Soon after, Ewing is ejected for throwing a punch at Mike Gminski.

The game roars to a finish. The big building pulsates with excitement, and erupts as Mark Jackson sends the game into overtime with two seconds left. Then Jackson scores eight points in overtime: the Knicks win by two. More important, they have won without Ewing, a great psychological boost for a young team that sometimes seems to stand around and wait for Ewing to win the game for them.

"Significant regular-season basketball returned to the Garden last night," writes Fred Kerber. "There were fights in the stands, obscene chants from fans, incredible plays, overtime, punches on the court, ejections, a roller coaster of emotional, gut-busting excitement."

It is the Knicks 24th win of the season, matching their total from a year ago. It's also their 12th straight win at the Garden.

Pitino stands in the hallway outside the Knicks' locker room. He's down about the impending fate of Billy Donovan. Bianchi has put subtle pressure on Pitino to let Donovan go, and bring in someone more experienced to back up Mark Jackson. Jackson is simply playing too many minutes. On three different occasions this past month Bianchi had deals lined up that fell apart at the last minute for various reasons: Franklin Edwards, Ennis Whatley, Leon Wood. And when each one fell through, Pitino breathed a sigh of relief. If he knew deep down that Donovan probably lacked the physical skills to be an effective backup, cutting him would be like cutting out a piece of his heart.

"A couple of weeks earlier, when Edwards supposedly was on his way, I was going to put Carlisle on the injured list, then see if Edwards was better than Donovan. If he was, Carlisle would have been activated and Donovan waived. Now Bianchi wants to being in Cedric Toney and release Donovan.

"I feel horrible about it. I asked Al if he could put it off a week. I don't want to waive him before the Big East tournament. Everyone'll be in town."

March 10–14

The Knicks against the Lakers in the Garden. The scalpers on Seventh Avenue say it is the toughest ticket of the season. It's one of those magical nights when the Garden is the home of the City Game.

The Lakers are a glamorous team. Magic Johnson with his smile that lights up the arena. James Worthy with his poker face and goggles and North Carolina pedigree. Pat Riley with his slicked-back hair, Italian suits, and matinee-idol looks. And, of course, Kareem Abdul-Jabbar in the middle. The game's old man river is still sky-hooking after all these years. Kareem, who grew up in Manhattan, played high school ball at Power Memorial. Back then he was Lew Alcindor, already living inside that fragile bubble known as fame. But that was many sky hooks ago, and now he comes into the Garden as laid back as a day at Malibu Beach.

Two nights earlier the Knicks beat Michael Jordan and the Chicago Bulls, and tonight they go up 12 in the second quarter, seven at the half. "Beat L.A. Beat L.A." chants the Garden crowd. For a while the Garden fantasy continues. The Knicks sock it to the Lakers. In the game's final six minutes, though, they miss some makable shots and lose by five. The 13-game win streak in the Garden is over. Even so, the Garden crowd gives them a standing ovation.

Afterward Magic is effusive in his praise for the Knicks. "Their press just took us out of everything in the first half." He says Jackson is "going to be great. He can pass and takes it in traffic and makes the shot." He says how he was shopping in Bloomingdale's earlier in the day, and "people were coming up to me and saying, 'Thirteen in a row.' You better watch out. The people of New York are excited about the Knicks again."

Just as effusive is Riley. "Madison Square Garden is the mecca of basketball. In the past three or four years it hasn't been like that. But it's coming back. Tonight you could feel the electricity. Basketball is back where it belongs. Boy, they make you play, I like, no, I *love*, what is happening in New York."

The Knicks are 25–34.

The next night Pitino goes to the Garden to watch Providence play Connecticut in the opening round of the Big East tournament. The Friars lose, ending their season. What a contrast to the year before, when Pitino brought his team into the Big East tournament and used a big victory over St. John's as a springboard to the NCAA. Rumors are rampant that first-year coach Gordie Chiesa has coached his last game. Last year seems like a time gone forever for Providence basketball.

The Knicks' roller coaster continues They lose to the Hawks on the road on Friday night, and come back in the Garden Saturday night to beat Utah. Win at home, lose on the road, almost as if they are two different teams. "Obviously I want to win on the road, too. That's how you build a team in the NBA. First you learn how to win at home. Then you learn how to be competitive on the road. Then you learn how to win on the road. Those are the NBA building blocks to success."

The Knicks have signed Scurry to a second ten-day contract, and have signed Sedric Toney to a ten-day contract. A former player at Dayton, who played in thirteen games for Atlanta and Phoenix two years ago, Toney has been playing AAU ball in Dayton. He comes in as a backup point guard. This was supposed to be the end of Billy Donovan, but Pat Cummings goes on the injured list with a bad ankle and Donovan dodges another bullet.

"Monday night against Cleveland in the Garden, the Knicks quickly fall behind, and Pitino knows quickly that they need a big coaching push. "Get after it," he yells, kneeling in front of the bench. "Come on, Dougie . . . Rotate, Rotate . . . work hard, big Sid . . . Get after it, Patrick . . . Rotate, Sid . . . Get tougher." He is coaching every play, bellowing across the Garden floor. Nothing works. The Knicks look lethargic, sloppy, a step slow in the press. At the half they are down 15 and look as gone as last year's hit record. Right before halftime he calls a timeout. "We're not even going to talk about what's going on here. We'll wait until halftime."

"I know you don't like to be yelled at," he tells them at

halftime, trying not to yell, "but I'm upset. You are starting to change people's perceptions, but a performance like this can bring everything back to square one. You have become fatheaded because you've won a few games." He leaves the room, trying to calm down, then changes his mind thirty seconds later and goes back. "I have more to say." Then he blasts them, college-style.

Once again their pressure defense and their hustle gets them back in the game. Pitino plays Ewing and Cartwright together, depending on the matchups, a strategy he is using more as the season wears on. "The decision to play Patrick and Billy together is based on matchups and how the game is playing, Obviously, we can't press when they're both in the game, so we are limited to how much we can play them together. But in certain situations playing them both puts a lot of pressure on an opponent's interior defense. It's very difficult to double-down on both of them. But we do suffer defensively when they play together because Billy has to play a forward who usually is quicker than he is. The point is, playing them together can be effective, but you have to pick your spots."

They cut the Cavalier lead to eight at the end of the third quarter, catch them midway through the fourth, and hang on for a 104–100 victory.

"What did you tell them at halftime?" Pitino is quickly asked as he comes into the hallway and is surrounded by the media.

"I'd rather not say. But what you saw tonight was a tremendous effort. All of New York should be proud of these guys."

Pitino goes on to say how great Trent Tucker is playing now. He's coming off the bench and sticking the jumper. Then he's asked about Mark Jackson, who has had another big game.

"He is in a class by himself. He is one of the toughest mentally I've ever seen."

The interview over, Pitino comes into the lounge. "Do you know that Sidney said after the game?" he asks with a laugh. "He asked me if they were still fatheaded."

March 17–26

The Greek chorus continues:

Jerry Sullivan in *Newsday* rates Sidney Green among his five least favorite NBA players. "Another one who puts up decent rebounding stats while hurting his team in other areas. If power is his game, someone should plug him in. Shoots layups like a bad CYO player. Full of phony bravado, but likes to disappear in big moments."

The next day a headline in the Post reads, "PITINO PLAN PAYS DIVIDENDS." It's a story written by Hank Gola, who took over the Knicks' beat after Kevin Kernan left for the *San Diego Union*. "Pitino's signature is all over this team and it's spelled w-i-n-n-e-r."

The Knicks beat Atlanta at home, then go off on a three-game Texas trip. They win at San Antonio and lose big at Dallas and Houston. A Knick highlight is Johnny Newman, who averages 21 on the trip. "We played Houston on the night after Akeem had blasted Bill Fitch in the papers," says Pitino. "We had no shot. They came out really fired up."

On Saturday night, March 26, the Knicks are back in the Garden against the Celtics. Ringling Brothers and Barnum & Bailey Circus is in town, and when Larry Bird comes out for his early shooting, the building isn't set up yet for basketball. Bird sits down in a seat, a disgusted look on his face. Later he will have 20 in the first half as the Celtics go up 18 and coast to a seven-point victory, only the Knicks' second home loss in over two months. Also watching the Garden being transformed into a basketball arena is Tim Walsh, the Knicks' assistant trainer. He is twenty-five and has a face that would be welcomed in County Cork. "I dreaded going to practice last year, because I knew something bad was going to happen. It was like an accident waiting to happen. Things were bad two years ago and just kept snowballing. Everyone was always trying to get out of practice. Patrick must have missed ninety percent of the practices the first year. The last few weeks of last season even Bob Hill was asking me how many practices we had left, because I always knew. I had a personal countdown going on."

"What's the worst part of your job now?" he is asked.

"Getting woken up on the road by guys wanting to know what time practice is," he says, grinning. "It happens all the time. I'm asleep and the phone rings at three in the morning. One of the players has forgotten what time practice is."

9 | The College Coach Redeemed

If we moved back to Providence, my wife would be so happy I wouldn't be just husband of the year, I would be husband for life. The other day she told me the house we used to have in Rhode Island hasn't been sold. That we could go back and live in the same house. I know that it would be a mess here in New York leaving my contract, but you can't react to what other people are going to think. The real question anyone has to ask is "What are you going to do with your life?" For me, I think that's going back to college.

I really have a better sense of worth as a college coach. The things I like to do—watch a player grow, help a player get better—I don't have enough time to do. I really miss the time you have to practice in college, to do all the little things that make your system better. Maybe what I miss most of all is the closeness to the players. No one knows what's going to happen in the future. In college you recruit a kid and know he's going to be there for four years. He almost becomes part of your family. Here, it's not the same.

I see people constantly making the same mistakes, but I can't really address them, or we'll get into a Houston situation where the players are complaining about Bill Fitch not letting them play their game. You always are walking a fine line. If you constructively criticize them, they say you are taking their game away. If you don't, you get the same mistakes over and over again. Knowing basketball is not the answer to keeping your job in the NBA. If you can't keep harmony on your team, everything you know about the game is irrelevent. But in a sense I feel I'm not being true to myself.

I first started realizing it when we started winning. I didn't get excited enough. Stu Jackson says he can't believe how much I've changed. I've had to adjust; that's the secret of success. Just like the defense, you have to adjust. It hasn't been easy. I've had to swallow things. I've had to learn how to live with certain mistakes. The one thing you learn is that guys will not criticize each other. Larry Bird is rare in that respect. He will get on his teammates and make them play harder. And you can't embarrass a guy in front of his peers. You embarrass Sidney and he goes into his shell. But you can't tolerate his mistakes or you can't win. It's a fine line. There are times when Dougie takes a foolish shot. In the timeout I say how our shot selection has to be better when what I'd like to do is tell him, "Don't you ever take that stupid shot again."

Like with Patrick. Now Patrick's been great, but one of the things he has to work on is passing the ball back out when he gets doubled. In the beginning of the year he wasn't doing that and our offense bogged down. We are starting to get him to be more cognizant of it, but it has to be done with care. I spent an entire timeout recently after he passed the ball out talking about what a great pass it was. When he scores I don't make much of it, but I heap praise on him when he kicks the hall back out. Patrick doesn't like criticism in public. One on one you can say anything to him, but not in front of anyone. Mark is the same way. You have to let him go, let him be creative. With Kenny Walker you constantly have to reinforce him, boost him. Conversely, you have to stay all over Newman or he'll fall asleep on you.

I thought the job would be more enjoyable. It is exciting and it is intense, but I thought it would be more fun. It's not. The travel, the traffic, the hassles of the big city: these things are not fun. I had more fun here as an assistant.

✝✝✝✝✝✝✝✝✝✝

It's a strange time for Pitino.

The Knicks are starting to win, and Pitino's methods have been redeemed. He said his team would get stronger as the season went on, and they are now stronger. He said the press would get stronger, and it has gotten stronger. He wanted to create more of a college atmosphere and the Knicks now resemble a rah-rah college team.

"The losing 29–37 record means little," Fred Kerber writes in the *Daily News*. "Pitino has done a terrific job. He won't be Coach of the Year, but if they gave a 'Best Coaching Performance with the Least Talent' award he'd win going away. Pitino's motivational skills should not be underestimated. He has drawn the team together, kept them enthused. Beyond the psyche, he has utilized every strength, hidden most weaknesses. He has made mistakes—what rookie coach hasn't?—but he has adjusted his philosophy."

Billy Donovan has been waived, and if this has been inevitable for weeks, it is still not easy for Pitino. A few weeks earlier Gordie Chiesa resigned at Providence. "I keep thinking of the day Gordie Chiesa stood in my driveway and I told him to forget about the Providence job and come with me to the Knicks as an assistant. The job had been open for a couple of weeks, and I tried to tell him that Providence did not really want him to be the coach. 'If that's the case, then you don't want the job. If they don't want you badly, it's not worth taking.' I knew that day in my driveway that if John offered him the job, Gordie—for economic reasons—would take it. And I thought Gordie should get the job because the players unanimously wanted him. I find it interesting that it was those same players' dissatisfaction that led him to resigning. But deep down I knew his taking the job was a mistake. It's terribly difficult for an assistant to become the head coach in the same program. The players know you in one role and all of a sudden you change roles completely, and they don't really understand why."

Soon after Chiesa resigned, Providence athletic director John Marinatto asked Pitino if he were interested in coming back. At first he said no way. He still has three years left on his Knick contract. But Marinatto keeps calling back and asking for Pitino to recommend possible coaches, and each time he does Pitino begins thinking more and more about the possibility of his own return. "The college game may be more geared to me physically and emotionally. The way I coach, I don't know if I can keep this pace up."

March 28–31

Al Bianchi is sitting in his office on the fourth floor of the Garden. On the wall is a chart with all the NBA teams and their players, color-coded by positions. Next to it is a similar chart of the CBA teams. In one corner are balloons left over from his fifty-sixth birthday a couple of days before. He is talking about the NBA life-style, how difficult it is on families, how difficult it is to coach in the NBA. "In this game it's the players, and you must understand that. If you lose the team, you're dead. Look at what happened to Kevin Loughery in Washington. Moses wouldn't play for him. The most important thing is the interaction between the coach and players. The X's and O's prepare your team, but if the guys don't play for you, there's nothing you can do. And if you lose them you're dead, 'cause you can't get them back.

"And you can't worry about the money the players are making. They're all overpaid, but you can't think about it. I've seen that drive coaches out of the game. They get so obsessed with what the players are making, they start letting that influence the way they deal with them. You can't do that. I didn't even want to know what they made.

"And it's tougher here than anywhere. The New York

mentality is impatience. You see people standing in lines every day, in the stores, at the movies. Listen to the cab-drivers. Everyone's impatient. It permeates the entire fabric of the city. You're fighting that constantly."

The day before at practice at SUNY Pitino has a long talk with his team. "We have 14 games left, and it's apparent we can't play good man-to-man defense. But it might be asking too much for you to press all the time. So I'll coach any way you want me to coach. Are you going to play better man, or are we going to press right from the beginning? I'll do whatever you want. But we have to do it together." He stops and looks at the players.

"I really think we should press," Cartwright says. "We have to dictate the tempo of the game, we have to be the aggressor, and the press makes us do that. Without the press we don't do much."

After Cartwright speaks, everyone agrees they should press the entire game. They are in a playoff race, and there is no time to hold anything back.

"You depend on me too much to be your leader," Pitino adds. "All twelve of you have to be leaders." They then go out and have a great practice.

"I was thrilled that it was Bill Cartwright who said we should press. Here's a guy who has spent much of the year wanting to be traded. Here's a guy whose individual game probably most suffered in a fast-paced, pressing style."

Tonight it is Dallas and the Mavs come in 46–21, first in their division. The week before they had beaten the Knicks by 20 in Dallas. Pitino starts Newman and Walker at the forward, and after a quick start the Knicks are down five at the half. The Knicks are ahead by one at the end of the third quarter, primarily because Cartwright has a big period, scoring seven of the Knicks final 11 points. Then Trent Tucker has 12 points in the fourth quarter. Once again he has come off the bench and stuck the jumper. The Knicks win 114–106.

The locker room afterward is jammed with reporters and TV cameras. Every game there seems to be more of them. They file in, move toward the back of the small, narrow room, to the lockers of Jackson and Wilkins. "I'm excited about coming to the Garden now," says Wilkins. "Not like last year when we almost had to sneak on the floor and keep our heads down in case people threw things at us."

Wilkins is a great chameleon. A reporter will suggest he took a bad shot and Wilkins will shake his head earnestly and say, I know, that was a bad shot. Then the next reporter will say it wasn't that bad a shot, and Wilkins invariably will say, no, it wasn't that bad a shot, I've been working on it. Part of it is con, but part of it is that he earnestly wants to be liked. Of all the Knicks he seeks the limelight like a moth to a flame. After all those years of growing up in brother Dominique's shadow, this is his moment.

He also is, perhaps, Pitino's greatest transformation. "It was tough in the beginning because I didn't know where I stood with him," Wilkins says. "He'd tell me, 'Gerald, you're a great offensive player, one of the guys we plan to rebuild around.' But then he didn't put any offensive plays in for me. He'd say, 'Gerald, you're going to be a great player.' Then he took my starting job away. I didn't know what to think. I kept reading in the papers that I was going and I didn't want to go. It was was sink-or-swim time. All I knew was that the man was playing with my head. But you know what? Maybe I needed something like that. Because right now I'm playing the best ball of my career, and I'm only going to get better."

Next door in the lounge Pitino is slumped on a leather coach. Now comes the exhaustion, you can almost see the life drain out of him, like steam slowly escaping through a manhole cover on Seventh Avenue. At a table nearby O'Brien is telling the other coaches how tonight was another character win, another game that they never would have won early in the year, as Sidney Green limps out of the training room, an ice pack on his ankle. Still wearing his white uniform with the orange trim, he starts walking across the room on his way to the locker room.

"You pussy," someone jokes.

Green smiles and shakes a fist in a mock gesture. "I'm tough. UNLV pride."

"Hey, Sid," says Pitino quietly. "I know your ankle was bad. I appreciate the effort tonight."

Green nods, goes into the locker room. As he gets undressed, he says that when he first came to the Knicks, he had not been a big Pitino fan. Pitino was just another coach who always was yelling at him. That's changed.

"I wasn't sure what to make of him in the beginning. I didn't really trust him. But now I like the guy, now that I know what kind of person he is. I wish I had played for him when I first came into the league. He stresses fundamentals, all the things I forgot. I can't wait to work with him this summer. Because I want to have the same kind of relationship with him I had with Tark. And when I heard what he's doing for Arturo Brown's brother, it brought tears to my eyes."

A Brooklyn kid from Nazareth High School, Arturo Brown was a senior at Boston University in the fall of 1982. He was the co-captain and their best player. Brown often would babysit for the Pitino's. One afternoon, while playing in a pickup game, he collapsed and died, the victim of an enlarged heart. After he collapsed, he leaned up for one last moment, then fell back again. Later, teammates said it was like Brown was taking one last look around. Pitino was at a hospital in Boston at the time; Joanne was giving birth to their son, Richard.

"I rushed to the hospital where Arturo had been taken, and I got there just as they were pumping his heart, trying to get it started. The entire team was in the waiting room. We went into a private room. Later, the doctor came out and told us that Arturo had died. We all started crying."

One of the players would later say that Pitino, tears streaming down his face, said, "It was simply a case of Arturo being a little too good for this place."

"For two or three weeks I felt paralyzed. The entire team did. It was a very tough time for all of us. We all went to the funeral and later that night we all ended up in a bar sobbing all night. I didn't want to coach anymore. I was incredibly down. We dedicated the season to Arturo, did a lot of things for him that year. And we went to the NCAA tournament that year.

"A few months later I bought a Mercedes because of him. When he used to babysit for us, I would be driving him back to campus and there was a Mercedes dealership near the campus that we'd drive by. I had a LeCar then, one of those little Renault things, and every time it hit a bump it would rattle. Arturo said that if I ever got to the NCAA tournament I had to get rid of the old LeCar and get a Mercedes. He must have said it four or five times, and it became a little joke between us. So one day I went out and did it. Kind of for Arturo, if that makes any sense. But four months later I had to get rid of it, 'cause I couldn't make the payments."

Pitino started a trust fund for Brown's younger brother, Rodney, to send him to private school and camps in the summer. The first year, between three and four thousand dollars were raised. But when Pitino left Boston University it withered away. So now every time he speaks at a camp, he puts his fee into the trust fund.

"When I found that out, it made me look at the man differently," says Green. "I know now that he cares for us."

Tucker enters the locker room still in his uniform, on his way back from a TV interview. He is humming that he's in a New York state of mind. Earlier in the season Pitino viewed Tucker as little more than deadwood, another symbol of the past that had to be cleared out. That opinion has changed. "I always knew Trent had leadership qualities. I just didn't think he placed a high priority on bettering himself as a player. He was too content to play tennis in the summer instead of working on his game. So I challenged him. Told him that he was afraid to be better."

"Rick put responsibilities on me, both as a player and as a person, and we had our spats," says Tucker. "There were some things said about me that I didn't think were true, and I had to prove they weren't true. On the court and off the court." Tucker believes the team started to believe in Pitino midway through the season. "Once we got in great shape, we began not minding playing all over the court. And once we started to see the press work, we began realizing we were getting better. We started to believe in one another. In a sport where you can't go your separate ways, we started to depend on one another. One of the reasons is that it's a younger team. Younger guys tend to hang out more together. They don't have families, so the team becomes their family."

"What about Pitino?" he is asked. "How much influence has he had in all this?"

"Pitino?" Tucker says. "He should be Coach of the Year. The guys didn't really know him in the beginning. A lot of guys were just trying to find out where they fit. But he adjusted, too. And once the guys saw that, I think that made all the difference."

The Knicks fly out that night to Cleveland, where they lose the next night to the Cavaliers. They take 20 three-point shots in the game, an NBA record. Before the game Pitino defends Mark Jackson, who is being sniped at by some of the Cleveland players for alleged hotdogging: Jackson's predilection for playing to the crowd when the Knicks are doing well in the Garden, for wagging his finger after big plays, throwing his fist in the air. Pitino says Jackson is a showman, someone who plays with enthusiasm. "Sometimes I think it hurts Mark in that he gets so pumped up after a big play, he tends to lose his concentration and forgets to get into the defense. But you don't want to take that away, either. Because that's one of the big things that makes him so special."

After the game Pitino says, "We are catching every bad break. The teams we are in contention with keep winning, and tonight we got a horrible whistle. But I want to make the playoffs in the worst way. Some people in New York think we would be better off in the lottery, and maybe get a Danny Manning. I totally disagree with that. Perception-wise, getting into the playoffs would be a great experience for the team. That experience would really benefit us next year."

April 2

The Knicks are now tied with the Bullets, 1-1/2 games back of Philly, 2 games behind the Cavs, after upsetting the Bucks in Milwaukee for their fifth road win of the season.

Ewing is averaging 19.3, is third in the league in blocks, 23rd in rebounding. Wilkins is at 17.3. Mark Jackson is averaging 13, is fourth in the league in assists and fifth in steals. Cartwright is at 11, Walker at 10, Green at nine, and Newman at eight.

Back in New York, they hang on to beat the Rockets by six after being up 18 at the half. It is another example of Pitino's theory that one of the most difficult things to do in basketball is play with a big lead. Ewing has 27 in first half, and ends with a season-high 36. It is the Knicks 18th win in the Garden in their last 20 games.

A few minutes after the game Ewing sits in front of his locker in a blue terrycloth robe, ice packs on both knees, his post-game ritual. He says, "It's not because my knees hurt, but because my knees are my future. They are my career."

He sips orange juice out of a cup and says, "I've never won 32 games since I've been here. So this is very exciting for me. I'm enjoying it. This is the feeling I've been waiting for since I came to New York. This is the feeling I had all my four years at Georgetown."

"Are you aware that you had a season high?"

He looks up. "We won and that's the bottom line. I've had season highs before and we didn't win."

Trent Tucker comes over and touches Ewing on the knee. "I'm proud of you."

Ewing nods.

Tucker goes back and stands in front of his locker. He always looks as if he just stepped out of *Gentleman's Quarterly*. Tonight is no exception: Sleek gray suit, Italian shoes, everything just so.

"What's the biggest difference between this year and last?" he is asked.

"This brings out more of the child in you. When you are winning and things are going good, it becomes more of a child's game than a business. It makes you remember how you used to play the game."

Right next to him on the wall is a large black-and-white picture of Tucker jumping into Ewing's arms in triumph, a freeze-frame of the joys of that child's sport.

Several reporters are crowding around Kenny Walker, whom Pitino has praised for having another good game, of doing a "lot of things that don't show up in the stats." Walker, who too often this year has been ignored in the postgame media crunch, is saying, "I heard people yelling, 'Put Walker in.' That was very gratifying to me. That wasn't happening earlier in the year."

Earlier in the year there was a stretch when Pitino didn't start Walker to spare him from the embarrassing boos when his name was announced. Now he says he thinks that the worst is behind him.

"How have you survived it emotionally?"

"If I had been surrounded by bad people, or had been in a bad organization, it would have been worse. But here there are good-quality people, and I'm just not talking about basketball." He looks over at Ewing. "Beast," he says, jutting out his chest and doing a little good-natured posturing, "I got Akeem's shot once tonight, and I got it last week in Houston too. Just so you know it was no fluke."

Ewing smiles his big smile, the one the public rarely sees.

This has been a great time for Ewing. He has played every game. He has practiced hard. He has become, along with Akeem Alajuwon, the best center in the game, and is poised to become a dominant NBA player for years to come. And if there are still times when you wonder why he's not a better rebounder, he has been willing, in Pitino's words, "to take us on his shoulders.

"Patrick does have problems with his hands. He still drops the ball more than he should. I think that's because he doesn't maintain eye contact with the ball long enough. That's mental. He also commits some silly fouls. But he's improved in that area recently. And he's also rebounded much better. His problem in the past was that he often got pushed too far under the basket. When he can take his athletic step in going for the ball, Patrick can rebound with anyone, and lately he is doing that more and more. Patrick has a tremendous attitude. I heard he didn't practice much, didn't work hard, didn't block shots. It's been just the opposite. He runs, he blocks, he has a great low-post game, and most of all he really wants to win. Winning is very important to Patrick, and in the past few weeks he has taken his game to a new level.

"Maybe the best thing about him is what a nice person he is. He's one of those people you want to bring home and tell your kids, 'Be just like Patrick Ewing.' I mean that sincerely. Once you get to know him, he's absolutely the nicest young man you'll ever come across."

Ewing's public image is starting to soften as well. In a recent article in *Inside Sports*, he has said his image doesn't matter to him, that it's a legacy from his Georgetown days when the Hoyas never won any popularity contests. Ernie

Grunfeld, the Knick broadcaster who played with the Knicks in Ewing's first year, says Ewing has gone through a remarkable transformation. Not only are the Knicks now clearly Patrick's team, it is a younger team, full of people Patrick is close to.

Across from him is Mark Jackson, who has had 17 assists in another great game. At one point he intercepted a pass near midcourt, went in for a layup, and just as two Rocket defenders converged on him, he flipped it back over his head, without looking back, to Wilkins for the easy basket.

"When did you see Wilkins?" he is asked.

"What do you mean?"

"It seemed like you never looked at him when you threw the pass. So when did you see him?"

"I saw him when I intercepted the ball at midcourt. So I knew he was there someplace."

It is a gift that Jackson has worked on. While watching television he looks around the room, then shuts his eyes, and tries to remember where everything is: the hands on the clock, where the newspaper was, every detail he can think of. Long ago he learned other kids could run faster and jump higher, so if he were going to be better he would have to be smarter. The other motivating force for Jackson, never far from the surface, is fierce pride.

He takes out a bottle of cologne and splashes some on his face.

"Are you aware of how lucky you are to be playing here in New York?"

"Most definitely. I think about it all the time."

The locker room begins to clear out. One of the last to leave is Wilkins. He runs a brush through his short hair, dabs some cologne on his face. He goes into the bathroom and smiles at himself in the mirror. The mirror almost smiles back. It is a Saturday night, the Knicks have won again, and Gerald Wilkins is ready to go out on the town.

"Woo, Billy Dee, you are a baaaad mother," says Tim Walsh.

Wilkins laughs as he puts on a silk striped jacket over a black outfit.

"I call him Billy Dee after Billy Dee Williams because he's so baaad," says Walsh.

"I am baad," laughs Wilkins. Getting ready to leave, he realizes he can't find his bracelet.

"See what I mean?" says Walsh. "Captain Video. I've got to bring extra sneakers on the road for him because he's always losing them. He loses everything."

Wilkins starts walking for the door, all sartorial splendor.

"Who takes care of you, Dougie?" asks Walsh.

"Timmy Walsh," he says in a grand exit out the door.

Walsh sits back and laughs. "I love him. The first time I ever went out with him on the road, we went to a mall. He stopped in the first store and spent three thousand bucks. He's got a shoe fetish. He just has to buy shoes. But we really don't have any jerks on this team. They're all good guys. Kenny Walker is without a doubt one of the nicest people you'll ever meet. He's very aware of other people's feelings, even down to the ballboys. He even offers to help me carry the bags and that's rare, believe me."

"Who else would help you carry the bags?"

Walsh thinks for a moment. "Louis Orr would help. Carlisle. Then, of course, the rookies always have to help carry the VCR. Mark does it now. Patrick did it when he was a rookie. They've all done it."

"Who are you the closest to?"

"Patrick. He's a great person. Very sensitive. He's like a brother to me. I wish more people knew that side of him."

"How has he changed since he first got here?"

"He was very shy in the beginning," Walsh says. "But he always said please and thank you. Patrick is very polite. In the beginning he was wary, like there was a wall around him. He wouldn't do many interviews. He wouldn't even go on our own network. He was just uncomfortable with it. Now I think he realizes that the media isn't the enemy. He's also very conscious of how well he plays. Very aware of getting rebounds. Not so much points, but definitely rebounds. Because he knows that's been the knock on him."

Walsh first became aware that something was happening with the Knicks on the trip to the West Coast in January. "I saw Bill Cartwright sitting in the training room before the game getting himself pumped up. He was holding his head in his hands, and his fists were clenched. I had never seen that before. It was like it had been so long since we had a big game."

The players are gone now. Walsh sits in front of a row of lockers. "These players like each other. It's not uncommon to go into the hotel coffee shop on the road, and see five guys eating together. I never used to see that before. You'd might see Trent and Louis eating together—because they're friends—but never five guys. Rick is very conscious of making it a family atmosphere, something he started stressing in training camp. Now everyone's cheering for each other, even in practice. And for the first time in three years I have seen five and six guys on the bench standing up and cheering during the games. Like a Rick Carlisle, who doesn't even play. And he's not just doing it for show. He's doing it because he means it. Now guys on the bench even stand up when someone comes out of the game. How many times do you see that in the NBA? I've never seen it. Not once. Now they even got me doing it."

April 5–10

The Knicks beat the Sixers in Philadelphia, scoring 45 points in the second quarter, 76 in the first half, 136 for the game. It is a season high. Pitino starts Cartwright and Ewing together, and when the Sixers double down on the big men, Johnny Newman buries the ball from the outside. The Knicks take 12 three-point shots and make half of them.

The Knicks don't press in the first quarter, largely because Cartwright is in the game, but in the timeout before the second quarter Pitino says, "Let's go with Custer, because this is Custer's last stand." This has become the Knicks' pressing quarter, the quarter when they have used their defense to spur their offense. It is part of Pitino's philosophy to "press from strength," not like many nights this year when the Knicks were getting burned in their man-to-man, and had to resort to the press to get back into the game.

It is an important victory for several reasons. It gives the Knicks a game advantage on Philadelphia in the the playoff race. It is their third straight win, their second straight on the road. And since February 1 they have had the third best record in the Eastern Conference.

Jerry Sullivan in *Newsday* writes, "It is the Knicks' relentless, pressing style that has gotten them this far. Neither K. C. Jones of the Celtics or Chuck Daly of the Pistons want to play the Knicks in a first-round playoff series."

"You can say that again," Dick Versace, a Detroit Piston assistant, tells Sullivan. "They're falling together. And I don't think there's any question that Rick Pitino has done a sensational job with that team. Maybe it's time to put away the reservations and give the guy a little credit. He's convinced guys not only to play his style, but to win with it."

The headline in Vecsey's column reads: "PITINO PRESS TAKES STARCH OUT OF FOES."

They lose Friday night in Chicago to Michael Jordan and the Bulls, even though Ewing goes for 42. Pitino feels they played well, and focuses on the Sunday game with the Bullets in the Cap Centre, another showdown game in the race for the playoffs.

On Sunday morning, in the *Boston Globe*'s sports page, Bob Ryan floats the rumor Pitino has told Providence College to hold off naming a coach until the Knicks conclude their season because "his wife is unhappy, and he is unhappy with Gulf & Western management." Ryan also writes

Pitino is acting as a power broker in the University of Massachusetts' search for a new coach.

That morning he meets with the Knicks at the hotel, where they go over the film of the Bulls games. The key message in the film is that they were outrebounded by the Bulls and need a much better collective effort on the boards this afternoon.

"I feel very fortunate to be coaching you because your attitude is great, and has been great all year. But you are meek, and because you are meek you don't talk enough defensively. Your personalities have to change on the court. You have to be serious in practice. When we have our walk-throughs you start to lose concentration after a while, and that's not professional. You have to concentrate more.

"But we're going to get into the playoffs. I'm convinced of that. And we're not going to get in because we have the easier schedule the rest of the way, or because the other teams are going to lose, but because we are playing as well as anyone in the NBA right now and we deserve to be in the playoffs."

They come out and jump all over the Bullets from the start of the game. They play great defense, crush the Bullets on the floor, place seven men in double figures, and cruise to an easy 20-point win. Pitino should be ecstatic. The Knicks have played great on the road against a team in the playoff race and won big. But a fly in the ointment emerges at the end of the game. "A few guys behind our bench were getting all over Louis Orr for not playing. I was feeling badly for him, so with about two minutes to go I put him in, not because I particularly wanted to play him, but because I wanted to shut the guys in the stands up. Then Louis comes up to me in the locker room, and says I embarrassed him by putting him in for garbage time. He said I don't encourage him enough. I encourage everyone else, pat everyone else on the back, but I don't do it to him. I suppose I shouldn't let it bother me, but he spoiled the win. Maybe the only way you can survive here is if you develop a pro attitude and not let any of it affect you. But I hope I never get one."

April 11–14

The next night the Knicks beat the Pistons when Ewing lets fly a fadeaway jumper with 23 seconds left in overtime. Around and around the rim it rolls before it drops. He has 36 points, once again, carrying the team. With his 13 assists Jackson breaks Oscar Robertson's all-time assist record for a rookie. Wilkins chips in with 23. Even better, the Knicks were down one with four seconds to play, but Ewing was fouled on the in-bounds pass and made the second foul shot, sending the game into overtime. It is a game played with playoff intensity, what Pitino calls a "halfcourt war."

Afterward Piston coach Chuck Daly calls the Knicks a "fearsome team." Vinnie Johnson calls them a "hungry team." Isiah says they're a "solid, maturing team."

Washington beats Atlanta, though, to remain in a tie with the Knicks for the eight playoff spot. Indiana beats the Nets on a last-second shot to remain a half-game ahead of both of them.

Two nights later the Knicks blow out the Pacers in the Garden. They get out to a quick lead, thanks primarily to an awesome Ewing explosion. Abusing Steve Stipanovich in the low post, he scores virtually every time he touches the ball, and completely dominates the game. This is coupled with a tenacious Knick defense that quickly has the Pacers in confusion. At one point in the second quarter the Knicks are up 21. When the Pacers call a timeout in the third quarter, the Knicks get a standing ovation. Early in the fourth quarter announcer John Condon says over the p.a. that Philadelphia has beaten Washington, and the Garden roars again. With about seven minutes left in the game Ewing scores on a jumper in the lane, then again on a sweeping hook across the middle. He has had 41 points in only 26 minutes. Mark Jackson has had 17 assists. The Knicks are now up about 20, get another standing ovation, and the rest is garbage time.

The Knicks are 36–41.

Pitino comes out of the locker room door and is immediately surrounded by microphones and minicams.

"How about Ewing?" asks Sam Goldaper of *The New York Times*.

"I taught him that dunk move the last few days," quips Pitino.

"Who's the most valuable player on this team?" he is asked.

Pitino looks at the questioner. "This is not track. There are no individuals here, this is the New York Knickerbockers. Some nights it will be Patrick. Some nights it will be Mark. Some nights it will be Dougie. That's not the point. Because every night it is the New York Knicks."

The Knick locker room is jammed. Johnny Newman is saying how this has been a fantasy year for him. Louis Orr is saying that one of the things he learned from Hubie Brown is that good defense keeps you in games. Ewing is saying that John Thompson used to say, "This is the time of year when the guys who can play start playing."

A few minutes later as the room begins to clear out, Mark Jackson is standing in the bright light before a TV camera. Nearby Ewing is getting dressed in front of his locker. Jackson says, "Patrick is the best center in basketball. He's the man. He's the one who will take the Knicks as far as we're going to go." Ewing gives no notice he can hear him, but Jackson is speaking loudly enough so that surely Ewing can. Every once in a while Ewing glances in his direction.

Jackson's gift to this Knick team is more than just his ability to make the highlight film pass. His presence has greatly aided Ewing. Not only can Jackson get him the ball to him in places where he can do something with it, he also has taken some of the pressure off him. Suzyn Waldman of WFAN remembers one time early in the season when Ewing was being interviewed on TV, a time when he is most uncomfortable. Sensing Ewing's discomfort, Jackson positioned himself behind the interviewer, and mugged in an attempt to put Ewing more at ease.

Peter Vecsey walks by and smiles at Jackson. "You make me proud to be from Queens," he says. Jackson laughs.

"How cognizant are you of keeping guys happy?" Jackson is asked.

He looks up. "Very," he says. "I've always thought that goes with being a point guard. I have to be conscious of who is getting the shots, and who hasn't seen the ball in a while. I've learned that certain guys need to be pumped up when they're down, need to feel that they're a part of it. I've always done that, ever since I started playing. It just comes from knowing people, from being around."

The next morning Pitino and his wife are driving through Mount Kisco, just down the road from their Bedford home. He has been up since about six, the time he gets up every morning he's home because he wants to spend time with his three sons before they go to school. He already has had several phone conversations, as he has every morning: Jersey Red, The Scout, all the guys checking in. Now he has just got off his car phone with John Marinatto, the Providence athletic director. Marinatto still has not found a coach.

"I think it will be this week."

Pitino turns onto a wooded road. Off in the distance his brick house is visible on a small hillside. He stops at the house to let Joanne off, then heads off towards Rye and the Arrowwood for a workout.

"We both would like to go back, we really would. But we can't. The timing's just not right. Joanne is the one who decided. She said, 'I'm not ready to move again so soon, it's too soon. We as a family need some stability. And you signed on to do a job here and that job is only half-finished.

You'll regret it if you left now." And I know that because of the whole Gordie Chiesa mess I couldn't go back.

"I realize Providence needs to move in another direction, to put the Rick Pitino era behind them and move into the future. I also understand that my goals have not been reached here in New York yet, that there are things unfulfilled. The other problem I would have leaving is that Dick Evans and Jack Diller gave me a tremendous opportunity here, and to leave so abruptly wouldn't be fair.

"But I really would like to go back. Some of the fans can be difficult. They sit behind the bench and throughout the game it's put this guy in, take this guy out. Put Cartwright in. Take Cartwright out. It never stops. It's a total distraction. The other night against Detroit some guy keeps yelling at me to put Ewing back in. Finally I yelled at him, 'Hey, pal, he's got four fouls.'

"I miss so many things about Providence: mingling with the student body, the players always coming in and out of the office, playing racquetball with Fast Eddie Jamiel, hanging out at the players' corner pub with Jody DiRaimo, a great friend, playing three-on three at midnight. The little things that really make you appreciate a job, but have so little to do with being a professional coach. But what am I going to do? Walk in and tell Dick Evans I want to leave because I miss playing three-on-three at Providence?"

In the *Daily News* this morning is a small item: "PITINO: NO TRUTH TO RUMOR ABOUT PROVIDENCE."

He calls his secretary, Barbara Kobak, on the car phone. She gives him a succession of messages. This guy wants to buy playoff tickets. This guy wants a letter of recommendation. This other guy wants tickets. This reporter wants an interview. That reporter wants an interview. All the behind-the-scenes demands of being the coach of the Knicks.

"You know, I went up to Louis Orr the other day and said that I was sorry if he didn't think I was giving him enough attention. "I'm not sorry that you aren't playing, because I don't think you deserve to play. But I'm sorry if you feel I don't encourage you enough." His voice seems to trail off. "I go back a long way with Louis."

He pulls into the long driveway leading to the Arrow-wood. "The two funniest guys through all this have been Dick McGuire and Fuzzy Levane. When we got 30 wins Dick said, 'Rick, that's enough. Don't get the fans spoiled.' Then we got 32 and he said, 'Rick, I mean it now. You're creating a monster.' Dick and Fuzzy have been around, they know New York. They help me keep things in perspective."

"Who else does that?"

"My family. Kids are the greatest for that. Early in the year when we couldn't win and I'd be getting paranoid that maybe we'd never win, my kids wake me up in the morning and say, 'Dad, you lost again, huh?' Or else they'd ask me, 'Are you ever going to win a game?' Jimmy O'Brien says his kids actually cry when we lose, but my kids? They break my shoes about it."

10 | Garden Party

People ask if I'm surprised we are doing so well. I'm always surprised. I was surprised we won so quickly at Boston University. I was surprised we won so quickly at Providence. I am surprised it turned around so quickly here. If people seem to be surprised, these things always surprise me as well. At the beginning of the year when we hadn't made any trades, I wondered just how good we could be.

The one thing I wanted to accomplish this first year was to establish enthusiasm and a work ethic. And we did that, even when we were losing. I told the players we might not be the best of friends early on, but I would never knock them to the media and that I would publicly take the blame when we lost. In return, I would expect them not to second-guess me, or knock Stu Jackson or Jimmy O'Brien. That has worked. Now you see guys raising their hands during a game and saying, "It's my fault." You never saw that earlier in the year.

The second thing I wanted to accomplish this year was to win at home. I thought if we could do that, we could get 30–32 wins and have a good foundation for the future. Learn to win at home this year, and next year learn how to win on the road.

But in the beginning we were never in the right place in the press. Sidney wasn't in training camp. Mark missed half of camp. Trent missed much of camp. Newman wasn't in camp. Plus, you don't have much time to practice once the season starts. You always are playing games, and if you're not you're either traveling or getting ready for the next game. So I knew the press would get better as the season went on. The more we played, the better we'd get at it. That happened at Boston University. It happened at Providence. And I knew it would happen here.

I think it was the Laker trip in January that I saw things turning around. It was a three-game trip, and though we didn't win any, we played the Lakers tough the entire game, then went to Sacramento and were in the game right to the end. That was really encouraging, because we had been getting blown out on the road. Just before the All-Star break in early February, I told them we had a chance for the playoffs. Everyone looked at me like I was very strange.

I've learned so much about these people. They're all so different. I've seen Mark Jackson change tremendously. At the beginning of the year he could be a bit temperamental. That's all gone now. He really is a born leader, and that's something you can't teach. And he has the great ability not to get down on himself when he makes a mistake. He fights through his mistakes. Only once in a while have I seen him get down on himself. It happened the other night against Detroit. He took three bad shots and I could see him start to get down. So the next day in practice I called him aside and said, "Even when things are not going well, you are a positive influence. You let your bad shooting affect you against Detroit. I don't ever want to see you get discouraged again."

Like with the jump suits. I'll kid him about them, say how when I first met him he wore blue blazers and penny loafers, and now he's wearing jump suits and white boots. I'm kidding, but there's a message there, too: don't forget where you came from. He also has a tendency to pass the ball behind him on the break. Let's say he's streaking down the court. Rather than give the ball to the lead guy, the obvious pass, the simple pass, every once in a while he'll make the more creative pass, the fancier pass, to the guy trailing, and sometimes this allows the defense to catch up to the play. When this happens, I don't say a word. I don't have to. He looks at me and he knows.

People are asking me now if I feel vindicated; do I feel that I silenced all the doubters? Well, the people who were doubting had no basis for their doubts. If I respected the people who were second-guessing me, I guess I would feel vindicated. If a coach had sat me down and said, "This won't work, and that won't work, and these are the reasons why," maybe I would feel vindicated now. But that never happened. In the beginning of the year everyone was quoting unnamed sources around the league who said my style of play couldn't work—but didn't say why. I said it could and gave reasons why, the shot clock and the three-point shot for example. Then there were others who heard the word "college," and said there was no way it could work. If I had changed the terminology and said "enthusiastic" or "aggressive style," maybe they would have believed it. It was like "college" was a dirty word in the pros. But no one ever gave any real reasons other than "pro guys won't do it." Well, pro guys have done it.

✝✝✝✝✝✝✝✝✝

April 15–19

Peter Vecsey asks, "Tell the truth now, does anybody, other than King Kong Bondy, care one iota these days how Bernard King is doing?"

Friday night the Bullets are in New York. The Knicks are 36–41; the Bullets and Pacers are 35–42. The Sixers are 34–42. A win tonight might just kayo the Bullets.

Pitino elects to start Ewing and Cartwright together, thinking the Bullets will have matchup problems. But from the beginning it's apparent the Bullets are fighting for their season. They constantly double down on Ewing, forcing him to kick the ball back to the guards, forcing them to shoot perimeter jumpers. And when the shots don't go down, the Knicks' offense starts to sputter, their Achilles' heel all season long. The Knicks are down four at the half, and in the fourth quarter they trail by a few all the way to the finish, only to lose 106–97. It is only the Knicks' third home loss since they lost to Phoenix in early January.

The first thing Pitino does with the team is blame himself for the loss. "I shouldn't have changed the starting lineup. It upset our rhythm. It's my fault."

Then he steps out into the hallway to meet the press.

"The Bullets deserve a great deal of credit. They stopped every phase of our offensive game. They beat our man defense to a pulp. They dominated us physically on the backboards. We played a very poor game. We were due for a game like this. Everybody's been saying we're a lock for the playoffs. That's ridiculous. Everyone's getting a little carried away."

The Knicks fly to Atlanta that night. Pitino is concerned because they have just blown a wonderful opportunity to put some space between themselves and the Bullets. "I think we're playing tight at home. It's like now we are expected to win, and the pressure has increased accordingly. So what does that mean? We're just going to have to win on the road."

The next night they get a lift from Pat Cummings, the forgotten Knick. Coming off the bench, he gets 10 points, his best outing in a long while. "I've prepared myself mentally," he says. "I know where everyone is coming from. They're rebuilding and I'm not a piece of the plan. But we're in a playoff chase, and it would be really selfish for me to put my feelings ahead of the team and start pouting. I just try to stay ready."

Cartwright's two free throws tie the game with 57 seconds left. Then after successive misses by Dominique and Antoine

Carr, Mark Jackson takes the ball down the court, and slices through the middle of the Atlanta defense for the go-ahead basket. When Dominique misses an off-balance 10-footer at the buzzer, the entire Knick bench erupts. The Knicks have come away with a big, big win.

"I could have called a timeout, and the worst that could have happened was the game could have gone into overtime," Pitino says. "But I have so much confidence in Mark doing the right thing to help us win that I let him go. His basketball IQ is off the charts."

At the end of the game the Knicks look in good shape for the playoffs. Then the next afternoon the Bullets beat the Celtics, and everything gets complicated again. The Knicks and Bullets are 37–42. The Pacers are 36–42. The Sixers are 34–44. Two of the teams will make it.

April 19

For the last home game of the season, the opponent is the Chicago Bulls. The Bulls come in having won five straight and 11 of their last 13, one of the hottest teams in the league. It is a sellout, the eighth of the year. About an hour before the game Mark Jackson is busy in the Knick locker room trying to find more tickets, the inevitable result of being the local entry. The next day Mike Lupica will write, "The Knicks are doing something again, and he is the reason. Jackson has been a rookie the way Lawrence Taylor was a rookie, the way Dwight Gooden was a rookie." The next day Walt Frazier will be quoted saying Jackson is becoming more like Clyde every day (Clyde being both Frazier's nickname and alter-ego). Red Holtzman will say, "At the same stage Jackson is ahead of Clyde. That's because he's been put in the role of handling the team by Rick Pitino."

Jackson has averaged 10 assists a game, something no rookie has ever done. More important, Jackson has electri-

fied the Garden. In a city whose heart has always belonged
to clever guards, Jackson has been the best one since Frazier.
Better yet, he is still living at home in Queens.

Stu Jackson is in the lounge talking about his boss. "He
never ceases to amaze me. The one constant thing about
him is constant change. He is always adapting, always looking for new ways to do things. The other night in Atlanta I
thought we had a good defensive game. So what does he tell
me and Jimmy O'Brien afterward? We have to come up
with new ways to play these guys next year. Next year. The
other thing that never ceases to amaze me about him is his
absolute confidence in his system. One night in Milwaukee
we were getting absolutely killed in the press. They were
flying through it. And Jimmy and I keep looking at each
other. Finally I suggest that maybe we should get out of the
press for a while. He just looks at me, gives me that look.
'We aren't doing it right,' he says. 'It will work, but we're
not doing it right.' Any other coach would have junked it."

Pitino comes in a few minutes later with Ralph Willard.
They have just come back from playing basketball at the
New York Athletic Club on Central Park South.

"How'd it go?" asks Jackson.

"We played one-on-one," says Willard. "I got hand marks
all over my body."

No more than Jordan is going to have by the time the
game's over. Pitino's strategy is not to press, thinking the
press will create too many transition situations for Jordan.
Instead, the idea is to trap him whenever he gets the ball.

The Knicks get a big ovation before the game. Michael
Douglas is sitting in the celebrity section across from the
Knick bench. Peter Falk, the most constant of the celebrities, is nearby, just as he has been through most of the
season. The luxury boxes that circle the Garden rafters are
all filled, not as in the past, when many of them stared down
on the polished floor like lonely sentinels.

The Knicks are down 50–49 at the half. They are doing a

good job on Jordan, making it difficult for him to get the ball, but he's made seven of ten shots from the floor, and already has 20 points. Shortly into the fourth quarter the Knicks are down 12, and Jordan is putting on a show. He takes an alley-oop pass from Sam Vincent on a break, rises over Mark Jackson, who is all but clinging to him, dunks the ball, then hangs on the rim for a few seconds in triumph as the Garden crowd erupts in a frenzy. Another time, trapped in the corner by two Knicks, he somehow knifes through them and goes in for a dunk. He will end up with 47 points, all the more incredible because every time he got the ball he was trapped.

With seven minutes left in the game, just when the Knicks appear to be out of it, they start to make a run. Their press starts to rattle Chicago. The Garden crowd chants, "Defense . . . Defense," and the Knicks cut the Bulls' lead to four with three minutes left. Back and forth it goes; Jordan, the Knicks, Michael Jordan, the never-say-die Knicks. The Bulls finally go ahead by three with 12 seconds left on two Jordan free throws. The Knicks call timeout and set up a three-point shot for the tie. Wilkins misses one from the left side. Trent Tucker ends up with the ball on the out-of-bounds line on the left side, the clock running down. He heaves up a prayer that misses badly. The ball somehow gets back to Mark Jackson, who has a decent three-point attempt from the top. It hits the front rim and bounces away. The Bulls have won, 121–118. Jordan has beaten the Knicks by himself.

"He's just an unbelievable basketball player. How can you yell at your players? They're trying to stop him. But he's Superman. How do you stop Superman? I don't have any kryptonite."

An hour afterward Pitino and Joanne leave the Garden, on their way to meet Jersey Red and some old friends at the Abbey Tavern. As soon as they enter the concourse that leads to Seventh Avenue, he's surrounded by a dozen kids

who want his autograph. He signs, starts walking. More
people want autographs.

"Rick, could you sign my jacket?" says a guy in his
twenties, wearing a white windbreaker.

"Your jacket? You can't be serious?"

"No, really. It will be an honor."

New York, New York.

A few minutes later he is in front of the Abbey Tavern.
"This is my old neighborhood," he says, standing on the
sidewalk. "I grew up right over there on 26th between
Second and Third." He points to the building next door.
"My father used to be the manager of that building right
over there. I used to work there summers as the night
watchman. Best job I ever had. Used to sleep all night. One
summer Dave Dibble and I lived there." He is silent for a
moment, running all the years through his mind. "Joanne
and I used to come here all the time."

The talk is of the playoff race. The consensus is it's all
going to come down to the game Saturday night against the
Pacers in Indiana.

"You know," says Pitino. "In a way that's how I like it.
One game for everything. That's the way it should be. It
reminds me of college."

"You do like it," says Jersey. "I know you do. That's why
you're sick. Because you really do like this."

The talk is casual for a while, and then almost inevitably
switches to Providence. In a sense everyone at the table
would love to see Pitino come back to Providence. They
know all it would take is one call from Pitino, and Providence athletic director John Marinatto would offer him the
job.

"What do you think I should do?" he asks each person.

Jersey Red says he should go back to Providence. In his
heart he is a college coach, and college is where his future
should be. Bobby Dempsey, who was a couple of years
ahead of Pitino at UMass, says Pitino should go back to

Providence. Sendek, who worked for him at Providence, says he should go back. He is, above all else, a teacher of the game, and there is more time to teach in college. Only Joanne says he should stay with the Knicks. Ironically, in all the published rumors, Joanne's unhappiness is always stated as the main reason.

"You know the real reason I would like to?" he says. "Because it would be better for my family. Rhode Island is a great place to raise a family. We loved it there. And I really would like my kids to have one place to grow up in, one place that was theirs. I never really had that. I lived here for a while. Then it was Queens. Then when I was about to go to high school it was Long Island. I was always moving, and I'd like it to be different for my kids." His voice is soft, almost wistful. "I would like my kids to have what I didn't. And I know it can't happen here. Sure, it's going great here now, but I know it can't last. Not in New York. The same writers who are being so great now will turn on me. I know this won't be the last move.

"But I know it can't happen now. Joanne is right. What I set out to do here isn't finished."

He falls silent. The talk eventually turns to the old times back at UMass. Then a guy in his mid-thirties comes over to the table.

"Coach," he says, sticking out his hand. "I just want to say thanks. Thanks for the job you've done. Because you've made us watch again."

April 22

"I think we've become very tight," Pitino says at the morning walk-through at the Mecca in downtown Milwaukee. "In important games the tendency is to play more conservatively, and that makes you tight. What we have to do is run up and down and be loose on offense; on the other end be very tough on defense. We have to open up the offense, not get more conservative. So there's no pressure on shooting. The pressure is on defense and rebounding.

"But the reason I know we are going to win tonight is because we have the two best centers. I know Sidney Green is going to get more rebounds than anyone else on the court. I know the small forwards, Kenny and Johnny, are going to play big. We have the best point guard. And outside of Michael Jordan—yes, Dougie, I have to give it to Michael over you—Gerald Wilkins is the best big-game player in the NBA at his position. So I know Gerald Wilkins will dominate tonight. And all the while I am talking to him, I see Dougie looking at me like I'm completely nuts."

Providence College has finally named a coach, Rick Barnes, the first-year coach at George Mason. Pitino is relieved. In a sense he is the reason why Barnes is the coach. Pitino had been asked by the University of Massachusetts to be on the search committee to find a new coach. Trying to come up with some names for the committee to interview, he called Barnes, whom he knew by reputation as being an up-and-coming young coach, an energetic recruiter. After Barnes said he wasn't interested in the UMass job, he told Pitino he was a big fan of his. He had heard him speak at camps, and used a lot of his things in his own coaching.

"I was surprised, because I didn't know Rick Barnes. So I told John Marinatto that he should talk to Barnes about the Providence job. At first John said no, that Barnes didn't have a big enough name. I said he ought to at least talk to him. About a week later Barnes called me and asked me about Providence. At that point I did a selling job, as good as any I ever did in trying to recruit a kid. I told him what a great school it was, what a great state it was, what a great situation it was. And the more I talked about it with him the more sad I became, because once again I realized what a great situation I had left behind."

Marinatto met with Barnes in Boston, and immediately was taken with the similarities between Barnes and Pitino.

Barnes has early-morning workouts. He has individual instruction for his players. His teams press all over the court and shoot three-pointers. To Marinatto, Barnes was a younger Pitino.

"I knew then it was finally over. I was never going back to Providence. I also knew then that it was better for everyone. It's was finally time to put the Rick Pitino era at Providence to sleep."

At the press conference announcing Barnes as the new Providence coach, Barnes says, "Outside of the three coaches I have worked for, I'd have to say that Rick Pitino has been the biggest influence on my coaching philosophy."

The Pitino era might be over at Providence. But the legacy endures.

The Bullets are 37–44. The Pacers are 37–43. The Sixers are 36–44. The Knicks, who have won eight out of their last twelve, are 37–43. Two of them will make the playoffs.

The game with the Bucks is their last regular-season game in the Mecca, drawing a sellout crowd. The Knicks lead by one with 7:36 to play, but only score 12 points the rest of the way and lose by nine. Ewing gets 25 and Wilkins 24, but Mark Jackson is 1–11, and once again the Knicks' lack of scoring punch from their forwards seals their fate. They are running out of chances. Making it worse is that the Pacers beat the Pistons, setting up tomorrow night's showdown game in Indianapolis. The Knicks charter to Indianapolis after the game.

"I don't think we can win," says Pitino quietly. "We aren't playing well. We're tight. It means too much, and most of these guys have never been through this before. The only one playing well is Patrick." He pauses, and sighs. "I don't know if we can win. Indiana is coming in hot. They won on the road at Atlanta and tonight at Detroit. But I don't even want to get in if we can't win tomorrow. I don't want to back in. Because if we're not playing well, what's the point?"

You know he doesn't mean it.

April 23

It has come down to this.

All the practices, all the travel, all the games, all the emotion. One game against the Indiana Pacers in Indianapolis. Ironically, it is on the road. The Knicks have been a disaster on the road much of the year.

Of course, they can sneak into the playoffs even if they lose, if the Bullets lose tonight at home against Atlanta, and the Sixers lose tonight at Cleveland and tomorrow at Detroit. They also can beat the Pacers tonight and still not make the playoffs, if the Bullets win tonight and the Sixers win both games.

Pitino brings his team to the arena late, as he has been doing the last two weeks on the road. The more time a young team spends hanging around the arena waiting for the game to start, the tighter they get.

"You have had a great season, whether you win or lose," Pitino tells the team before the game. " 'You have won thirteen games more than you did last year. You have brought the crowds back to the Garden. You have changed the writers' attitudes. You have brought the excitement back. You have had a great season, and nothing that happens tonight can take that away. That's the thing to remember. So go out and have fun tonight, because these are the moments to cherish, ones you will remember when your careers are over."

He walks onto the court and sees who the referees are. "I keep a log on all the officials and the tendencies they all have. For instance, when you get Earl Strom, you know he's going to let you play. So we make our last-minute adjustments accordingly. Tonight I know that one of the officials is going to be tough on post-up play, while the other is going to let us play more."

He looks around at the large, boisterous crowd. "This reminds me of going into a Villanova, or a Syracuse. It's like a college road game. One of those crowds that's going to do everything in its power to help the home team win."

The Knicks miss their first eight shots, and trail 17–8. Once again they have come out tight, a young team going through their first playoff race. They don't make their first field goal until midway through the first quarter. At the quarter they are down four, at the half they are down one, 47–46. Nothing is going to come easy tonight; both teams playing frenzied defense. The Pacers have taken away the Knicks' transition game, and once again they are struggling in their halfcourt offense. They continually get the ball inside to Ewing, he is continually double-teamed. When he kicks it out, the Knicks don't often convert the perimeter jumper.

At the half the Knicks learn the Sixers have lost. Their fate has now become very simple: win this game and they make the playoffs. Lose and go home.

"During the first half the guy who was monitoring the scores from the other games was sitting at the table right next to me," Pitino says. "So I always knew what was going on. I knew before the half that there wasn't going to be any three-way tie. We have to win now."

At the start of the fourth quarter, the game is tied. The arena is in bedlam. A meaningful game brings out the best of professional basketball. In an unusual twist the two contenders are going head to head. Pitino and Jack Ramsey are coaching every play. At one point referee Jess Kersey nullifies a Knick basket, saying Ewing's hand went up through the basket to tip in a Mark Jackson miss. Pitino goes berserk and is on the verge of getting a technical when Ewing rushes over.

"Not now, Coach," he says, holding Pitino back. "You know he's just waiting to give you a T. Don't worry, we're going to win anyway."

Pitino elects to plays Ewing and Cartwright together, and it begins paying dividends. As has happened so many times in the past months, the presence of Cartwright takes some pressure off Ewing, and he sparks the Knicks to a 81–72 lead. The Pacers come right back and tie the score at 81. The thunderous crowd keeps rising to its feet. The Knicks again take control of the game, Ewing and Cartwright carrying them, and go up five with 3:32 remaining. But once again the Pacers come back. Back and forth they go. After all the games and all the travel, the last playoff spot in the East will be decided these few minutes.

Cartwright's two free throws with 2:15 left give the Knicks their last points. It also gives them an 88–84 lead. Steve Stipanovich makes two free throws nine seconds later. Then the Knicks come back down the court with the ball. Walker misses a jumper, but the Knicks get the rebound. Wilkins misses a shot, but gets in his own rebound. The clock continues to wind down. Wilkins then misses again, and in a wild scramble for the ball he throws the ball back over his head as he is going out-of-bounds. Later he will say he hoped the ball was going to stay up in the air for ten minutes. It doesn't. But when it's caught by Vern Fleming of the Pacers, there are only four seconds remaining in the game. The Pacers call timeout.

"No threes," Pitino tells his team. "Don't let them beat you with a three." Recently Stipanovich and John Long have made three-point shots in crucial situations for the Pacers.

When the teams go back on the court, Pitino sees who the Pacers have in the game and calls another timeout. The tension builds. Pitino's strategy is to force Indiana's entry pass into the middle of the floor. He thinks Stipanovich probably will get it. "Don't let him take a three," he tells Ewing. "Leave your feet if you have to, but don't let him take a three."

All year Pitino and the coaching staff have been telling Ewing not to leave his feet on defense, something he has a bad habit of doing when ball-faked. Now they are telling him to jump at will.

"No threes, Patrick," yells Pitino as the Pacers get ready to in-bound the ball. "No threes."

As expected, Stipanovich gets the ball near the top of the key on the in-bounds pass. As expected, he turns to shoot a three-point shot. Ewing rushes at him. He fakes the shot, and Ewing goes high in the air to contest it. Stipanovich steps around him and begins to drive down the lane, hoping to draw a foul. Mark Jackson fakes as if he's going to jump into Stipanovich's path, and Stipo seems to stumble. Walker gets a piece of the shot, the ball misses the basket, and the entire Knick bench jumps off the bench and runs on the court in jubilation. The Knicks are in the playoffs.

A pile of players roll around on the floor, a timeless scene direct from Central Casting. Underneath one of the piles is Ewing. Worried about his sore ankle, he frantically tries to push people off him. It's a wild and wonderful scene in a building that now has gone quiet. The people are dazed, the Pacers shell-shocked. Their season is over.

"All I could think about was last year and the Georgetown game that got us to the Final Four," Pitino will say later. "It was the same feeling."

It's a page from the same script.

Rick Pitino promised in July that he hadn't become the Knicks coach to go through another 24-win season. He promised in training camp that this was a team that was going to the playoffs. He promised at the first exhibition game that someday the Knicks would be cheered in the Garden. He promised in the beginning of the year that someday "they will talk about Knick pride."

Only nine months later, he stands on the Market Square Arena court, all the promises delivered.

11 | A Knickerbocker Fantasy

Patrick has really developed as a player. He's no longer just a great athlete. He is becoming a great basketball player. He's also becoming a great leader. I really like Patrick Ewing. It's great when your superstar is such a sensitive person. He always comes to practice with a smile on his face. He always says "Good morning." He is the total opposite of what I'd been led to believe about him. A lot of people thought that he never was going to be the player he was at Georgetown. There was too much focus on him when he first came to the Knicks, as though he could take them out of the lottery all by himself. The one thing about Patrick is he'll be better as you surround him with better players, because he is very team-oriented. He helps out on defense. He does a lot of the little things players do who have come out of good programs.

Listen to him when he talks about Georgetown, how much pride he has. I tell him that one day he will talk about the Knicks with the same kind of pride.

Mark Jackson has maintained the same mental attitude all year. The only difference is his confidence has grown. He has a great ability to say the right thing about everyone, almost as if he is a press agent. He obviously has been great all year, better than any of us had the right to expect, but he can be even better. He needs to get better defensively, and needs to learn to make the simple pass. But he is a born leader, and that's why I feel so good about the future. Now we have two leaders—Patrick and Mark—and that is something the Knicks didn't have last year.

I think I'm most pleased with Gerald Wilkins. In one short season he's changed from an "I" person to a "we" person. That's a big adjustment to make in one year. I had to get him to understand that if he were to continue to be a New York Knickerbocker, he was going to have to change. He has been the best surprise of all, because everyone told me he was a potential attitude problem. But he is a really nice kid, he's fun to be around. Sure, I have to sit on him a little bit for his own good. He still needs more discipline in his life, but he's never complained, even though, given NBA standards, he's not making a lot of money. He's also gotten much better as a player. He still needs to be more of a physical player, but he's made great strides this year.

These are the three building blocks. Three young players that can be the cornerstones of this franchise for years to come.

Bill Cartwright has gone from someone who didn't have a great deal of enthusiasm to someone who feels rejuvenated. I think he's been caught up in the youth of the team, can see that things are changing, and can see that maybe there is a place for him in the change. He is still a great trade commodity, and as Patrick gets better and decreases his silly fouls, it becomes easier to trade Billy. But he proved this year he is very valuable.

Evaluating Sidney is difficult because he's a good guy, and he's highly motivated. His problem is he has a power forward's body in a small forward's game. His entire game is taking jump shots and fall-away shots. He has no inside moves. He needs individual instruction desperately. He needs to learn a Buck Williams game. But he says he wants to live in the gym this summer. He's willing to work to transform his game. In retrospect, it was not easy for Sidney to miss training camp and have to start the season not knowing the coaches or the system. And vice versa. I've always said that improving the individual weaknesses of college players gave me the most satisfaction of anything in coaching. Now I want to do the same thing with Sidney, because, like Hubie Brown, he's misunderstood. Sidney is a person who has a lot of quality. My challenge is to have his game catch up to his character.

Kenny Walker works very hard, but has a fragile psyche. You have to stay positive with him. He is someone you always want on the team because of his attitude—he has a great attitude for working—but he is never going to be a main player.

Trent Tucker was a little sour on the situation in the beginning, but when he saw all the positive things happen he became a very good leader. He really helps the younger players. He has a great deal of good in him. He's also career-oriented, wants to be around and do well. He's a perfect second-line player because he shoots so well and he can play good man-to-man defense.

Louis Orr is a lot like Trent. There is a lot of good in him, you just have to get it. He is very sensitive, sometimes over-thinks things and reads into things that aren't there. I questioned whether he could play in the league anymore because of his back injury, but in the past two weeks in practice he's proved me wrong. I think now that if he really works over the summer he might be able to hook on some-where else for a couple of years.

Johnny Newman is a great waiver pickup. He can shoot and he has an explosive quick step to the basket. He's not going to rebound, he doesn't handle the ball well, and he's not going to get any assists, but he can score. Surround him with better players and he will be better, because then his deficiencies won't matter so much.

Sedric Toney is a wonderful kid. He's the perfect elev-enth man, a delight to have around. I was a little dejected when I had to let Billy Donovan go, but if it had to be anyone to replace him I'm glad it's Sedric. He's really more of a two guard than a point, but he's enthusiastic and he pushes Mark in practice. I hope he's around next year.

Pat Cummings has been much better than I thought he was going to be. Once he didn't play, I thought he would be a total pain in the neck, but he hasn't been. He has a pro attitude in that all he really cares about is minutes, and he may have some negative things to say once he's out of here at the end of the year, but he's handled it very well. I have to commend him for that. He knows he won't be here next year, and the second part of the year he's seen the backup power forward role go to Billy Cartwright, yet he has been no problem. He gets along with the rest of the players, and when he does get in he plays hard.

And you know what's unbelievable?

We have not had one incident in practice the entire year. Not one fight. Not one incident between a player and a coach. And that is unbelievable. Not just in the NBA, but anywhere.

My personal goal was to get into a situation the second half of the year when the games were important, when there was playoff pressure on this team, because that will only make it easier in the future. The key with the team now is take it one step further. I've always tried to keep looking at what has to be done, not what's been done. I want to stay hungry. I want to develop a strong basketball team here in New York. Sure, this year's been great, but we can't go into next year with the same team. We need more help at forward and we need a backup point guard. Right now we are not a strong team. We are a team that played as hard as a professional team can play, but we have to get to the next level.

✝✝✝✝✝✝✝✝✝✝

The first thing Pitino tells the team Monday morning at SUNY is to seize the moment. "Right now we have fabulous chemistry. We have worked hard all year and pulled together, and now we have something special. But we don't know if it will last. So let's seize the moment and win now. Because who knows what's going to happen?"

It has become like waking up on the far side of the rainbow.

Harvey Araton in the *News* says: "PITINO: A FLEXIBLE FLIER." Pitino has turned the "the Knicks into a serious professional basketball team in six months, while convincing people he's actually been coaching Madison Square Garden University." He also says Pitino is more flexible than Hubie Brown, whose "game plan was inflexible, and would change over his dead body."

Filip Bondy in the *Daily News* writes that he has gone from thinking the Knicks stink, that they're the same team as last year and Pitino is a "raving, substituting lunatic" to believing Pitino should be the Coach of the Year and "I look like an idiot."

On the back of *Newsday* is a picture of Pitino crouching down in front of the Knick bench, complete with the caption: "RICK PITINO: HIS WAY WORKS AFTER ALL." The *Boston Globe* runs a story about Pitino with a headline: "HE'S DONE IT AGAIN," and Lesley Visser calls him the "sorcerer with an angel's face."

Every day there are more media at practice at SUNY.

"How are you going to prepare for the Boston Garden?"

"Three ways," Pitino quips. "We are going to spray dust all over our locker room and turn up the heat. We are going to contaminate the oranges. And we're going to tell our family members to sit behind a pole in their living rooms while they're watching TV to get used to the seats they're probably going to be sitting in."

So much has changed since training camp. Bob Thornton is gone. Chris McNealy, Jawann Oldham, Gerald Henderson, Rory Sparrow, Ray Tolbert are gone. Bernard King never arrived. Tony White, Billy Donovan, and Carey Scurry have come and gone. It is a long way from training camp at SUNY. Back then the playoffs seemed as far away as Uranus.

Now the Knicks have qualified for the playoffs for the first time in four years. More important, they did it by winning three out of their last four road games after starting off 1–23 on the road. After being 14–28 at the All-Star break, they have gone 24–16 to reach the playoffs, the third best record in the Eastern Conference. For three straight months they played better than .500 basketball, the first time in four years they even had had one month with a winning record. Their 14-game jump to 38 wins is the biggest one-season jump in their history. Now they are a team no one wants to play.

On Thursday the Knicks fly to Boston and their playoff date with the Celtics. "I would have loved to have played Detroit. I think we could have been competitive with them. And I know they didn't want to play us. Brendan Malone was scouting there the night we were playing Milwaukee, and says they were checking on our game every few minutes. Then again, maybe it's best we play Boston. If we're going to get playoff experience, it will help us down the road to go against the Celtics now. And I think we can win. Or at least I am telling the team we can win. You have to do that. You never can let them see that you have doubts, or else they will have an excuse."

April 29

The banners are in the rafters. The parquet floor has been laid down. The orange seats look dirty. The Boston Garden is ready.

In Pat Riley's recently released book, he says, "The Boston mystique isn't leprechauns in the floorboards. It isn't blood and guts. It's a willingness to use any technique to upset an opponent. . . . Boston is supposed to be the Athens of America. But from our experience, it's more like Beirut."

Pitino agrees: Boston management goes out of their way to make things difficult for the visiting team. "In other places in the league they make you feel like a guest. Here they make you feel like the enemy."

The once great rivalry of the Celtics and Knicks has been revived. All the form charts point to a mismatch. The Celtics have been to the NBA finals four straight times. Their starters have seemingly played since Naismith put up the peace baskets. In contrast, the Knicks start Ewing in his third year, Wilkins in his third year, Walker in his second year, and the rookie Jackson. Their first forward off the bench is Johnny Newman, claimed off the waiver wire.

Pitino's strategy tonight is not to press. He is concerned about the Celtics' ability to pass the ball. In addition, they have had several days to prepare. He also remembers that when the Knicks beat the Celtics in Madison Square Garden in January, they did it primarily playing aggressive man-to-man.

The Knicks are up three at the quarter, down two at the half. At one point Sedric Toney has the ball on the sidelines in front of the Knick bench. Danny Ainge is guarding him.

"Take it, Sedric," says Pitino.

"Yeh, take it," says Ainge.

Toney takes the shot. It goes in for a three.

"What do you have to say now?" Pitino says to Ainge.

Ainge turns back and laughs.

Pitino laughs back.

With four minutes to go in the third quarter the Knicks are leading by three. Then the Celtics put their game in overdrive, go one a 26–5 run, and lead 96–79 with 6:26 left in the game. Bird leaves the game with four minutes left with 29 points. McHale also has 29. Wily veteran Dennis Johnson has 16, and has taken Mark Jackson to school.

"I've seen it here so many times," Pitino says amid a crush of media. "A team is right in the game in the third quarter, maybe even ahead, then comes a Celtic run and the game is over. And there's nothing you can do about it. You can call all the timeouts you want, but it doesn't make any difference. We played very well for three quarters, but the thing about the Celtics is you have to play well for 48 minutes, or you have no chance. All in all, though, I would rather get beat by 20 than three or four. Psychologically it's better. If you lose by three or four you stay up all night second-guessing yourself. Twenty, and you sleep better." He rolls his eyes.

"Why didn't you press tonight?"

"Two reasons. One, they're a great passing team, and the other is that they've had three or four days to prepare, and I have tremendous respect for their coaching staff and their players."

The faces in front of Pitino keep coming. The questions stay the same.

"I don't think the score was indicative of the way we played. We played Larry Bird about as well as we can play him. He had to earn all his points, and that's all you can do with him."

Inside, the locker room is beginning to clear out. The reporters have come and gone. Pitino has left. Only a few of the players remain. Stu Jackson sits on a bench. Nearby is trainer Mike Saunders and Johnny Newman, who has had another in a string of bad shooting nights, 3–12. Newman is wearing a silky-looking black outfit.

"Johnny, what is that you're wearing?" says Jackson, a sly smile on his face. "Is that what you call a leisure suit? What is that made of? Pleather?"

"Pleather?" asks Newman.

"Yeh, it's like a combination of plastic and leather," says Jackson. "Pleather."

"Well if you like it, you better get more than one," says Newman, getting up to leave. "Because if you only get one, you'll wear it every day."

Jackson laughs and shakes his head. "I wouldn't wear that to a walk-through."

Newman walks out of the room, followed by Green and Cartwright. A few minutes later Ewing leaves. They are large men in expensive suits, businessmen on the road after a long and frustrating day.

May 1

Pitino sits in the locker room about an hour before the game. "I'm not really nervous. I don't get nervous before playoff games. I didn't get nervous before college tournament games either. Even last year in the Final Four. In a sense, tournaments and playoffs are all gravy, especially for teams that have overachieved. I feel the pressure is to get into the playoffs and that the playoffs are a reward. They should be enjoyed. These are the moments that should be treasured. Sure, I want to win, and sure, I hope we play well, but I really don't think this is the time to be uptight."

He walks out into the hallway and chats with Billy Minardi, his brother-in-law and one of his closest friends. He is a bond broker in Manhattan and goes to every Knick home game. Going to Pitino's games is nothing new to Minardi. He was a student at Boston College when Pitino started coaching at nearby Boston University and went to all the BU games, often bringing twenty friends with him, because back then you could buy beer that came in large containers.

"Some nights we probably made up forty percent of the crowd," he says.

When Pitino was at Providence, he flew up from New York for most of the games. "I'd fly in from New York after work, stay over, take a six o'clock plane out the next morning, and be back at work at eight. The best one was when I went to Louisville last year for the regionals. I flew down Thursday afternoon, checked into the hotel, went to the game. Then I flew back to New York the next morning at six without ever checking out of my room, and flew back to Louisville Saturday morning."

Pitino's strategy for this game is to vary his defenses: a little press, a little man-to-man. Despite that, the Knicks fall behind early, and by halftime already are down 15. Already Bird and McHale have 30 points between them; Green and Walker have four. Early in the third period the Celtics have increased their lead to 17, all the Knicks warts are showing, and it's just a matter of how much.

"You see this and you realize what an unbelievable job Pitino did with this team," mutters Fred Kerner at the press table.

At one point McHale comes by the Knick bench. "Hey, Rick," he says with a laugh, "will you stop breaking Danny's balls? He's losing his confidence."

It's about the only laugh Pitino's going to get.

With about five minutes to play and the Celtics leading by 19, referee Hue Hollins calls a foul on Ewing.

"Hue, they're the Boston Celtics," yells Pitino. "They don't need any breaks."

"I've had it, Rick," says ref Ed Rush, standing near the Knick bench.

"I've had it with you too. I can't take any more of this bullshit."

"Stop it, Rick, or you're gone," Rush answers.

"The only way you're going to get rid of me is to bounce me," Pitino yells back. "I'm not going to stop it."

Rush gives him a second technical: automatic expulsion. Pitino starts walking toward the runway and yells, "This is bullshit" to Rush as the Garden crowd erupts.

Bianchi later says the only thing he would have done differently is he would have gotten thrown out after the first ten minutes.

"I respect the Celtics, but that doesn't mean I got to like them," mutters Bianchi. He has lost to the Celtics too many times in his long NBA career, as a player at Syracuse and Philadelphia and later as an assistant coach at Phoenix. "Everyone talks about those ghosts in Boston

Garden. I can't tell you how tired I am of those goddamn ghosts."

"It was a message to the officials," Pitino says afterward. "Did they get the message? I hope they did. The Boston Celtics are a great team. They don't need any edges. They'll do it by themselves."

It's not the only controversy.

Johnny Most, the long-time radio broadcaster for the Celtics, has decided Pitino is his villain for the series. He is especially upset that Pitino closed his practice the day before to everyone except the New York media. When Pitino got his first technical in the first quarter Most said, "He'll say a lot more. He has a big mouth. He's been popping off and doing a lot of unethical things. That's his style. The things he did to give an advantage to the New York media were almost disgusting. In fact, it is disgusting. Maybe someday he'll grow up."

Meanwhile, Pitino is in the hallway engulfed by TV cameras and reporters.

A radio reporter sticks his microphone into Pitino's face. "Rick, even though you're now down two games, you must be enjoying this."

"I am not enjoying this," Pitino says, his voice high. "I am losing my hair and I am dying."

"But surely you are a little," the reporter presses.

"I enjoy other things more than watching the Boston Celtics, thank you very much." He pauses to gather his summing-up statement. "Boston dominated us in every facet of the game. Once the Celtics get into their halfcourt game, they are the best team in basketball. Everyone should appreciate watching Bird play, for someday it will be like your father telling you about Babe Ruth." He praises the play of Dennis Johnson, who once again has raised his game a notch in the playoffs. If the word around the league during the season had been that DJ was entering the twilight of his career, he has had two great games. But Pitino also defends

Mark Jackson whenever a reporter tries to press the issue that DJ has outplayed Jackson in the two games. Jackson has shot 3–11 from the floor, the Knicks have not run, and DJ has posted him up inside.

"It's not DJ versus Mark. It's the Celtics versus the Knicks."

"And you had seen enough of that, right?" says Peter Vecsey . "I mean, when you got tossed."

"Let's just say I didn't think that changing defenses was all that important at that point."

Later that night, back home in Bedford, Pitino is more reflective. "I'm really amazed we have come as far as we have. We play a team like the Celtics, and all our weaknesses show up. The only positive is how Patrick is responding." He pauses, and then voices an idea he's been mulling over. "I'm thinking of starting Johnny Newman. I was thinking of not playing him at all because he's been such a disaster. The first game he was 3–13 and today he was a non-factor. He hasn't been shooting well the past few weeks, even in practice. I've even thought of playing Louis Orr there because he's been playing well in practice. We got to get some offense out of the three spot. The best Kenny can give us is maybe 12 points. We need more. Maybe Johnny can get hot and get 20. So I'm going to tell him tomorrow I'm going to start him because I know he is going to have a great game."

His starting forwards, Walker and Green, have been outscored by Bird and McHale by the unbelievable margin of 118–24. It has, of course, been the Knicks' Achilles' heel. All year Pitino has tried to camouflage the fact the Knicks' starting forwards were last in the NBA in total points. As the season has gone on, he has become more overt about it: he merely played them less and less in important situations.

"Do you have any reaction to what Johnny Most said about you?"

"Not really. Johnny Most is the all-time homer. He sees the game through green-colored glasses. It is a total distortion. When I was at UMass, we used to turn the sound down on the TV and listen to Johnny because it really was like two different games. He turns basketball into professional wrestling, complete with good guys and villains. It's an act. No one takes him seriously. I take it as a compliment that I've now become one of the Boston Celtics' villains."

May 2–3

One of the questions to Pitino after practice at SUNY is about the referees.

"Let me put it this way: one of my favorite fairy tales is Robin Hood. And what makes it good is that he stole from the rich and gave to the poor. Now wouldn't it have been a bad fairy tale if he had robbed from the poor and given it to the rich?"

The big news is K. C. Jones has prematurely announced his retirement, effective at the end of the season, and become a part of the Celtic front office. Even in Boston, the dignified exit of a storied coach has been trampled in the scramble for a scoop. He will be replaced by assistant coach Jimmy Rodgers, sought by the Knicks to be their coach before they came back to Pitino.

With Jones' retirement, Pitino will begin next year, oddly enough, as the dean of the Atlantic Conference coaches. Dave Wohl of the Nets has been fired, replaced by Willis Reed. Kevin Loughery of the Bullets has been fired, replaced by Wes Unseld. Matty Guokas of the 76ers has been fired, replaced by Jimmy Lynam. "It makes you realize what a perilous profession this is."

May 4

Madison Square Garden the way it used to be: scalpers outside on Seventh Avenue. The "Boston sucks" chants. The celebrities in the front rows: Michael Douglas, Bill

Murray, Peter Falk, John McEnroe, Jimmy Buffet. The City Game on display. The crowd is waving white towels, a last-minute promotional idea. They boo the Celtics in the pregame introductions. When the Knicks are introduced, a roar reverberates throughout the Garden.

"I haven't seen it like this all year," says Pitino, kneeling in front of his bench moments before the game starts. He smiles. "I brought the towels."

The game plan is to jump all over the Celtics, constantly pressure them, whether it's in fullcourt man-to-man or in the press. I want to create chaos. They have been able to run their plays the first two games, and we can't allow that. If they are able to run their plays and get into their rhythm, we can't beat them."

As soon as the game begins Pitino is coaching every play. "Bird . . . Bird," he yells at Newman every time the Knicks go from offense to defense. He wants Newman to overplay Bird at all times to discourage the pass to Bird. He constantly yells at Newman to pick him up higher, not to let him get the ball. "Johnny, get to Bird . . . Bird . . . Bird."

Another of Pitino's strategies is to have Wilkins, not Mark Jackson, guard Dennis Johnson. Not only does the bigger Wilkins make it more difficult for DJ to post-up his defender, a tactic he tends to resort to more in the playoffs, it also makes it tougher for DJ to make the entry pass into Bird and the other Celtic big people.

Pitino is nonstop on the sidelines, admonishing and encouraging as the frantic action swirls in front of him, "Sid, I'm not going to tell you again," Pitino yells as Green runs by. "Get in the press quicker." "Work him, Dougie, work him." "On the glass, big." He is constantly off the bench, screaming out defenses, calling plays, clapping his hands, raising his fist, the intensity dripping off him.

Yet there are moments of levity too. At one point Pitino yells, "Green, green," telling his team what defense they're in.

"Green?" Danny Ainge asks, standing nearby, a perplexed look on his face, "You don't have a green."

Pitino laughs. "We do now. It's a new halfcourt trap just to cut off your threes."

The game is tied at 45 at the half. Once again the Knicks are shooting a low percentage, 42 percent, but Bird only has 10 at the half, McHale 14. On other side, Newman already has 16, a Pitino dream come to life.

The Knicks fall behind by eight shortly into the third quarter before making one of their patented Garden comebacks, one sparked by Mark Jackson. When a timeout is called with 4:06 left in the third period, the Knicks are given a resounding, standing ovation. Bill Murray is introduced to the crowd, and he stands and frantically waves a white towel over his head. The Garden roars. Then Michael Douglas is introduced, and he waves two towels. Pandemonium.

In this quarter Pat Cummings has played the most since the Atlanta game two weeks ago. He comes in when Sidney Green goes to the bench with four fouls, a night when he again appears lost in one of his funks. The Knicks end the quarter leading by three, and when Cummings comes out a few minutes later he gets a standing ovation.

The Knicks go up 10 shortly into the fourth quarter. The Garden is rocking, the towels waving; the noise rolls onto the court in every increasing waves. The Celtics look frazzled. Bird is missing. They never seem to be able to get into any offense. Still, they come inching back until they finally tie the game at 94 with just under two minutes to play. After Ewing makes two foul shots, the Knicks' press traps Dennis Johnson in the corner, where he throws a desperation pass up near mid-court. Mark Jackson intercepts, and in the ensuing action Ewing gets fouled again. He makes two more foul shots. The Garden is in absolute mayhem. The Knicks never look back and win 109–100.

It's been a perfect execution of Pitino's game. Constant defensive pressure has prevented the Celtics from ever settling into an offensive rhythm. The tempo of the games has been increased, the chaos Pitino was looking for has been found. The Celtics have turned the ball over 19 times. The Knicks also have outrebounded the Celtics for the first time in the series. Newman has been instant offense, ending with 34 points, a career high. Ewing finishes with 31, dominating Robert Parish inside. Mark Jackson has 14 assists.

In the locker room Cummings stares in the TV lights, a rare sight this year. He is naked except for his red underwear. "I'm like a dog that hasn't eaten in a week," he says, smiling, his hangdog face all creases, "and I'm looking forward to my next meal."

"How tough has this been for you?"

"It's been an adjustment, because I still think I can produce. I am finally healthy for the first time in two years and playing is fun again. Sure, it's a tough feeling when you don't get in. You feel like you're chained to the bench. What you have to tell yourself is that there are seven other guys on the bench who all want to be in the game, too."

This is the same Pat Cummings who, as Knick rumor has it, came into the locker room in a rage after the big Knick win on Christmas day two years before because he hadn't played enough at the end of the game. Now he is sounding like Jack Armstrong, all-American team player.

"Do you expect to be here next year?"

"I really don't want to go into that. Right now this is fun, what you play all year for. Nobody really knows where they're going to be next year."

A few feet away is Sidney Green. Next to him is Louis Orr. Both are in varying stages of getting dressed. "I'm happy to see that," says Green, glancing over at Cummings being interviewed. "Next to winning the game, that's the best thing I've seen all night." he nudges Orr. "Look at Cakes," he says with a laugh. "He hasn't stopped talking yet."

Among the Knick beat writers he's viewed as one of the best interviews; personable, perceptive, engaging, cooperative.

"So it doesn't bother you that he might have played in your place tonight?"

"Not at all. That's all part of being a team. If it weren't for what Pat did in the Atlanta game, I would be in Las Vegas on vacation now. The guys who don't play much— Pat, Louis here—they maintain an attitude. The first thing Louis said to me when he came in here was that us guys on the first unit are going to work our tail off tomorrow in practice. That's their attitude. That's because we've come together as a team."

The room is crowded with media. Newman is saying that even when Pitino had him on the first team the past two days, he still wasn't sure he was going to start. "Then I heard my name being announced and I said, 'Hey, that's me,' " he says, the wide-eyed wonder in his voice.

Wilkins is saying that the decision to put him on DJ defensively, plus having him bring the ball up the court once in a while, took some of the pressure off Mark Jackson.

"Does it bother you that you didn't score much tonight?" he is asked.

"Last year I'd score my 25, and we'd lose by 25. Now I know I can contribute in other ways too."

"Gerald, are you guys going to be able to press the entire game Friday night?"

Wilkins smiles, his dark eyes dancing. "You know, man, we're in great shape. And we'll be pressing Friday. Because it's now or never."

Jackson stands in front of the next locker. He has played well, once again the on-court leader, as he's been all year. It's been a redemption game for him. He heard all the knocks, that DJ was taking the rookie out behind the wood-shed and rapping his knuckles.

"Too much has been said about this being a learning experience. I've learned from the first time I stepped out onto a court. People who put emphasis on that, I question their knowledge of the game. After the two games in Boston I was very angry. There was too much talk of that. I am not a rookie. I am not inexperienced. That's no excuse, and I don't want to hear about it anymore."

"Did it bother you that you weren't on DJ tonight?"

Jackson juts out his jaw, a subtle gesture he makes when his feels his pride is under attack. "I have total confidence in Coach Pitino's decisions and what's best for for the New York Knicks." After a few moments he cools down, and smiles. On his way into the Garden before the game, he was stopped in traffic in a cab about seven blocks from the Garden, so he got out and started walking. "Some people must have thought I was crazy, but I just wanted to get out there with the fans. I wanted to become part of the people. To get hungry again, like they are hungry. I always make myself try to feel like I'm playing for the people who can't play, or never had the chance. Maybe it's corny, but I'm out there and I believe it. When I'm in an empty gym, I sometimes feel like the worst player in the world. I get pumped up by the crowd."

Pitino is completely drained. For one of the few times all year, he and Joanne decide to go right home rather than go out to eat in the city. By chance he and Ainge end up in the elevator together.

"Thanks, Rick," says Ainge. "I had plans to play golf tomorrow. You messed them up. But you know what? I rescheduled for Saturday."

"Better put those on ice, too."

"I don't think I've ever seen the Garden that electric," Pitino says later that night. "I was here in 1973, when everyone talks about how electric the Garden was, but I don't remember it being any better than this. I feel good about this game tonight for two reasons. The obvious one is that we're still alive. The second is that a lot of people thought we should have been in the lottery instead of the playoffs, especially after we got blown out those first two games in

Boston. Now those critics have been silenced. Now everything has been accomplished this year that could have been accomplished. They did everything we wanted them to do in the game plan. We have been on them all year to pay better attention during the walk-throughs, to be more focused, and in the past three weeks they have done all you could ask. I couldn't be more proud of them and the staff."

He falls into silence.

"But you know the thing that's the toughest to change about professional athletes? Their refusal to accept any blame for a poor performance. Like Mark having problems with DJ in the first two games. Rather than say I didn't play that well, but I've learned some things that I'll be able to use in New York, he gives that 'I am not a rookie' stuff. Or Johnny Newman. On the way home I hear Johnny saying on WFAN that the reason he hasn't been playing well is that we haven't been running a lot of motion offense, and when we don't do that he doesn't get very good shots. The thing is, we didn't run very much motion offense tonight. The reason he hasn't been playing well recently is he hasn't shot well, and he hasn't made good offensive decisions. And rather than say he had a good night, he has to make excuses for how badly he's played the past couple of weeks.

"That's the thing I don't understand. As much as I tell them it's all right to accept blame, as much as I tell them sometimes that because of my coaching we lost the game, it doesn't sink in. Rather than admit their deficiencies and work to correct them, they look for excuses. I think it's the last hurdle players have to get over."

May 6

It is two and a half hours before the game, and trainer Mike Saunders is in the locker room, getting ready. "I've never felt so proud to be a part of the Knicks as I did the other night," he says, "and I've been here ten years. I looked out on the court at our players and they looked eight feet tall. I've seen every guy grow this year, even a guy like Louis Orr. He's more a part of this team now, even though he doesn't play anymore. But I see his attitude, how much a part of it he is. They all are. Wilkins has become more mature. His ability to concentrate is better. Before all he cared about was the points column. Now he understands that's just part of it."

The players are starting to drift in, the room still quiet.

"Patrick has emerged as a leader. He sets a great example at practice. He works hard, he's enthusiastic. I think he's only had one day all year when he didn't practice. I've seen him grow as a person too. You know, all the players always liked Patrick. From the first day when he was a rookie, he was great in the locker room. He joked with the other guys, he kibbitzed. His walls were never up in the locker room. Now he's taken it a step further. Now he's become their leader.

"And you know, it's all because of Rick. I hope he understands that. Sometimes I don't think he does. He wasn't here last year, doesn't realize how completely it's changed. But right from the first day of training camp it's been night and day."

The big, empty arena is in murky twilight. A few TV cameramen are setting up their equipment. Rick Carlisle is casually shooting at one end of the floor while talking to a couple of Boston sportscasters. At the other end of the floor five Knicks ballboys, including Mark Jackson's brother, Troy, are playing a rag-tag pickup game.

A few minutes later Jackson walks out onto the court, joins the pickup game. He plays on the same side as his brother and hoists up a few shots before leaving to do a TV interview.

Pitino is going with the same game plan that worked so well Wednesday night: induce chaos. Pressure and attack. Pressure and attack.

The Celtics come on the court first in their kelly green warmups, the most distinctive colors in basketball. Immediately the "Boston sucks" chants start. Then the Knicks come out in their white warmups to a deafening roar. It is another Garden love-in, another night of celebrities in the first row, another affirmation the Knicks are New York's new darlings. Stu Jackson looks around and rolls his eyes in amazement. "The Providence Civic Center was never like this."

The Knicks quickly fall behind 8–2. Pitino calls a twenty-second timeout. "You got to win tonight," he says loudly, eyes darting from player to player. "You. The crowd is not going to win this game. You have to do it."

The Knicks fall behind 16–4. Several times the Celtics have beaten them down the court for easy baskets. Pitino calls a full timeout. He is furious. He starts screaming at the forwards and center to get back on defense quicker. One of them starts to say it was someone else's fault.

"I don't care whose fault it is," he bellows, his face flushed. "I don't care. Get back on defense. They should never beat you down the court. Never. And they've already got five layups. You're making McHale look like he's Herschel Walker." He slams his clipboard on the court, and starts in again. The ten little figures on his clipboard scatter at his players' feet.

The Knicks get back in the game. By the end of the quarter they are down 28–21, down six at the half. On the verge of being blown out in the opening minutes, they have scratched their way back, even though they only have shot 38 percent of the first half, compared to the Celtics' 53 percent. Newman, off to another good start, has 14 points, the only Knick in double figures. Bird has 11 and McHale 12. Once again the Celtics' two big guns have been kept under control.

By the end of the third period the Knicks trail by only one, and it seems like a page from the other night. The

Knicks' pressure is bothering the Celtics. Bird has been kept in check. Mark Jackson is in the midst of having a great half. With 9:31 left, a Wilkins drive knots the game at 77, and begins a run of eight straight Knick points. With 6:20 left, the Knicks are up 83–77, the Celtics call a timeout, and the Garden is going crazy.

Just when it seems the Knicks finally are in control, the Celts make one more run at them. They narrow the lead to one. Then, with the shot clock winding down, Dennis Johnson strokes a three-pointer from right in front of Pitino, and the Celtics lead by three with 3:18 left to play. They never trail again, even though a Newman three-point play puts the Knicks within one with 2:43 to go. The Celtics win it, 102–94. Bird ends with 28, McHale and Parish 20, Johnson 19. Jackson has 28 for the Knicks, Newman 25, Wilkins, 18. Ewing, a monster on the boards all night long, is held to only 10 points, but has had 20 rebounds.

With two seconds remaining and Jackson at the foul line for two meaningless shots, it becomes a celebration. The game is over, the Knicks' season is over. Pitino takes out Ewing to thunderous applause. He takes out Wilkins and Newman to more applause. They have come a long way since the first exhibition game when the Knicks were roundly booed after the first four minutes. Such a long way since boos almost chased the Knicks off the court as soon as they fell behind. A long way since Pitino decided to announce Jackson's name first because he knew Jackson wouldn't be booed. Now the entire Garden is on their feet.

"Anybody who is down right now is leading a foolish life," Pitino tells his team in the locker room. "You had a great season, and now is the time to celebrate. What we wanted to do was to make the playoffs and go as far as we could go, and we have done that. There are no losers when you get this far, especially you people. This is the first step for the future. You brought the excitement back to New York, and it's only going to get better. So go out and celebrate."

In the interview room Pitino gives all credit to the Celtics.

He says that the Celtics dug down in the closing minutes and showed their greatness. He hopes the Celtics now "win it for K. C.

"I'm as proud of this team as any team I've ever coached. We gave a great effort tonight. We have accomplished a lot this year. We have played the last month in a lot of pressurized games. And we learned to win on the road. These things are invaluable. And the most important thing we accomplished is we have created a 'we' attitude."

The Celtics return the compliments:

"They're going to kick some butt next year," says Jones. "We had to fight for our lives. The Knicks will never be the same after this. They will come back next year on a different level. Going through this sort of experience makes a young team much, much tougher."

"If the Knicks pick up a few players and continue to play as well as they have this year, they're going to be one tough team," says Bird.

"This was as tough a first-round series as we've had in a long time," says McHale. "The Knicks just wouldn't die."

"With Mark and Patrick, fans are going to be coming here for a long time to come," says Dennis Johnson.

The Knicks' locker room is mobbed with media. The Knicks have lost, but there is little remorse. They have played well. They were in the game right to the end. They have served notice that they are a team to be reckoned with next season. Already the talk is of next year, the future.

"We have grown and matured together, and now we have the talent to build a dynasty," Ewing says. He is sitting in his blue terrycloth robe with ice packs on both knees. Rivulets of sweat roll down his mahogany face. The faces crowd around him with their similar questions and Ewing gives thoughtful answers to every one. He smiles. If the Knicks have come so far since the beginning of the year, so has Patrick Ewing. The two are finally linked together. His stamp is all over this young team.

"Do you think the fact that you had 20 rebounds tonight

will end the perception that you're not a good rebounder?" asks Jerry Sullivan of *Newsday*.

Ewing's dark eyes get instantly cloudy. "I don't care about the perception," he says, turning away to get undressed. "I am a winner. That's it." Then he says again, almost to himself. "A winner."

The locker room resembles the last day of school. The Knicks are going home for the summer, now is the time for good-byes. The mood is bittersweet. Pitino has told them to celebrate, and celebrate they should. Yet there's also the realization that when a season ends, it closes a chapter in their professional lives. Next year some of their teammates will be gone. There will be new faces to blend in, a new chemistry to assemble.

Mark Jackson peers into the glare of the TV camera. In just one short season, he has become the most loved Knick guard since Walt Frazier, the kid who sprang from the city's mean streets. In a few days he will be named the NBA Rookie of the Year. More important, he is the Knicks' future, someone destined to team with Ewing to anchor the Knicks for years.

"What about Pitino?" he is asked.

"He is a great coach. He is a great motivator. He is full of enthusiasm. And he has a never-say-die attitude. He's the key to my success. He handed me the ball from day one and said, 'This is your team. Run it.'"

"What about the Knicks?"

Jackson pauses a beat, running all the games and all the months through his mind. This long, winding season is finally over. "Right now we're a very good basketball team. Very soon we're going to be a great one."

✝✝✝✝✝✝✝✝✝

May 8

I was sitting in the backyard today, relaxing for the first time in I don't remember when, and I started thinking about the past year and a half. How unbelievable it's been. It started when Daniel was born in September of '86. Every morning Joanne would get up and drive to Boston to be with him in the hospital. I admired her dedication and perseverence. Every day she went. For a while he couldn't get any nourishment, then they rectified that. It always seemed to be one problem after another. We were devastated. But we told ourselves that at least he was going to be all right, that we were going to have him. This went on for five months.

Finally Daniel came home. For the first time since he had been born, he had a clean bill of health. We couldn't believe how fortunate we were. I told Joanne that she had to take a couple of days off and come to New York with me for the Big East tournament. She had been dealing with the strain every day since Daniel was born, and she needed a little vacation. We had a nurse there, and she went to New York with me. The next time we saw him, he was lying in the hospital. Our six months of prayers ended with Daniel dead. Through it all I realized God made Daniel and took him back with Him; I had to be thankful for such a devoted wife.

The decision to leave Providence followed. People thinking we were villains, even people we thought were our friends. So when we moved here to New York, we didn't really feel good about ourselves.

Then my father got sick.

One minute everything is going to be all right, and the next my father is dead. It's been an emotional roller coaster.

And now? The only bad thing about this job is I know it's going to end. I am thirty-five and I know that a New York coach can't last forever in the pros. You know, it's funny. Joanne and I are fixing up the house, but in the back of our minds we know this will not be our last house. For example, last year in our Rhode Island house we had built-in bookcases. Now we're putting in portable ones, so we can take them with us. Little things like that. Knowing that you really can't get too emotionally involved with the house because we're going to have to move someday.

"You realize it in every aspect of your life, whether it's fixing up your house, future plans for your children, or joining certain clubs. You realize that you aren't going to be here forever, and that's the uneasy feeling I don't want to live with. I want roots for my children, so they can go back to their high school reunions, can go back to places where they grew up and feel it's theirs. But I know with this job that might not happen. But I'm going to enjoy this job, because I've come to learn that these are fleeting years. One day they're going to end.

All year in the back of my mind I wondered if I had made the right decision in coming here to New York, especially when things started going badly in Providence. Obviously some of it has been a guilt trip. But what I've come to realize is that I'm not going to know for a long time whether it was a good decision or not. Maybe I'll never know. It's like you're walking through a long, dark tunnel, and you don't know where the tunnel is going to end. Then in the middle of the tunnel someone gives you a match. Now you have hope, you know you're going to have some light. But you still don't know where the tunnel is going to end.

12 | My New Kentucky Home: An Update One Year Later

Everything started when Kentucky called my business consultant, Mitch Dukov, in early February and asked if I would have any interest if the Kentucky job opened up. I told him to tell them I had none. The four people Kentucky was pursuing at the time were Pat Riley, Lute Olson, Mike Krzyzewski, and myself. Riley told them he might be interested at some other time in his career but not now. Krzyzewski told them he had no interest. Olson later was interviewed, then said he wasn't interested.

Then their coach, Eddie Sutton, resigned and C. M. Newton, the new athletic director, called me. I told him that I couldn't even start thinking about coaching at Kentucky until the NBA playoffs were over. I had to keep totally focused on coaching the Knicks. The guy he should go after, I told him, was P. J. Carlesimo of Seton Hall. He was coming off the Final Four, he was hot, and Kentucky could probably get him. C. M. couldn't gamble on me, because the Knicks season could go all the way to June, and he couldn't wait that long.

It was no secret that if the right college offer came along that I would be interested in listening. But the timing was just not right.

Then after P. J. bowed out, I got a call from C. M. again.

I was at the Ryetown Hilton in Westchester County, near where we practiced, getting ready for the playoffs. He said I was still his choice. I still wasn't interested and told him that, but I also thought I should keep Al Bianchi—the Knicks general manager—informed, because I didn't want him to hear it through the grapevine and think I was doing anything behind his back. So I went over to SUNY-Purchase, where we have our offices, and told him. I also said I really wasn't interested. Al said, "Look, Rick, you should never close the door. You should keep your options open. I saw what happened to John McLeod in Phoenix. After all the years there, at the end they still didn't have any loyalty to him. You have to keep your options open." I knew right then that Al didn't want to keep me as the coach. It wasn't like I went to him and said I was interested. But he never said anything to tell me he wanted me to stay.

Then a couple of days later I got a call from David Roselle, the president of the University of Kentucky. He told me he was getting mixed signals. C. M. was telling him I wasn't interested, but other people were telling him I was. I told him about the conversation I had had with Al. We talked for forty-five minutes, and when we got off the phone, I started seriously considering it for the first time. Roselle said he wanted to make Kentucky's program like North Carolina's or Duke's, one that everyone could be proud of. He was the one who sold me on it. If he hadn't called me, I believe I'd still be with the Knicks today.

What really shook me was what happened with coach Michel Bergeron and general manager Phil Esposito of the New York Rangers, who also are owned by Gulf & Western. They were at each other's throats, in what had become a very public feud. Then right before the playoffs Esposito fired Bergeron. Then after the season the Rangers fired Esposito.

Al and I were never like those two—we were in a kind of cold war—but I could see that happening to us, locked in a philosophical struggle where we both end up losing our jobs. I wanted no part of a power struggle. I had never never been in a situation like that before, not with John Simpson at Boston University or Lou Lamoriello at Providence. I always had worked for people who I knew were behind me at all times.

I had felt all along that Al had settled for me. He had wanted Jimmy Rodgers. Then when he couldn't have him, he had a choice of Larry Brown, Jimmy Valvano, or me. He felt that Brown was too much of a nomad, that Valvano was too much a college coach. Given the three of us, I was the best choice. Yes, I was a college coach, too, but I had worked in the pros. And I was coming off the Final Four. The Knicks brass was split. Dick Evans wanted Valvano; Jack Diller wanted me.

So I became the alternative candidate, and I never really felt Al stood by me. For all his toughness with the media, I never felt he backed me with them. And I could have lived with that, mind you. If I had had ninety percent of the media against me and Al totally believing in me, I would have felt great. But I felt insecure about my job, and I thought that was wrong. I'm not going to gamble on my career with three small children.

What makes it more difficult is that I like Al as a person, and I respect the job he's done as general manager. But we had very strong philosophical differences about how the game should be played, and I didn't think they were going to get better. In a sense, I guess we both got what we wanted. He gets a chance to hire a coach he wants. I get to return to college basketball, even if it came quicker than I had expected. So maybe we both got the best of all possible worlds, and we both can live happily ever after.

✝✝✝✝✝✝✝✝✝✝

The irony is the year started so well.

Pitino inherited a team that seemed stuck on a treadmill of futility, playing in a Madison Square Garden that had become a tomb full of sullen, unhappy fans and empty seats. Pitino instituted his pressing style and changed all that.

By January 1988 the Knicks had started to win in the Garden. Soon after the crowds started to come back, complete with the celebrities in the front row. In the second half of the year the Knicks began to be almost unbeatable at home, serving notice they were an NBA team on the rise. They qualified for the playoffs on the last night of the season, and even though the Celtics eliminated them in the first round, it had been a storybook year. In the dying seconds of the fourth game with the Celtics, when it was apparent the Knicks season was ending, the entire Garden stood and cheered them.

It only got better over the summer.

Charles Oakley of the Chicago Bulls, who had led the NBA in rebounding the past two seasons, came to the Knicks in June, traded for Bill Cartwright, who had been dangled as trade bait since the fall of 1987. Oakley, a bruising 6-foot-8 forward, would help Patrick Ewing with the rebounding and give the Knicks more of a physical presence inside. The comparisons to Dave DeBusschere were inevitable. In the early seventies it had been the acquisition of DeBusschere that supposedly was the missing piece of the puzzle that enabled the Knicks to win two world championships. Now Oakley was coming. The general consensus was the trade was a Knick steal, getting arguably the best rebounder in the game, approaching the prime of his career, for an aging center with a history of foot problems.

Then in the draft the Knicks selected Rod Strickland, a point guard from DePaul. He was expected to be the backup to Mark Jackson, something the Knicks had sorely lacked the year before when it often seemed as if their offense seemed to downshift the minute Jackson went out of the game.

So when they opened in November, the Knicks were an improved team.

The only real problem area was the backup center slot behind Ewing. They had only Eddie Lee Wilkens, an NBA journeyman trying to resurrect his career after knee surgery and some time playing in Europe, second-round pick Greg Butler, known in NBA parlance as a "project," and Sidney Green, who at 6-foot-9 could play center for a few minutes to give Ewing a breather. Other than that, it was a much deeper team than it had been a year earlier. It also was a team that faced greatly heightened expectations.

The Knicks lost their first two games of the year, on the road to the Celtics and the New Jersey Nets, but rebounded to go 9–5 for the month of November. The highlight was a romp of the Detroit Pistons on the road, a game in which the Knicks hit nine three-pointers and scored 133 points against the NBA's best defensive club. This was evidence of Pitino's new philosophy to open up the offense, to run more and take more three-point shots. Wilkins, Newman, Jackson, and Tucker he nicknamed the "Bomb Squad," and all were encouraged to take the three-pointer at virtually every opportunity. It was a strategy Pitino had employed at Providence College, where his team had led the country in three-pointers taken and rode the shot all the way to the Final Four. It was all part of his philosophy of putting constant pressure on the opposition, trying to control the pace of the game. Defensively, it was with traps and fullcourt pressure, the idea being to get opposing teams out of their set offense. Then at the other end of the floor, run and shoot three-pointers, not let the opposition set up defensively.

December was more of the same. They continued to win at home, continued to sit on top of the Atlantic Division as Larry Bird went out for the season with surgery on both heels, a loss that crippled the Celtics and left the Philadelphia 76ers as the main competition for the divisional race. The only down moment came on a road loss to the Charlotte Hornets, an expansion team. Afterward, Pitino said, "We're nowhere near a championship team."

True to form, Al Bianchi criticized him for his remark. The Knicks continued to breeze along nonetheless. Ewing was having an MVP type year. Jackson was all flair and savvy in the backcourt, and when he went to the bench the explosive Strickland was often a quick pick-me-up off the bench. If he didn't run the team as well as Jackson, or pass nearly as well, he displayed a marvelous ability to penetrate to the basket. Newman and Wilkins still could be as on and off as a light switch, but both still had nights when they scored by the bucketfuls. Tucker was a great role player off the bench: a great deep shooter, a determined defender. Green and Walker were effective role players off the bench, both seeming to benefit from lowered expectations. The Garden continued to be full and alive.

In early January, the Knicks overturned a 17-point deficit and beat the Nets in the Meadowlands. But the big news was not the score. At one point, dissatisfied with Strickland's effort, Pitino pulled the rookie and said angrily, "I'm sick of your Joe Cool act." This would not have been any big deal except for the fact that the press table in the Meadowlands is situated behind the bench, so the remark was overheard and repeated by several of the New York writers. Pitino's remark angered Bianchi, who questioned in print Pitino's public critique of Strickland.

This brought to the surface the sometimes strained relationship between coach and GM. Maybe it was inevitable. Pitino never had been Bianchi's choice to be the Knicks coach. Bianchi had been hired, then ordered by Garden management to go talk to Pitino. Not exactly the ideal way to start a working relationship.

The problem lay deeper than that, though.

Bianchi is an NBA lifer. Pitino promised to bring more of a "college atmosphere" to the Knicks. Bianchi never actually said so, but it was apparent even last year that he never agreed with Pitino's coaching philosophy. He looked at the

Knicks pressing fullcourt and he saw college ball, not pro ball.

Then, too, he also believes that rebuilding takes time, that the worst thing that can happen is to go for a quick fix. Pitino, on the other hand, wanted to win right away, for he knew New Yorkers didn't want to hear about rebuilding; they only wanted to hear about winning.

If Pitino had philosophical differences with Bianchi, though, he did his best to downplay them. He never criticized Bianchi. He kept up the pretense he and Bianchi had a good working relationship. His public posture was that though he and Bianchi didn't socialize together, they both wanted the same things from the New York Knicks, to build a team that could one day win the championship.

The Strickland affair brought their differences into the open. Pitino countered by saying that if he wasn't appreciated as a coach, he would go elsewhere, a story splashed across the back of the New York *Post*. Bianchi later apologized to Pitino, saying his remarks were taken out of context, but it all added spice to the rumors that Pitino was looking for a college coaching job. (Not that Pitino's desire to go back to college basketball should have come as any surprise. When this book came out in November 1988, Pitino made no secret in it of his desire to one day return to college coaching. All the same, the news he was considering going back to college coaching was treated in the *Post* as if it were an exclusive.)

In January the Knicks made a seven-game swing to the West Coast, the kind of road trip that used to leave them bloodied, all their warts showing. This time they were 2–5, but came from 20 down to beat Portland, and beat the Lakers in the Forum, ending the Lakers' long winning streak on their home court. Despite the losing road trip, they still went 10–6 for the month and now were 27–16, with a three-game lead in the Atlantic Division.

February saw the arrival of Kiki Vandewehge, traded for

the 1989 first-round draft pick. Vandeweghe had been rumored to be coming to New York since the start of the season, and when he finally arrived, he was called the final piece of the puzzle. He was trumpeted as a proven scorer in the half-court game, despite the fact that he hadn't played in over a year because of his chronically bad back. In fact, the reason why the trade took so long to consummate were the conflicting stories about the severity of his condition. One theory was it was career-threatening. The other was it was going to get remarkably better as soon as he got out of Portland.

While the Knicks waited for Vandeweghe to get in some semblance of shape, they had another good month. Ewing and Jackson went to the All-Star game. As did Kenny Walker, who won the slam-dunk contest and immediately became a folk hero in the Garden. How different from the year before, when he had been booed for not living up to the expectations as the sixth player selected in the 1986 draft!

The highlight came on February 26, when the Knicks dismantled the Celtics on national television. It was their 21st straight win in the Garden, a club record. They were now cruising along at 37–18, with a commanding six-game lead over Philadelphia. (The Garden winning streak eventually reached 26, before Philadelphia ended it.)

Then the troubles started. Mark Jackson missed 10 games with a torn cartilege in his knee, and when he came back, the Knicks shortly afterward went through an 8–11 stretch, their worst of the season. There were all sorts of rumors about back-biting and dissension, complete with a report that Jackson and Wilkins had gotten into a loud and ugly argument on a plane flight. Jackson also started being criticized for his flamboyance: his finger-pointing after scores, the spreading out of his arms and turning around like he was an airplane after an exceptionally good move to the hoop. Last year it was called the flair of an emerging great young NBA point guard. Now, more and more, it was being called "hot-dogging." All of a sudden the world started getting more complicated for Mark Jackson. He had gone through an extended contract renegotiation. He had gone through the trauma of arthroscopic surgery, the first time in his career he was ever hurt. Now there were also rumblings of discontent among the fickle Garden crowds. Pitino constantly defended Jackson. If in private he occasionally told him to curtail the flamboyance, in public he reminded people he was only a second-year player.

All this came at a time in the season when it was obvious the Knicks had become bored. The division title had been won. They couldn't catch Detroit for the best record in the East. In a sense they were in limbo, playing out the final weeks of the season with nothing to play for, waiting for the playoffs to start.

"We are a team that sets short-term goals," Pitino said shortly before the end of the season. "The home-court streak. The division. Fifty victories. We have to keep a goal in front of us, and we haven't had one in a while."

Unfortunately, the bad stretch seemed to take away some of their luster. In the long, arduous NBA season that always has its shares of ups and downs, the Knicks' fate was to have a down stretch on the eve of the playoffs.

"They stumbled and bickered and finger-pointed through an 8–11 stretch," wrote Fred Kerber in the New York *Daily News*. "Their home-court dominance was a tattered memory. Such weaklings as Charlotte and Miami punched out their lights. Kiki Vandeweghe, who should have been greeted with open arms, instead met cold shoulders. Relying on a treasure chest of psychological ploys designed to rekindle the fires, coach Rick Pitino was again rumored to be heading for a college job. Mark Jackson, who already had undergone a messy contract affair, underwent knee surgery and was KO'd for 10 games. Through it all the Knicks, worried to the core, said, 'Don't worry. Be happy.' "

What was also obvious is that Vandeweghe's arrival had upset the delicate chemistry of the Knicks.

"I wanted Kiki, too," said Pitino, "because I thought he would make us a better team. But as soon as he came in, the chemistry changed. It shouldn't have, but it did. And it wasn't Kiki's fault. He couldn't have handled things any better. It was our fault. It was immaturity on our part."

One of the sore spots happened inadvertently. One of the promotions run on the Madison Square Garden Network showed the Knicks of the early seventies being compared to this year's team: Ewing to Willis Reed, Oakley to DeBusschere, Jackson to Walt Frazier, Wilkins to Dick Barnett, and Vandeweghe to Bill Bradley. Not Johnny Newman, the actual starter, to Bradley. But Vandeweghe, the new guy, the white guy.

"Johnny came to me and he was upset," Pitino said. "He said he had seen the thing on television and he wanted to know what the story was. I joked that maybe it was because they needed a white guy, trying to diffuse it. I had nothing to do with it, and wasn't even aware of it until Johnny came to me. But he was upset, so I had it changed. But Johnny was still upset by Vandeweghe's coming. He shouldn't have been, because I told Johnny that he was my starter for the rest of the year. Next year the job was open, but for the rest of the year he was the guy and not to worry about it."

This unrest was unusual because until Vandeweghe's arrival the Knicks were known as an extremely close team, rare in the NBA. "One day we had a team meeting after an argument in the locker room about Gerald Wilkins not passing the ball. At one point Sidney Green said that he knew that some of the Lakers didn't get along, either, and that good teams can overcome that. I told him that I didn't want a situation like that. I would rather lose in Eastern Conference finals as a team together than win the NBA title with dissension. That's just the way I am. It's the foundation upon which my coaching philosophy is based."

In the last few weeks of the regular season Pitino's offensive philosophy began to be questioned more and more, particularly by Steve Pate in the New York *Post*. While running and three-pointers were all fine and dandy during the regular season, he noted the Knicks lacked a good halfcourt offense, a liability that would haunt them in the playoffs. Pitino not only felt the criticism was unfounded, he also felt that it had been leaked from Bianchi.

"We run the same plays everyone else does," Pitino said. "We have weaknesses, and one of the things any coach does is to camouflage those weaknesses and accentuate the positives. If you asked me the two things we have to work on next year, it would be a better halfcourt defense and a better halfcourt offense. For instance, we are not a good passing team. Everyone says we never pass the ball to Kiki. Well, I can show you tapes where we often miss Gerald and Johnny when they are open too. But no one mentions that. They just mention Kiki, implying that it's intentional."

"Al went to probably five practices in two years. And it's in practices, not games, where you can see the deficiencies. The obvious fan can go to the games and see what's wrong. Experts have to watch practices to know why. But what I came to learn is that Al Bianchi never wanted to like the style of play."

Some of the New York media also kept insisting that all the ingredients were there for a championship team. They seemed not to know that only sixteen months before this had been a team stuck in a quagmire of ineptitude. Or that it was still only the second year of what only a year earlier was perceived to be a long-range rebuilding program. No one remembers how far this team had come in such a short time. "We have some writers this year who weren't around last year and don't know what it was like," said Pitino. "They keep talking about what good guys we have, but they never understand the amount of work that went into making them good as a team. They weren't here for that."

When the regular season ended in April, the Knicks truly

had had a memorable season. They won over 50 games for the first time in eight years. They won the Atlantic Division for the first time in 18 years. They were the only team to sweep the Pistons, going 4–0 against the team that eventually won the championship. In NBA history, only nine teams have improved by 10 games two years in a row. The Knicks are now one of them.

The first playoff series was against the Philadelphia 76ers. Pitino felt good about the playoffs, seeing his club turn it around in the last week and become focused again. The first two games were played in the Garden. The Knicks won the first when Jackson threw in a three-point prayer. In a sense it was a shot that would come back to haunt them later, when Jackson would take a similar shot in the dying seconds of the first game of the Chicago series, resulting in an airball.

The Knicks won the second game with an unbelievable comeback, 107–106. Down 10 with just over two minutes to play, Mark Jackson, who had been held to six points, came back with a three-pointer, a free throw, and jumper to make it 106–102 with 50 seconds to go. Gerald Wilkins then stole the ball and hit a baseline jumper, cutting the lead to two. The Knicks then prevented the Sixers from crossing the halfcourt in the allotted 10 seconds, and got the ball back once again, setting up Tucker's game-winner.

"I was watching a baseball game on TV in the locker room before the game, and Rick came in and told me he dreamed I hit a game-winning three-pointer," said Tucker afterward.

Pitino confirmed the story. "I couldn't sleep and then had this bad nightmare about two-thirty in the morning, in which Charles Barkley made a three-point play to win the game. I woke up and said, 'Hey, I better have another dream.' So then I dreamt that Trent had a three-point shot to win us the game."

They closed out the series in the Spectrum in Philadelphia, 116–115, when Gerald Wilkins hit an 18-foot jumper with six seconds to play in overtime. Afterward, several of the Knicks took a broom and pretended to sweep the court. This obvious symbolic swipe at the Sixers was criticized afterward. Pitino chalked it up to "youthful exuberance."

Their next opponent was the Chicago Bulls, upset winner over the Cleveland Cavaliers when the wondrous Michael Jordan, who averaged 39.8 in five playoff games, hit a miraculous shot at the buzzer of the deciding contest. The Bulls' win assured the Knicks of the home-court advantage of this best-of-seven series, something they wouldn't have had with Cleveland.

In the first game the Knicks held Jordan to only 12 shots in regulation, 15 below his average, and with a 12-point lead in the fourth quarter appeared to be in control of the game. With 3:42 remaining, the Knicks still led by eight, but the Bulls scored eight straight points as the Knicks self-destructed. Even then they had a chance to salvage the game in the closing seconds, but an ill-advised three-point attempt by Mark Jackson in the dying seconds missed, and the game went into overtime. From there things fell apart. Jordan pulled out the stops, the Bulls scored the final 11 points and won, 120–109. The Knicks home-court advantage was over.

The Knickerbockers came back in the second game to even the series at one apiece with an impressive performance, winning 114–97. Ewing led the way with 23, Jackson added 20, and Vandeweghe came off the bench for 18, a page from the script the Knicks had envisioned when they had acquired him. More important, they held Jordan to a season-low 15 points.

"Our defense played Michael as well as he can be played," Pitino said.

The series shifted to Chicago Stadium, where the Knicks got stomped, 111–88. Jordan scored 40, with 15 rebounds and nine assists, then limped off with a recurrence of a groin injury. Pitino said afterward he was confident the Knicks could come back and shoot better than 38 percent, then added that the only consolation was that maybe Jordan would be a little fatigued for the fourth game, scheduled for the next afternoon.

He wasn't. He went for 47 points and led the Bulls to a 106–93 win. Bill Cartwright, the ex-Knick, also had a big afternoon, scoring 19 of his 21 points in the first half and generally outplaying Ewing, the man he had played against in practice for the past three years. "We knew we were in trouble when we heard Michael was hurt," Pitino said. "He came to New York once with an upset stomach and scored 47 points."

The series then shifted back to the Garden, the Knicks one game from being eliminated. Ewing came through with 32 points and the Knicks stayed alive, trying to become only the fifth team in NBA history to come back after trailing 3–1 in a series.

The sixth game was scheduled for the Chicago Stadium. Beforehand, however, Pitino responded to a public statement by C. M. Newton that he would approach Pitino as soon as the Knicks ended their season. It was the first time anybody at Kentucky had publicly said Pitino was their choice to be their new coach. "Right now I'm not thinking about anything except the playoffs," Rick said. "We are trying to get to the championship round in the Eastern Division, and that is the only thing I am concerned about."

Would he be interested in Kentucky after his season ends?

"I'm not sure," he said. "I know very little about Kentucky. I was there when Villanova beat Georgetown for the national title in 1985, and I once did a clinic there when Kenny Walker was a senior, but I was only there for a few hours. So I don't really know a lot about it. It's something I will investigate when the season ends."

Pitino's interest in Kentucky was not surprising. Sure, the Knicks had been a dream job, coaching the team he had rooted for as a kid growing up in New York. But he missed college basketball more than he ever thought he would. He missed the players always being around, missed all the hours spent in the gym helping kids improve their games. He couldn't do this in the pros. There are too many games. The players practice, then leave for the day. They have their own lives, not like in college when the players' lives so often revolve around the gym and the players' lounge.

So even as the Knicks made their remarkable turnaround last year, Pitino reached the conclusion that he had made the wrong choice. If the Knicks had given him more than two days to make up his mind, he never would have left Providence.

And now legendary Kentucky was wooing him. Kentucky, one of the great names in the history of college basketball, with a tradition as rich as the horse country that surrounds Lexington, complete with a 23,000-seat arena, and Adolph Rupp, the old Baron of the Bluegrass himself, staring down from the heavens. Even more attractive to Pitino was the fact that this was to be another resurrection job, the kind he had made his reputation on. If it was now a program in disgrace, complete with a recruiting scandal, it also was one with tremendous potential.

One night he and Joanne had gone out in New York with P. J. Carlesimo, the Seton Hall coach wooed by Kentucky, only to drop out at the last minute. "P. J. said he had loved it, and thought it would be a great place to live. The only reason he backed out was he liked his job at Seton Hall and liked being in the Big East Conference. But he said if I didn't like my job, I should go to Kentucky because there was no reason not to."

On the day of the sixth game between the Knicks and the Bulls, the NCAA announced it had put Kentucky on probation for three years and banned them from appearing in the NCAA Tournament for the next two years due to recruiting and academic rules violations. The Wildcats also were banned from appearing on television the following year and limited to three scholarships for the next two years. The NCAA also said it would have been justified in shutting down the entire program for a year.

The sixth game was another big night for Jordan. He scored 40 points, including eight free throws in the last 1:18, as the Bulls hung on to eliminate the Knicks 113–111.

The Knicks season was over.

Not to mention the Rick Pitino era. But no one knew that yet.

Bianchi gave Pitino permission to go to Kentucky, and the following Monday he and Joanne flew by University of Kentucky jet to Lexington. The first day he was shown the community, hidden from the hordes of media who were searching for him. Right away he was impressed, not only with the physical facilities, the lifestyle in Lexington, the potential of Kentucky basketball to be a perennial Top 10 program, but also with the obvious obsession the people in the state have with Kentucky basketball.

"I thought I was a basketball junkie, but I've never seen anything like the enthusiasm here. Take the enthusiasm that surrounds Providence College basketball and multiply it by ten," he told a friend while there. "I'm impressed with everything about it, and I know it would be great for the family. But thinking about moving so soon is difficult."

Also in Lexington, on the Pitino watch for the New York *Daily News*, was Fred Kerber. "It's obvious down here now how badly they want Rick Pitino," Kerber said. "Every place you go, there are people looking for him. Every hotel has a TV truck parked out in front, just waiting. Camera crews are tripping over each other all over town. If he wants to be loved and adored, this is the place."

C. M. Newton said Pitino fit his description of the ideal new Wildcat coach. "This guy can really coach," he said. "He can motivate. He can teach. He has discipline in his program. He does all those things that I think are important in a basketball coach."

The first night of his stay, though, Pitino was having

dinner with Newton in a local restaurant when Jerry Tipton, a sportswriter for the *Lexington Herald-Leader*, approached the table and showed Pitino a copy of a story. It stated that while a graduate assistant at Hawaii in 1974–75 he had been cited for eight NCAA violations—ranging from arranging free flights for players to helping players receive free meals at McDonald's. Pitino replied that he only had been a grad assistant at the time and had had nothing to do with the violations. (They eventually led to the resignation of both the Hawaii head coach and athletic director.) He said later that the allegations were not new. The athletic directors at both Boston University and Providence had been aware of them before they hired him.

That same day Newton said at a morning press conference, "I have absolutely no question about Rick Pitino's integrity. And had we had any, he would not have been invited to the campus." But after the news conference Newton admitted that because of the Hawaii allegations he did not feel as strongly about Pitino as he had the day before.

Later in the day a source told *Newsday* that Newton had made a phone call to the NCAA to "doublecheck" Pitino's standing with the NCAA. Then he said Pitino had gotten "a clean bill of health from the NCAA, and the job is his if he wants it."

In a press conference the next morning, Pitino said, "There is no one in the business with more integrity than I have. The one thing you won't have to worry about is cheating. And it didn't happen in Hawaii, as far as I was concerned. I've made mistakes before, but Hawaii was not one of them. If there's any doubt about the character of Rick Pitino, don't hire him. Forget him."

Soon after, a Hawaii district attorney sent Newton a letter saying Pitino had had nothing to do with the allegations, that it had been guilt by association.

Rick and Joanne flew back on Thursday, three days after arriving. When he left, he had officially been offered a reported six-million, seven-year contract. He went back to New York to think it over. After all, he still had three years left on his Knicks contract.

"I've learned from experience that the best thing to do is go back and think about it and not get carried away," he said. "I'm going to spend some time with my family over the weekend thinking about it."

All the while many New York writers were lining up to take shots at him. He was called everything from another coaching gypsy, à la Larry Brown, to just another sweet-talking salesman who comes to town saying all the right things, then leaves a trail of empty promises, always on the way to the next job. For over a week he dominated the sports pages of the three New York tabloids.

The Pitino Watch continued over the long Memorial Day weekend.

Knicks spokesman Dennis D'Agostino said the Knicks had had no contact with Pitino after he returned from Lexington, and that the Knicks had no idea what he was going to do. Pitino publicly said he hadn't yet made up his mind, and though that was true, he certainly was in favor of going to Kentucky. The Knicks' cause wasn't helped any when they announced over the weekend that they had changed their minds and now wanted compensation if Pitino left his contract and accepted the Kentucky job. Specifically, they wanted Kentucky to pay for their search for a new coach. C. M. Newton said he wouldn't pay, but Pitino said he would pay the Knicks himself if it came to that.

Yet he was in no rush to announce his final decision, even if he already had arrived at one. He had done that two years ago and had come to regret it. He also was not looking forward to moving Joanne and his three young sons so soon. They already had moved twice in four years.

"This is a career decision and I want to make sure it's the right one," he said. "I don't want this to be another of those bing-bang things. It's difficult uprooting your family. I want the decision to be the best one for my family. It's different moving from Providence to New York than it is moving from New York to Kentucky. It's not only a more difficult move, it's subjecting your family to a totally different lifestyle."

A few days later he made up his mind. It was going to be Kentucky. The only obstacle left was one last meeting with Knick management. Pitino said the meeting with Knick officials was not a smokescreen for him to renegotiate his Knick contract, for money wasn't the issue. He met with them on May 30 at the Garden, and when the meeting was over it was all but official.

"I wish it could have lasted longer with the Knicks," Pitino told the media afterward, "but you have to know who you are and I am a college basketball coach. This is where my heart is, and I think it's best for everyone concerned."

Bianchi was later asked if there had been any attempt to keep Pitino in New York. "No, that was not the purpose of the meeting. He wasn't interested in that." Bianchi also said he wasn't bitter or upset, adding that he was well aware of Pitino's desire to return to college coaching. He did add, however, "In spite of what people say, I didn't plan on a coaching change after two years."

Two days later Pitino was introduced at a press conference in Lexington. Accompanied by Joanne, he walked into a conference room on the University of Kentucky campus that had 15 camera crews and the 22-member university athletic board. Dressed in a gray suit, his dark hair neatly in place, he still looked young enough to pass for a postgraduate doctoral student. He said, in his unmistakable New York accent, "We missed the college community and dealing with young people. Every day for the past two years we've looked back and missed Providence. I almost went back there last year. We're New Yorkers and the New York Knicks are a class organization that will win a championship, but emotionally and physically I needed to get back to college.

"We may speak differently, but I believe people are people wherever you go and we're all the same. We wanted stability and roots. I want my children to go through the same grammar school and high school, something I didn't have. I hope that Kentucky basketball and the city of Lexington will be part of our lives for a long time."

He also gave the press conference a sneak preview of his motivational skills. The setting was Lexington, Kentucky, but it just as easily could have been Boston, or Providence, or New York. He talked about winning, and doing it quicker than anyone thinks possible. And yes, even words about one day cutting down the nets and advancing to the Final Four.

Perhaps Rick Pitino is at his best when he enters a downtrodden situation as the advance man for a dream. It's then he's at his motivational best, juicing everyone up to believe as he believes, a basketball version of a tent evangelist.

"I don't want people here thinking of coal and horses, but of Kentucky basketball tickets," he said. "I want them to be the most precious thing in life someday."

Rick Pitino and the Knicks were officially in the past tense.

Everyone always tells you not to look back, but for the past two years that's all I've done. It's been a tumultuous two years for me. We were very successful on the court, but I wasn't very happy personally. I wanted to get back to college basketball.

I'm glad I had the opportunity to coach Patrick Ewing and Mark Jackson. I'm glad I had the opportunity to coach in the pros. And I'm glad I was a part of bringing pro basketball back in New York. That's something that I'll always feel good about. But I was never really happy there. The difference is I know that Kentucky wants me. That makes all the difference. If you don't get the love of the people who you are working for, what's the point? Everyone has to be in it together.

I think Kentucky is going to be the greatest challenge of my coaching career. It's going to take at least three years because of the sanctions, but I think I've had enough expo-

sure to last me the rest of my life. What I'm after now is happiness for me and my family. A few weeks ago I had a reunion in New York for some of my former players from Boston University and Providence. It was a great night, and driving home afterward, I realized that those are relationships that last a lifetime. That is what I've missed the last two years. And I know that I'll have that experience again in Kentucky.

For two straight years I've been looking back every day, but I don't think now that I will ever look back at New York.

Statistics for the 1987–88
New York Knickerbockers Season

Roster

NO.	PLAYER	POS.	HT.	WT.	BIRTHDATE	COLLEGE
3	Rick Carlisle	G	6-5	210	10-27-59	Virginia, '84
25	Bill Cartwright	C	7-1	245	7-30-57	San Francisco, '79
42	Pat Cummings	F-C	6-9	230	7-11-56	Cincinnatti, '79
33	Patrick Ewing	C	7-0	240	8-05-62	Georgetown, '85
44	Sidney Green	F	6-9	220	1-04-61	UNLV, '83
13	Mark Jackson	G	6-3	205	4-01-65	St. John's, '87
4	Johnny Newman	G-F	6-7	190	11-28-63	Richmond, '86
55	Louis Orr	F	6-9	200	5-07-58	Syracuse, '80
11	Sedric Toney	G	6-2	178	4-13-62	Dayton, '84
6	Trent Tucker	F-G	6-5	190	12-20-59	Minnesota, '82
34	Kenny Walker	F	6-8	217	8-18-64	Kentucky, '86
21	Gerald Wilkins	G	6-6	195	9-11-63	Tenn.-Chattanooga, '85

HEAD COACH—Rick Pitino (Univ. Mass., '74)
ASSISTANT COACH—Stu Jackson (Seattle Univ., '78)
ASSISTANT COACH—Jim O'Brien (St. Joseph's, '74)
ASSISTANT COACH—Brendan Malone (Iona College, '62)
TRAINER—Mike Saunders (New York Univ., '77)

NUMERICAL ROSTER

3-Rick Carlisle
4-Johnny Newman
6-Trent Tucker
11-Sedric Toney
13-Mark Jackson
21-Gerald Wilkins

25-Bill Cartwright
33-Patrick Ewing
34-Kenny Walker
42-Pat Cummings
44-Sidney Green
55-Louis Orr

Rick Carlisle—3

Signed to a one-year contract as a free agent on November 30 . . . Was waived by Boston Celtics in training camp . . . Played six games with the Albany Patroons of the CBA, averaging 17.3 ppg before signing with the Knicks.

Made his Knickerbocker debut a memorable one, pouring in a career-high 21 points December 1 vs. Seattle . . . Shot 9–12 from the field that night, adding six assists, two steals, and two rebounds in 34 minutes.

Rick averaged 2.8 points, 1.2 assists, and 7.8 minutes in 26 games off the bench this season . . . Career high scoring average . . . Shot .433 this season (29–67 FGA) . . . Hit on 6–17 from three-point range, good for 35 percent . . . Was a DNP (CD) 31 times this season.

Placed on the injured list with a strained groin muscle on March 2, and was activated on March 27.

Following his career-best 21 points, his best scoring total was 10 at Detroit on December 12 (4–7 FGA) . . . Was scoreless in seven of last eight games played . . . His 34 minutes in first game as a Knick was season high.

Only Knick player who owns an NBA Championship ring, earning one as member of 1985–86 world champion Boston Celtics . . . Averaged 1.9 points in 10 playoff games that year for Boston . . . Injuries kept him out of playoffs in two other years with Celtics, including last season.

NBA RECORD

Sea.-Team	G	MIN	FGA	FGM	PCT	FTA	FTM	PCT	OFF	DEF	REB	AST	PF	DQ	STL	BS	PTS	AVG
84-85—Bos.	38	179	67	26	.388	17	15	.882	8	13	21	25	21	0	3	0	67	1.8
85-86—Bos.	77	760	189	92	.487	23	15	.652	22	55	77	104	92	1	19	4	199	2.6
86-87—Bos.	42	297	92	30	.326	20	15	.750	8	22	30	35	28	0	8	0	80	1.9
87-88—NY	26	204	67	29	.433	11	10	.909	6	7	13	32	39	1	11	4	74	2.8
Totals	183	1440	415	177	.427	71	55	.775	44	97	141	196	180	2	41	8	440	2.4

Three-Point
Field Goals: 1984-85, 0-for-2 (.000); 1985-86, 0-for-10 (.000); 1986-87, 5-for-16 (.313). 1987-88: 6-17 (.353). Totals: 11-45 (.244).

PLAYOFFS

Sea.-Team	G	MIN	FGA	FGM	PCT	FTA	FTM	PCT	OFF	DEF	REB	AST	PF	DQ	ST	BS	PTS	AVG
84-85—Bos						ON INJURED LIST												
85-86—Bos.	10	54	15	8	.533	4	3	.750	3	2	5	8	9	0	2	0	19	1.9
86-87—Bos.						ON INJURED LIST												
87-88—NY	2	8	4	1	.250	2	0	.000	1	1	2	0	1	0	0	0	2	1.0
Totals	12	62	19	9	.473	6	3	.500	4	3	7	8	10	0	2	0	21	1.8

Three-Point
Field Goals   Totals 0-for-0 (000).

Bill Cartwright—25

Big Bill enjoyed one of the most rewarding seasons of his nine-year pro career . . . Stayed injury-free, playing in all 82 regular-season games for the first time since 1982–83 . . . Averaged 11.1 points, 4.7 rebounds and 20.4 minutes this season.

A .553 career shooter prior to this season, Bill shot .544 in this campaign, his best mark since 1983–84 (.561) . . . Scored 914 points this year, the first time he missed the 1,000 plateau during an injury-free campaign . . . Scored his 9,000th career point in the season finale at Indiana on April 23 as the Knicks vaulted into the playoffs.

Climbed several all-time Knickerbocker career lists this season . . . Has now played in 537 games to rank eighth all-time for New York (Earl Monroe is seventh with 596) . . . Finished the regular season with 9,006 points, also eighth all-time in club annals (Senator Bill Bradley is seventh with 9,217) . . . His 16,791 minutes played once again is good for the eighth in Knicks history (Earl the Pearl is again seventh with 17,552).

Had six 20+ point games this season . . . Posted three double-doubles, those being his only three double-figure board efforts of the campaign . . . Knickerbocker scoring leader in three games, and led the team in rebounding on nine occasions.

Twice honored as the Sharp Electronics Knick Sharpshooter of the Month, taking laurels in December and February . . . Shot .556 (60–108) in December and at a .613 clip (38–62) in February.

Started in only four games this season . . . First starting assignment on December 26 in Atlanta, and he responded with club-high 21 points (7–10 FGA) and six rebounds against the Hawks . . . Final start of the season came on April 15 against the Bullets at the Garden, with just two points (1–1 FGA) and three caroms in 13 minutes.

Season scoring high 23 points twice in back-to-back games in mid-December . . . On December 8 he tallied 23 points on 7-for-12 shooting in 24 minutes . . . Just two nights later again scored 23 once again on 8–10 FGA in 21 minutes against Denver.

Rebound high this season was 11 at Seattle on January 20 . . . Season-high 36 minutes against the Cavs on February 13, pouring in 20 points (8–9 FGA) with six rebounds . . . Knicks senior player in terms of continuous service. . . . Bill, Louis Orr, and Trent Tucker are lone holdovers from previous Knicks playoff squad in '84.

NBA RECORD

Sea.-Team	G	MIN	FGA	FGM	PCT	FTA	FTM	PCT	OFF	DEF	REB	AST	PF	DQ	ST	BS	PTS	AVG
79-80—NY	82	3150	1215	665	.547	566	451	.797	194	532	726	165	279	2	48	101	1781	21.7
80-81—NY	82	2925	1118	619	.554	518	408	.788	161	452	613	111	259	2	48	83	1646	20.1
81-82—NY	72	2060	694	390	.562	337	257	.763	116	305	421	87	208	2	48	65	1037	14.4
82-83—NY	82	2468	804	455	.566	511	380	.744	185	405	590	136	315	7	41	127	1290	15.7
83-84—NY	77	2487	808	453	.561	502	404	.805	195	454	649	107	262	4	44	97	1310	17.0
84-85—		DNP, Injured																
85-86—NY	2	36	7	3	.429	10	6	.600	2	8	10	5	6	0	1	1	12	6.0
86-87—NY	58	1989	631	335	.531	438	346	.790	132	313	445	96	188	2	40	26	1016	17.5
87-88—NY	82	1676	528	287	.544	426	340	.798	127	257	384	85	234	4	43	43	914	11.1
Totals	537	16,791	5805	3207	.552	3308	2592	.783	1112	2753	3838	792	1751	23	313	543	9006	16.8

Three-point
goals: 1980-81, 0-1: 1983-84, 0-1. Totals 0-2.

PLAYOFFS

Sea.-Team	G	MIN	FGA	FGM	PCT	FTA	FTM	PCT	OFF	DEF	REB	AST	PF	DQ	STL	BS	PTS	AVG
80-81—NY	2	49	17	6	.353	12	8	.667	4	9	13	1	7	0	1	1	20	10.0
82-83—NY	6	172	43	25	.581	22	17	.773	9	25	34	4	25	0	3	7	67	11.2
83-84—NY	12	398	126	70	.556	80	69	.863	27	72	99	5	44	0	2	14	209	17.4
87-88—NY	4	76	18	9	.500	15	10	.733	8	11	19	6	12	0	8	3	29	7.3
Totals...	24	695	204	110	.539	129	104	.806	48	117	165	16	88	0	14	25	325	13.5

ALL-STAR

Sea.-Site	MIN	FGA	FGM	PCT	FTA	FTM	PCT	OFF	DEF	REB	AST	PF	DQ	STL	BS	PTS	AVG
1980—NY	14	8	4	.500	0	0	.000	1	2	3	1	1	0	0	0	8	8.0

Pat Cummings—42

Played in 62 games this season, most since he appeared in 63 in his first season as a Knick in 1984–85 . . . Pat averaged 5.5 points, 3.8 rebounds, and 15.3 minutes this season . . . Logged 946 minutes, first time he missed the 1,000 mark since his rookie season in 1979–80 with Milwaukee . . . Career .499 shooter coming into season, Pat hit on .456 from the field this year.

Started in nine games, including the first four games of the season . . . Season-high 17 points on 6–11 shooting in season opener on November 6 at Detroit . . . Made final start of season on December 23 vs. Chicago, going scoreless with one rebound in 10 minutes.

Posted seven double-figure point games . . . His lone double-figure rebound effort was his season-high and club-high 16 boards against the Nets on December 19, falling just four rebounds short of career-high 20 (for Dallas in March '83).

Placed on injured list on March 13 with sprained right ankle . . . Activated on March 23.

DNP (CD) in seven of 16 games upon return, but played major role in Knickerbockers' key win at Atlanta on April 16, coming off the bench for 10 points (4–8 FGA) and eight rebounds in 19 minutes.

Has most playoff experience of any Knick, averaging 5.7 points in 27 playoff contests . . . Appeared in 1980, '81, and '82 playoffs with Milwaukee and in 1984 with Dallas.

NBA RECORD

Sea.-Team	G	MIN	FGA	FGM	PCT	FTA	FTM	PCT	OFF	DEF	REB	AST	PF	DQ	ST	BS	PTS	AVG
79-80—Mil	71	900	370	187	.505	123	94	.764	81	157	238	53	141	0	22	17	468	6.6
80-81—Mil	74	1084	460	248	.539	140	99	.707	97	195	292	62	192	4	31	19	595	8.0
81-82—Mil	78	1132	430	219	.509	91	67	.736	61	184	245	99	227	6	22	8	505	6.5
82-83—Dal	81	2317	878	433	.493	196	148	.755	225	443	668	144	296	9	57	35	1014	12.5
83-84—Dal	80	2492	915	452	.494	190	141	.742	151	507	658	158	282	2	64	23	1045	13.1
84-85—NY	63	2069	797	410	.514	227	177	.780	139	379	518	109	247	6	50	17	997	15.8
85-86—NY	31	1007	408	195	.478	139	97	.698	92	188	280	47	136	7	27	12	487	15.7
86-87—NY	49	1056	382	172	.450	110	79	.718	123	189	312	38	145	2	26	7	423	8.6
87-88—NY	62	946	307	140	.456	80	59	.738	82	153	235	37	143	0	20	10	339	5.5
Totals	589	13,003	4947	2456	.496	1296	917	.708	1051	2395	3446	747	424	9	319	148	5873	10.0

Three-point
goals: 1980-81, 0-2; 1981-82. 0-2; 1982-83, 0-1; 1983-84, 0-2; 1984-85, 0-4; 1985-86, 0-2. 1987-88; 0-1. Totals 0-14.

PLAYOFFS

Sea.-Team	G	MIN	FGA	FGM	PCT	FTA	FTM	PCT	OFF	DEF	REB	AST	PF	DQ	STL	BS	PTS	AVG
79-80—Milw	6	57	17	11	.647	6	5	.833	4	12	16	2	9	0	1	0	27	4.5
80-81—Milw	5	25	11	3	.273	4	3	.750	3	3	6	0	2	0	1	0	9	1.8
81-82—Milw	6	44	11	4	.364	2	1	.500	3	8	11	2	7	0	0	2	9	1.5
83-84—Dallas	10	300	115	47	.409	15	14	.933	26	46	72	15	30	0	4	2	108	10.8
87-88—NY	3	28	5	2	.400	4	3	.750	2	5	7	3	11	0	0	0	7	23
Totals	30	454	159	67	.421	31	26	.839	38	74	112	22	59	0	6	4	160	5.3

Patrick Ewing—33

Emerged as a force to be reckoned with this season, particularly down the stretch when Patrick was a dominant force . . . During the finest season of his three-year pro career, Ewing established career highs in games played (82), minutes (2,546), rebounds (676), field goal percentage (.555), points (1,653), and established a club record with 245 blocked shots . . . Ranked among the NBA leaders in scoring average, field goal percentage, and blocks . . . Selected to the NBA All-Star game (in Chicago) for second time in three years.

Season averages: 20.2 points, 8.2 rebounds, 2.99 blocks, and 31.0 minutes (he averaged 35.2 minutes in his two prior seasons) . . . Started in all 82 regular season games, and posted double-figure scoring in all but one (eight points at Atlanta on March 11).

Registered 27 double-doubles (points-rebounds) on the season (had 22 last year) . . . Paced Knickerbockers in scoring 31 times; led in rebounds on 37 occasions . . . Posted 40 20+ point games, five 30+ point games, and a pair of 40+ point games.

In the All-Star Game at Chicago Stadium, he posted nine points and six rebounds . . . Named to the All-Star team for the second time, but it was his first game appearance (injury prevented him from appearing in the 1986 game).

Patrick's 245 blocks broke his own club record of 147 set in 1986–87 . . . Had seven games with at least six blocked shots.

His two 40+ point games came within six days of each other . . . Recorded 42 points (16–20 FGA), the high performance for a Knick this season, on April 8 at Chicago . . . Also went 10–13 from the line in that game, as he fell one point shy of his career high (43 points against Atlanta on December 13, 1986) . . . Then on April 13 against Indiana at the Garden, he poured in 41 points (18–24 FGA) in just 26 minutes to lead the Knicks to victory.

Established a career high with 21 rebounds against Philadelphia on January 16 . . . His previous best was 20 rebounds against New Jersey at the Garden on December 12, 1985.

Established another career high with a pair of eight-block games . . . Recorded eight blocked shots on January 23 against the Kings and again on April 15 against the Bullets . . . Fell just two blocks shy each time of Joe C. Meriweather's club mark of 10 blocked shots vs. Atlanta in 1979.

Had a season full of honors . . . Besides being named to the league All-Star squad, Patrick was also named Met Life

Knick of the Month for November and Sharp Electronics Knicks Sharpshooter of the Month for November.

Spearheaded the Knicks' drive for the playoffs as he put together perhaps the best sustained stretch of his career in the season's final weeks . . . He shot at least 50 percent from the field in each of the season's last 22 games, shooting .623 (210–337 FGA) in that span . . . Raised his overall shooting percentage in that stretch from .527 to its final .555 . . . He averaged 25.9 points (285) in the year's final 11 contests . . . Led the Knicks in scoring seven times in the last 11 games, with four games of at least 36 points . . . And over the final 13 games of the season, he pulled down an average of 9.6 rebounds (125), with nine double-figure rebound games in the last 13.

NBA RECORD

Sea.-Team	G	MIN	FGA	FGM	PCT	FTA	FTM	PCT	OFF	DEF	REB	AST	PF	DQ	STL	BS	PTS	AVG
85-85—NY	50	1771	814	386	.474	306	226	.739	124	327	451	102	191	7	54	103	998	20.0
86-87—NY	63	2206	1053	530	.503	415	296	.713	157	398	555	104	248	5	89	147	1356	21.5
87-88—NY	82	2546	1183	656	.555	476	341	.716	245	431	676	125	332	5	104	245	1653	20.2
Totals . . .	195	6433	3050	1572	.515	1197	863	.721	526	1156	1682	331	771	17	247	495	4007	20.5

Three-point
goals: 1985-86, 0-5; 1986-87, 0-7. 1987-88; 0-3. Totals 0-15.

PLAYOFFS

	G	MIN	FGA	FGM	PCT	FTA	FTM	PCT	OFF	DEF	REB	AST	PF	DQ	STL	BS	PTS	AVG
87-88—NY	4	153	57	28	.491	22	19	.864	16	35	51	10	17	0	6	11	75	18.8
Totals . . .	4	153	57	28	.491	22	19	.864	16	35	51	10	17	0	6	11	75	18.8

ALL-STAR

Sea.-Site	MIN	FGA	FGM	PCT	FTA	FTM	PCT	OFF	DEF	REB	AST	PF	DQ	STL	BS	PTS	AVG
1986—Dallas					(INJURED-DID NOT PLAY)												
1988—Chicago	16	8	4	.500	1	1	1.000	1	5	6	0	1	0	0	1	9	9.0

Sidney Green—44

Acquired by Knickerbockers from Detroit for Ron Moore and a second-round pick on October 28 . . . Was club's second leading rebounder this season behind Patrick Ewing, helping to shore up team's rebounding efforts.

Played in all 82 games this season, a career high . . . Averaged 7.8 points, 7.8 rebounds and 25.0 minutes this season . . . Shot .441 from the field (a .460 career shooter coming into the season), although Sid showed a soft touch facing the basket. Started in 65 games.

Led Knicks in rebounds 33 times this season . . . Posted 12 double-doubles and 21 double-figure rebound games.

Sid's single-game rebound high this season was 18 caroms, pulled down twice . . . Grabbed 18 boards on January 5 against Phoenix, and again on February 4 against his former Piston mates . . . Each time fell five rebounds short of his career high, 23, established with Detroit vs. Milwaukee on December 30, 1986 . . . Had 10 games with at least 12 rebounds.

Scored season-high 20 points (8–11 FGA) vs. Boston on January 9 at the Garden . . . Had 18 points (9–14 FGA) against the Kings on February 18 . . . Posted 25 double-figure scoring efforts this season.

Another Knick who contributed mightily to playoff drive . . . Led the Knicks in rebounds in five of season's last 10 games . . . Averaged 8.4 rebounds (84) in that span, with four double-figure rebound games . . . Started in eight of the season's last nine.

NBA RECORD

Sea.-Team	G	MIN	FGA	FGM	PCT	FTA	FTM	PCT	OFF	DEF	REB	AST	PF	DQ	STL	BS	PTS	AVG
83-84—Chicago	49	667	228	100	.439	77	55	.714	58	116	174	25	128	1	18	17	255	5.2
84-85—Chicago	48	740	250	108	.432	98	79	.806	72	174	246	29	102	0	11	11	295	6.1
85-86—Chicago	80	2307	875	407	.465	335	262	.782	208	450	658	139	292	5	70	37	1076	13.5
86-87—Detroit	80	1792	542	256	.472	177	119	.672	196	457	653	62	197	0	41	50	631	7.9
87-88—NY	82	2049	585	258	.441	190	126	.663	221	421	642	93	318	9	65	32	642	7.8
Totals	339	7555	2480	1129	.455	877	641	.731	755	1618	2373	348	1037	15	205	147	2899	8.6

Three-point
goals: 1984-85, 0-for-4, 1985-86, 0-for-8, 1986-87, 0-for-2, 1987-88 0-2. Totals:0-16.

PLAYOFFS

Sea.-Team	G	MIN	FGA	FGM	PCT	FTA	FTM	PCT	OFF	DEF	REB	AST	PF	DQ	ST	BS	PTS	AVG
84-85—Chicago	3	54	24	12	.500	11	7	.636	10	5	15	2	8	0	0	1	31	10.3
85-86—Chicago	3	53	20	6	.300	12	6	.500	7	5	12	0	9	0	1	1	18	6.0
86-87—Detroit	9	42	10	6	.600	6	5	.833	3	6	9	1	2	0	1	2	17	1.9
87-88—NY	4	93	17	8	.471	0	0	.000	8	25	33	7	14	0	9	1	16	4.0
Totals......	19	242	71	32	.450	29	18	.621	28	41	69	10	33	0	11	5	82	4.3

Mark Jackson—13

The Knickerbockers' floor general, Mark Jackson, has taken the NBA by storm this season, winning NBA Rookie of the Year honors while enjoying one of the finest rookie seasons in the franchise's 42-year history . . . Swiped Rookie of the Month in November, December, and February with classic, precision passing . . . Selected Met Life Knick of the Year award, the team MVP, in ballot of media covering Knicks . . . Had collared monthly honors three straight months.

Dished out 868 assists for an NBA rookie record, knocking the legendary Oscar Robertson (690 in 1960–61) from the books . . . Averaged 10.6 assists per game for another NBA rookie standard; the Big O's previous mark was 9.7 . . . His 205 steals fell just shy of NBA rookie record 211 set by Indiana's Dudley Bradley in 1979–80.

Ranked third in the NBA in assists and fifth in steals (2.52), playing with the poise of a veteran beyond his years.

His 868 assists also established a Knicks' club record (the former record was 832 by Michael Ray Richardson in 1979–80) . . . Smashed the team rookie assist mark of 386, ironically erasing Knick legend Dick McGuire, the man who selected him in the '87 draft, from the books in only his 40th game . . . Mark's 3,249 minutes played set a Knick rookie standard, the previous mark of 3,150 set by Bill Cartwright in 1979–80 . . . "Action" became only the fifth Knick rookie in in club annals to play in every game on an 82-game schedule, joining Cartwright, Larry Demic, Lonnie Shelton, and Darrell Walker.

Averages this season: 13.6 points, 10.6 assists, 2.50 steals, 4.8 rebounds, and 39.6 minutes, another category in which he ranked among NBA leaders.

Started in 80 of 82 games . . . Inserted into the starting lineup in third game of season, and remained there the rest of the way, as veteran point guards Rory Sparrow and Gerald Henderson were dealt away . . . Led New York in scoring in 11 games . . . Led or tied Knicks in assists in all but one game, February 10, when Gerald Wilkins edged him, six assists to five.

Had 11 games this season with at least 16 assists: five with 16, four with 17 and two with 18 . . . Achieved season-high 18 twice, both at Chicago (January 30 and April 8) . . . Fell three assists shy of club record 21 set by Carl Braun against St. Louis on December 12, 1958 . . . Posted 48 double-figure assists games (59 percent of club's schedule).

Poured in season-high 33 points against Bulls at the Garden on March 7 (10–20 FGA) to lead Knicks to victory . . . Had 10 games of 20+ points.

Posted a pair of triple double: 11 points, 13 assists, 10 boards on January 18 vs. Atlanta, New York's first triple double since Bernard King's on March 9, 1985 . . . Followed with April 15 three-bagger vs. Washington: 25 points, 10 assists, 10 boards.

Showed flair for the dramatic in closing seconds: Jumper at the buzzer gave New York a 98–96 win over Indiana on March 1 . . . Three nights later, his close-in shot with two seconds left tied Philadelphia, setting up 110–108 overtime victory . . . In-the-paint floater with three seconds left in Atlanta gave Knicks vital 95–93 win on April 16.

Shot .254 from three-point range, but was 13–38 from long distance (.342) in final 14 games.

Another stellar Knick performer down the stretch . . . Averaged 15.8 points in last 12 games . . . Averaged 12.7 assists (140) in final 11 contests . . . Had at least 16 assists four times in final 11 games . . . Shot .854 from the free-throw line (35–41) in last 11 contests.

COLLEGE STATISTICS

Season	G	FGM	FGA	PCT	FTM	FTA	PCT.	REB.	AST.	POINTS	AVG.
1983-84	30	61	106	.575	53	77	.688	59	108	175	5.8
1984-85	35	57	101	564	66	91	.725	44	109	180	5.1
1985-86	36	151	316	.478	105	142	.739	125	328	407	11.3
1986-87	30	196	389	.504	125	155	.806	110	193	566	18.9
Totals	131	465	912	.510	349	465	.750	338	738	1328	10.1

NBA RECORD

Sea.-Team	G	MIN	FGA	FGM	PCT	FTA	FTM	PCT	OFF	DEF	REB	AST	PF	DQ	STL	BS	PTS	AVG
87-88—NY	82	3249	1013	438	.432	266	206	.774	120	276	396	868	244	2	205	6	1114	13.6

Three-Point
Goals: 1987-88 32-126 (.254)

PLAYOFFS

	G	MIN	FGA	FGM	PCT	FTA	FTM	PCT	OFF	DEF	REB	AST	PF	DQ	STL	BS	PTS	AVG
87-88—NY	4	171	60	22	.357	11	8	.727	6	13	19	39	13	10	14	0	57	14.3
Totals.....	4	171	60	22	.357	11	8	.727	6	13	19	39	13	10	14	0	57	14.3

Johnny Newman—4

Added new dimension to Knickerbocker team—fine outside touch and strong moves to the basket—when New York signed him as free agent on November 12 . . . Outstanding pickup by GM Al Bianchi . . . Averaged 10.0 points in 77 contests . . . Shot .435 from the field this season . . . Started in 25 games.

Led Knicks in scoring eight times . . . Had nine 20+ point games.

Season marked by two memorable streaks . . . Connected on club-record 19 straight field goals, January 1–8 . . . Included in that hot string was an 11-for-11 effort at Boston on January 6, in which he paced the Knicks with 24 points . . . Had gone 5 for 5 from the field in previous game against Phoenix on January 6 . . . For his efforts was named Sharp Electronics Knick Sharpshooter of the Month for January.

Had second outstanding streak, this time from the free-throw line a month and a half later when he connected on 31 straight free throws, February 13–March 1 . . . That fell just five shy of Henry Bibby's club-record 36 straight November 10–December 15, 1973.

Established career scoring highs in steady progression . . . First, with 24 points at Boston on January 6 . . . Then scored 27 points on 9-for-12 shooting against Hawks on March 19 . . . Poured in 28 points at Dallas on March 22 before finally establishing yet another regular-season career best with 29 points (12–17 FGA) in scoring barrage to secure significant road victory vs. 76ers on April 5.

Registered career-high seven rebounds vs. San Antonio on March 21.

Another Knick who rose to the occasion during the playoff drive . . . Averaged 14.9 points (283) over season's final 19 games, including four 20+ point games . . . In final 11 games of season, J. New was 8–23 from three-point range, after going 1 for 23 in prior seven . . . Averaged 20.6 minutes on season, but 25.5 in last 13 games . . . Shared Met Life Knick of the Month for March with Trent Tucker, first co-winners in three-year history of award.

NBA RECORD

Sea.-Team	G	MIN	FGA	FGM	PCT	FTA	FTM	PCT	OFF	DEF	REB	AST	PF	DQ	STL	BS	PTS	AVG
86-87—Cleveland	59	630	275	113	.411	76	66	.868	36	34	70	27	67	0	20	7	293	5.0
87-88—NY	77	1589	620	270	.435	246	207	.841	87	72	159	62	204	5	72	11	773	10.0
Totals	136	2219	895	383	.428	322	273	.848	123	106	229	89	271	5	92	18	1066	7.84

Three point field goals: 1986–87, 1-for-22 (.045). 1987-88: 26-93 (.280). Totals: 27-115 (.235).

PLAYOFFS

Sea.-Team	G	MIN	FGA	FGM	PCT	FTA	FTM	PCT	OFF	DEF	REB	AST	PF	DQ	STL	BS	PTS	AVG
87-88—NY	4	113	68	31	.456	16	14	.875	8	3	11	7	16	0	6	1	76	19.0
Totals	4	113	68	31	.456	16	14	.875	8	3	11	7	16	0	6	1	76	19.0

Louis Orr—55

Season shortened by injury . . . Missed all of preseason and first 20 games of regular season after undergoing off-season surgery to correct herniated disc . . . Activated on December 16 . . . Scored three points in five minutes the following night against Philadelphia.

Averaged 1.4 points and 6.2 minutes in limited role in 29 games off the bench . . . Career .470 shooter shot only .320 this season . . . Career lows in virtually every category due to limited action . . . After he was activated, Lou DNP (CD) in 33 of 62 games.

Season-high five points vs. Atlanta on January 18 . . . Longest playing stint was 17 minutes at Seattle on January 20, scoring four points . . . Played 14 minutes and scored two points vs. Pacers on April 13 . . . Was a DNP (CD) in each of the season's final five games.

NBA RECORD

Sea.-Team	G	MIN	FGA	FGM	PCT	FTA	FTM	PCT	OFF	DEF	REB	AST	PF	DQ	ST	BS	PTS	AVG
80-81—Ind	82	1787	709	348	.491	202	163	.807	172	189	361	132	153	0	55	25	859	10.5
81-82—Ind	80	1951	719	357	.497	254	203	.799	127	204	331	134	182	1	56	26	918	11.5
82-83—NY	82	1666	593	274	.462	175	140	.800	94	134	228	94	134	0	64	24	688	8.4
83-84—NY	78	1640	572	262	.458	211	173	.820	101	127	228	61	142	0	66	17	697	8.9
84-85—NY	79	2452	766	372	.486	334	262	.784	171	220	391	134	195	1	100	27	1007	12.7
85-86—NY	74	2237	741	330	.445	278	218	.784	123	189	312	179	177	4	61	26	878	11.9
86-87—NY	65	1440	389	166	.427	172	125	.727	102	130	232	110	123	0	47	18	458	7.0
87-88—NY	29	180	50	16	.320	16	8	.500	13	21	34	9	27	0	6	0	40	1.4
Totals . . .	569	13,353	4539	2125	.468	1642	1292	.787	903	1214	2117	853	1133	6	455	163	5545	9.7

Three-point goals: 1980-81, 0-6; 1981-82. 1-8; 1982-83. 0-2; 1984-85. 1-10; 1985-86, 0-4; 1986-87, 1-5. 1987-88; 0-1 Totals: 3-36 (C83).

PLAYOFFS

Sea.-Team	G	MIN	FGA	FGM	PCT	FTA	FTM	PCT	OFF	DEF	REB	AST	PF	DQ	STL	BS	PTS	AVG
80-81—Atl	2	56	25	9	.360	7	6	.857	6	4	10	4	4	0	5	1	24	12.0
82-83—NY	6	105	47	18	.383	10	10	1.000	8	13	21	3	10	0	5	4	46	7.7
83-84—NY	12	229	70	29	.414	19	15	.789	22	28	50	6	32	1	4	1	73	6.1
87-88—NY	2	3	1	0	.000	2	1	.500	0	0	0	0	0	0	0	0	1	0.5
Totals	22	393	143	56	.391	38	32	.842	36	45	81	13	46	1	14	6	144	6.5

Three-point goals: 1981-82, 0-for-1. 1982-83, 1-for-5 (.200). 1983-84, 2-for-6 (.333). Totals, 3-for-12 (.250).

Sedric Toney—11

Signed to a 10-day contract as a free agent on March 13 to give Mark Jackson breather at point guard position . . .

Inked for remainder of season on March 23 . . . Averaged 2.7 points, 1.1 assists, and 6.6 minutes in 21 contests off the bench.

Sedric shot at .438 clip (21–48 FGA) as a Knickerbocker in limited action . . . Season-high point total of 11 scored against Indiana on April 13 (4–6 FGA).

Scored six points in his second game as a Knick on March 16 at Philadelphia . . . Then tallied six again in next contest, March 19, vs. Atlanta . . . Shot .533 (8-15) in his first four games.

Season-high six assists (with five points) against Houston on March 24 . . . Hit on 91 percent from free throw line (10–11).

The 26-year-old guard was born on April 13, 1962 . . . Toney played in 13 games for Atlanta and Phoenix in 1985–86 . . . Averaged 6.2 points, 2.0 assists, and 17.7 minutes that season . . . Career-scoring high 22 points for Suns vs. Rockets on April 12, 1986 . . . Had been playing AAU ball out of hometown of Dayton, Ohio, when Knicks signed him . . . Third-round draft pick (59th overall) by Atlanta in 1985 draft . . . No relation to Andrew.

NBA RECORD

Sea.-Team	G	MIN	FGA	FGM	PCT	FTA	FTM	PCT	OFF	DEF	REB	AST	PF	DQ	STL	BS	PTS	AVG
85-86—Atl-Phoe	13	230	66	28	.424	31	21	.677	3	22	25	26	24	0	6	0	80	6.2
88-88—NY	21	139	48	21	.438	11	10	.909	3	5	8	24	20	0	9	1	57	2.7
Totals	34	369	114	49	.430	42	31	.738	6	27	33	50	44	0	15	1	137	4.0

Three-point goals: 1985-86: 3-10 (.300); 1987-88: 5-14 (.357) Totals 8-24 (.333).

PLAYOFFS

	G	MIN	FGA	FGM	PCT	FTA	FTM	PCT	OFF	DEF	REB	AST	PF	DQ	STL	BS	PTS	AVG
87-88—NY	3	15	6	3	.500	2	2	1.000	0	2	2	0	1	0	2	0	11	3.7
Totals	3	15	6	3	.500	2	2	1.000	0	2	2	0	1	0	2	0	11	3.7

Trent Tucker—6

Sharpshooting three-point specialist was once again among the NBA leaders from long range . . . Shot at a .413 clip from Downtown (69-167) . . . Established a Knickerbocker club record with 69 three-point field goals in a single season, smashing his own club mark of 68 set last season.

Trent averaged 7.1 points and 17.6 minutes in 71 games this season . . . Started in only four games . . . Placed on the injured list on November 30 (sprained left knee) and activated on December 15.

Scored season-high 18 points (7–12 FGA) at New Jersey on November 19 . . . In last game before being placed on injured list, he started and scored 16 points at Cleveland on November 25.

Got off to slow start from three-point range . . . Shot only 11–38 (.289) from Downtown in his first 18 games . . . From that point on, he hit a sizzling 45 percent from long distance (58–129 FGA), hitting at least one three-point bomb in 38 of 53 games . . . Finished with the hot hand, with at least one three-pointer in each of season's last five contests, shooting 44 percent (7–16) in that span.

Trent is a .423 shooter from three-point range (227–537) during his career, the highest long-range percentage among active players . . . Participated in Long Distance Shoot Out at All Star Weekend in Chicago.

Shot 42 percent from three-point distance in March to share Met Life Knick of the Month honors with Johnny Newman . . . Overall from the field, Trent shot 46 percent (86–187) in his last 27 games.

NBA RECORD

Sea.-Team	G	MIN	FGA	FGM	PCT	FTA	FTM	PCT	OFF	DEF	REB	AST	PF	DQ	STL	BS	PTS	AVG
82–83—NY	78	1830	647	299	.462	64	43	.672	75	141	216	195	235	1	56	6	655	8.4
83–84—NY	63	1228	450	225	.500	33	25	.758	43	87	130	124	138	0	63	8	481	7.6
84–85—NY	77	1819	606	293	.483	48	38	.792	74	114	188	199	195	0	75	15	653	8.5
85–86—NY	77	1788	740	349	.472	100	79	.790	70	99	169	192	167	0	65	8	818	10.6
86–87—NY	70	1691	691	325	.470	101	77	.762	49	86	135	166	169	1	116	13	795	11.4
87–88—NY	71	1248	455	193	.424	71	51	.718	32	87	119	117	158	3	53	6	506	7.1
Totals.....	436	9604	3589	1684	.469	417	313	.751	343	614	957	1007	1048	5	428	56	3908	9.0

Three-point goals: 1982-83, 14-30 (.467); 1983-84, 6-16 (.375); 1984-85, 29-72 (.403); 1985-86, 4-91, (.451); 1986-87, 68-161 (.422). 1987-88: 69-167 (.413). Totals: 227-537 (.423).

BORN TO COACH

PLAYOFFS

Sea.-Team	G	MIN	FGA	FGM	PCT	FTA	FTM	PCT	OFF	DEF	REB	AST	PF	DQ	ST	BS	PTS	AVG
82-83—NY	6	85	15	9	.600	10	7	.700	2	7	9	5	7	0	2	0	26	4.3
83-84—NY	12	254	84	42	.500	10	6	.600	6	12	18	27	32	0	11	3	91	7.6
87-88—NY	4	71	19	8	.421	4	3	.750	0	2	2	4	4	0	1	0	25	6.3
Totals.....	22	410	118	59	.500	24	16	.666	8	21	29	36	43	0	14	3	142	6.5

Three-point goals: 1982-83, 1-for-2 (.500). 1983-84, 1-for-5 (200) Totals, 2-for-9 (.286).

Kenny (Sky) Walker—34

Sky came into his own in the second half of this season . . . Played in all 82 games this year, after logging 68 games as a rookie when he was dogged by a pulled back muscle . . . Started in 61 contests, averaging 10.1 points, 4.7 rebounds, and 26.1 minutes on the season.

Led New York in scoring seven times this season . . . Posted five 20+ points games, along with a pair of double-doubles.

Best single-game scoring effort was 25 points, registered in back-to-back games . . . rang out '87 with 25 points (10–17 FGA) on December 29 vs. Portland . . . Rang in the new year with same total on 7–12 from the field, adding four boards, against the Clippers on New Year's Day at the Garden.

Rebound high this season was 11, at Chicago on January 30 . . . Tallied 11 points in same contest.

Major contributor with steady play during Knickerbockers' late-season playoff push . . . Shot .525 (73–139 FGA) in March to earn Sharp Electronics Knick Sharpshooter of the Month . . . During the final two months of the campaign, Kenny shot .498 (114–229) to raise overall shooting percentage to .473 (from .461).

His free-throw shooting improved in the latter stages as well, hitting on a sizzling .810 clip (51–63 FTA) in his last 35 games.

Averaged 5.3 rebounds in final 15 games . . . Had three

games with at least seven boards in that span . . . Came up with biggest defensive play of the season when he stifled Steve Stipanovich on his close-in attempt in final second to preserve Knicks' playoff clinching 88–86 win in Indiana on April 23.

NBA RECORD

Sea.-Team	G	MIN	FGA	FGM	PCT	FTA	FTM	PCT	OFF	DEF	REB	AST	PF	DQ	STL	BS	PTS	AVG
86-87—NY	68	1719	581	283	.491	185	140	.757	118	220	338	75	236	7	49	49	719	10.4
87-88—NY	82	2139	728	344	.473	178	138	.775	192	197	389	86	290	5	63	59	826	10.1
Totals.....	150	3858	1309	627	.479	363	278	.766	310	417	727	161	526	12	112	108	1536	10.2

Three-point goals: 1986-87, 0-for-4 (.000). 1987-88: 0-1. Totals: 0-5 (.000).

PLAYOFFS

Sea.-Team	G	MIN	FGA	FGM	PCT	FTA	FTM	PCT	OFF	DEF	REB	AST	PF	DQ	STL	BS	PTS	AVG
87-88—NY	4	80	24	8	.333	2	2	1.000	3	6	9	5	11	0	2	3	18	4.5
Totals.....	4	80	24	8	.333	2	2	1.000	3	6	9	5	11	0	2	3	18	4.5

Gerald Wilkins—21

Was the Knickerbockers second-leading scorer during regular season behind Patrick Ewing . . . Averaged 17.4 points, 4.0 assists, and 33.4 minutes on the year.

Led the Knicks in scoring 25 times this season . . . Posted a pair of 30+ point games and 30 20+ point efforts.

Tied career-high 81 games played . . . Only contest he missed was March 22 at Dallas due to a strained back . . . Marked only the fourth game he has missed in three pro seasons.

Tallied season-high 39 points (14–28 shooting) on February 18 against Sacramento . . . That capped a superb month for Doug E. . . . In 12 games during February, he averaged 21.8 points, raising his scoring average from 16.0 to 17.3 . . . Led Knicks in scoring seven times in those 12 games and enjoyed four efforts with at least 25 points . . . Ended the month by equalling career-high nine rebounds at Denver on February 28

Led New York scoring attack five times in six-game stretch, March 21-31 . . . Averaged 20.8 points during that span and shot .509 from the field on 57–112 FGA.

Ended the season with career-high 90 steals.

Shot .302 from three-point range this season (39–129) . . . Was 11–25 (.440) from Downtown in 13-game stretch, March 12–April 8.

Three games with at least nine assists . . . Season-high 10 assists on New Year's Day win against Clippers . . . Led New York with six assists at Detroit on February 10, only game all season that Mark Jackson did not pace or tie club lead in assists.

Keyed several of Knicks' important late-season wins . . . Hit for 20 points, (9–14 shooting) and had nine assists in key road win at Milwaukee on March 31 . . . Then, on April 5 at Philadelphia, poured in 27 points in convincing win over 76ers.

NBA RECORD

Sea.-Team	G	MIN	FGA	FGM	PCT	FTA	FTM	PCT	OFF	DEF	REB	AST	PF	DQ	STL	BS	PTS	AVG
85-86—NY	81	2025	934	437	.468	237	132	.557	92	116	208	161	155	0	68	9	1013	12.5
86-87—NY	80	2758	1302	633	.486	335	235	.701	120	174	294	354	165	0	88	18	527	19.1
87-88—NY	81	2703	1324	591	.446	243	191	.786	106	164	270	326	183	1	90	22	1412	17.4
Totals.....	242	7486	3560	1661	.467	815	558	.684	318	454	772	841	503	1	246	49	3952	16.3

Three-point goals: 1985-86, 7-25; 1986-87, 26-74; 1987-88: 39-129 (.302). Totals 72-228 (.316).

PLAYOFFS

	G	MIN	FGA	FGM	PCT	FTA	FTM	PCT	OFF	DEF	REB	AST	PF	DQ	STL	BS	PTS	AVG
87-88—NY	4	149	69	33	.478	14	12	.857	1	7	8	19	12	0	11	0	80	20.0
Totals.....	4	149	69	33	.478	14	12	.857	1	7	8	19	12	0	11	0	80	20.0

Knicks 1987-88 Highs & Lows

KNICKS INDIVIDUAL
MINUTES, GAME—51 (Jackson at Chicago, January 30)
POINTS, GAME—42 (Ewing at Chicago, April 8)
REBOUNDS, GAME—21 (Ewing vs. Philadelphia, January 16)

ASSISTS, GAME—18 (Jackson at Chicago, January 30; at Chicago, April 8)

STEALS, GAME—7 (Jackson vs. Milwaukee, Dec 15; Wilkins at Chicago, Jan 30)

BLOCKS, GAME—8 (Ewing at Sacramento, January 23; vs. Washington, April 15)

KNICKS TEAM

MOST POINTS: GAME—136 (at Philadelphia, April 5)

HALF—76 (at Philadelphia, April 5, first half)

QUARTER—45 (at Philadelphia, April 5, second quarter)

FEWEST POINTS: GAME—85 (at New Jersey, March 5)

HALF—32 (at Boston, November 18, second half)

QUARTER—11 (at Boston, Nov 18, 4th; vs. Phila, March 4, 4th)

HIGHEST FG PCT, GAME—.610 (at Philadelphia, April 5)

LOWEST FG PCT, GAME—.371 (at Atlanta, April 16)

LONGEST WINNING STREAK—3 (three times)

LONGEST LOSING STREAK—5 (November 6–13, first five games of year)

BIGGEST WINNING MARGIN—32 (vs. New Jersey, December 19, 125–93)

BIGGEST LOSING MARGIN—28 (at Detroit, December 12, 96–124)

HIGHEST ATTENDANCE, HOME—19,591 (eight times)

HIGHEST ATTENDANCE, ROAD—28,676 (at Detroit, November 6)

Odds 'N Ends About the 1987-88 Knicks

THE RECORD: The Knicks finished the regular season with a record of 38–44, and qualified for the NBA playoffs for the first time since 1983-84 . . . This year's record is their winningest since that '83–84 season (47–35) . . . The Knicks' 38 wins were a 58 percent improvement over last season (24–58) . . . They exceeded last year's win total in game no. 58.

THE WIN JUMP: The Knicks' 14-game jump in the win column from last season to this season is the biggest one-season jump in their history . . . Twice before, they'd jumped 11 games in the win column from one season to the next (from 43 to 54 from 1967–68 to 1968–69; and from 39 to 50, 1979–80 to 1980–81) . . . The Knicks showed the second-best improvement in the NBA this season (Denver jumped 17 games in the win column from last year to this year).

THE STRETCH DRIVE: In just getting under the wire for the playoff berth, the Knicks won eight of their last 12 games, 13 of their last 22, and 24 of their last 40.

THE LOW POINT: On January 30 the Knicks lost in over-time at Chicago, 97–95 . . . Their record fell to 14–28, 14 games under .500 and their lowest point under .500 on the season . . . They were 5 ½ games behind the final playoff spot . . . But from that point on, they sported a 24–16 record to reach the playoffs.

BY THE MONTHS: Coming into this season, the Knicks hadn't had a winning month since March of 1984 . . . But they highlighted the playoff push by closing the season with *three straight* winning months . . . They went 8–4 in February, 9–8 in March, and 7–4 in April.

THE FRIENDLY CONFINES OF MSG: Knicks' success at Madison Square Garden played a big part in the playoff story . . . Knicks finished the regular season with a 29–12 home record, their best record at the Garden since 1983–84 (also 29–12) . . . Their home season was highlighted by a 13-game home winning streak, January 9–March 7, the longest home win streak since 1972–73, when the Knicks won a club-record 20 straight home games (they also won 20 in a row at home in 1968–69) . . . The 13-game home win streak ended with a 104–99 loss to the Lakers on March 9.

ATTENDANCE: Knicks showed a marked jump in home paid attendance . . . They drew 586,752 to the Garden, an average of 14,311 per date . . . Last season, they drew a total of 538,058 for a 13,123 average.

SELLOUTS: But the real attendance story was told in the number of times the Knicks sold out the Garden . . . They recorded *eight* sellouts during the regular season (with the magic number of 19,591), as opposed to just *one* sellout last season . . . This season's eight sellouts marked the most for the Knicks since 1974–75, when they recorded 19 sellout houses at MSG.

ON THE ROAD: The Knicks went 9–32 on the road this season, their best road mark since 1983–84 (18–23), but that's only half the story . . . At one point the Knicks were 1–23 on the road, after losing a club-record 18 straight road games (December 3–February 22) . . . They snapped the road losing string with back-to-back road wins at Los Angeles over the Clippers (106–96 on February 25) and at Golden State over the Warriors (125–119 on February 26) . . . Starting with the losing-streak-ending win over the Clippers, the Knicks won eight of their last 17 road games.

AND ON THE ROAD THEY CLOSED IT OUT: With the playoffs berth on the line, the Knicks responded by winning three of their last four road games, and five of their last seven . . . including the last-gasp, 88–86 victory in Indiana in the season finale on April 23 that nailed down the playoff spot.

Revised and updated with over 75 all
new sports records and photographs!

THE ILLUSTRATED
SPORTS RECORD BOOK
Zander Hollander and David Schulz

Here, in a single book, are more than 350
all-time sports records with stories and
photos so vivid it's like "being there." All the
sports classics are here: Babe Ruth, Wilt
Chamberlain, Muhammad Ali ... plus the
stories of such active stars as Dwight Gooden
and Wayne Gretzky. This is the authoritative
book on what the great records are, and
who set them—an engrossing, fun-filled
reference guide filled with anecdotes of
hundreds of renowned athletes whose
remarkable records remain as fresh as when
they were set.

GAME TIME!

YOU DON'T SIMPLY TELL CHILDREN TO
SAY NO, YOU TEACH THEM HOW—
AND GIVE THEM REASONS TO WANT TO

WHEN SAYING NO ISN'T ENOUGH

HOW TO KEEP THE CHILDREN YOU LOVE OFF DRUGS

By Ken Barun and
Philip Bashe

Ken Barun, the nation's leading fighter against drug abuse, tells parents how to guide their children safely through their drug susceptible years, 8 to 20:

Why kids go on drugs * The facts about the drugs they use * Parents' all-too-common mistakes * How to make your child *want* to say no to drugs * The tell-tale signs of drug use and exactly how to respond to them * The names and addresses of drug abuse programs all over the country * And so much more—in a book your children want you to read!

"THIS IS A WONDERFUL BOOK, ONE THAT IS SORELY NEEDED."

—Abigail ("Dear Abby") Van Buren

"READING THIS COULD SAVE A LIFE!"

—*Hudson Daily Sun*

27 million Americans can't read a bedtime story to a child.

It's because 27 million adults in this country simply can't read.

Functional illiteracy has reached one out of five Americans. It robs them of even the simplest of human pleasures, like reading a fairy tale to a child.

You can change all this by joining the fight against illiteracy.

Call the Coalition for Literacy at toll-free **1-800-228-8813** and volunteer.

Volunteer Against Illiteracy. The only degree you need is a degree of caring.